MCSE Exam Notes™:
NT® Server 4 in the
Enterprise

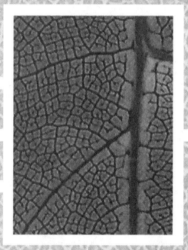

Robert King and
Gary Govanus

San Francisco • Paris • Düsseldorf • Soest

Associate Publisher: Guy Hart-Davis
Contracts and Licensing Manager: Kristine Plachy
Acquisitions & Developmental Editor: Neil Edde
Editor: Ronn Jost
Project Editor: Emily Wolman
Technical Editor: Ron Reimann
Book Designer: Bill Gibson
Graphic Illustrator: Michael Parker
Electronic Publishing Specialist: Bill Gibson
Production Coordinator: Eryn L. Osterhaus
Indexer: Rebecca Plunkett
Cover Design: Archer Design
Cover Illustrator/Photographer: FPG International

Library of Congress Card Number: 98-85466
ISBN: 0-7821-2292-2

Manufactured in the United States of America

10 9 8 7 6 5 4 3 2

To my best friend, and my wife, Bobbi.
—Gary

To my wife Susan.
—Bob

Acknowledgments

People keep trying to teach me patience. Someday it may take! There are many people who have been tried severely during the writing of this book, and I'd like to thank them all: my loving wife Bobbi; my two daughters, Dawn and Denise; Brandice and CJ for giving up time with their grandfather; Mom and Dad for understanding why we couldn't visit; Neil Edde, for giving Bob and me the chance; Ronn Jost, our Editor, for nursing us through; Ron Reimann, our tech Editor, for making sure we didn't lie to you; and Project Editor Emily Wolman, Production Coordinator Eryn Osterhaus, and Designer and Desktop Specialist Bill Gibson, for all the hard work they put in over the course of this project. To all, thank you.

—Gary Govanus

I always thought that writing a book would be easy—it's just teaching on paper, right? Little did I know just how much sacrifice would be involved. Unfortunately, most of the sacrifices were made by my family. For that (and more), thanks first go to my wife, Susan, and my daughter, Katie.

I'd also be remiss if I didn't thank the guys at The Endeavor Group in Reno (www.endeavor-net.com) who donated a couple of their great computers to my home lab so I could test before I typed.

Lastly, thanks to the fine folks at Sybex for giving me the opportunity to write this book.

—Bob King

Table of Contents

Introduction

If you've purchased this book, you are probably chasing one of the Microsoft professional certifications: MCP, MCSE, or MCT. They are all great career builders. When you glance through any newspaper's want ads, you'll see employment opportunities for people with these certifications; finding qualified employees is a challenge in today's market. If you are certified, it means that you know something about the product, but more importantly, it means that you have the ability, determination, and focus to learn—the greatest skills any employee can have.

You've probably also heard all the rumors about how hard the Microsoft exams are—believe us, the rumors are true! Microsoft has designed a series of exams that truly test your knowledge of their products. Each exam not only covers the materials presented in a particular course, but also covers the prerequisite knowledge for that course. This means two things for you—that the first exam can be a real hurdle and that each exam *should* get easier since you've studied the basics over and over.

This book has been developed in alliance with the Microsoft Corporation to give you the knowledge and skills you need to prepare for one of the key exams of the MCSE certification program: *Implementing and Supporting Microsoft Windows NT Server 4.0 in the Enterprise* (Exam 70-068). Reviewed and approved by Microsoft, this book provides a solid introduction to Microsoft networking technologies and will help you on your way to MCSE certification.

Is This Book for You?

The *MCSE Exam Notes* books were designed to be succinct, portable exam review guides that can be used either in conjunction with a more complete study program (book, CBT courseware, classroom/lab environment) or as an exam review for those people who don't feel the need for more extensive preparation. It isn't our goal to "give the answers away," but rather to identify those topics on which you can expect to be tested and provide sufficient coverage of these topics.

Perhaps you've been working with Microsoft networking technologies for years now. The thought of paying a lot of money for a specialized MCSE exam preparation course probably doesn't sound too appealing. What can they teach you that you don't already know, right? Be careful, though. Many experienced network administrators have walked confidently into test centers only to walk sheepishly out of them after failing an MCSE exam. As they discovered, there's the Microsoft of the real world and the Microsoft of the MCSE exams. It's our goal with these *Exam Notes* books to show you where the two converge and where they diverge. After you've finished reading through this book, you should have a clear idea of how your understanding of the technologies involved matches up with the expectations of the MCSE exam makers in Redmond.

Or perhaps you're relatively new to the world of Microsoft networking, drawn to it by the promise of challenging work and higher salaries. You've just waded through an 800-page MCSE study guide or taken a class at a local training center. It's a lot of information to keep track of, isn't it? Well, by organizing the *Exam Notes* books according to the Microsoft exam objectives, and by breaking up the information into concise, manageable pieces, we've created what we think is the handiest exam review guide available. Throw it in your briefcase and carry it to work with you. As you read through the book, you'll be able to identify quickly those areas you know best and those that require more in-depth review.

NOTE   The goal of the *Exam Notes* series is to help MCSE candidates familiarize themselves with the subjects on which they can expect to be tested in the MCSE exams. For complete, in-depth coverage of the technologies and topics involved, we recommend the *MCSE Study Guide* series from Sybex.

How Is This Book Organized?

As mentioned above, this book is organized according to the official exam objectives list prepared by Microsoft for the *Implementing and Supporting Microsoft Windows NT Server 4.0 in the Enterprise* exam. The chapters coincide with the broad objectives groupings, such as Planning, Installation and Configuration, Monitoring and Optimization, and Troubleshooting. These groupings are also reflected in the organization of the MCSE exams themselves.

Within each chapter, the individual exam objectives are addressed in turn. And in turn, the objectives sections are further divided according to the type of information presented.

Critical Information

This section presents the greatest level of detail on information that is relevant to the objective. This is the place to start if you're unfamiliar with or uncertain about the technical issues related to the objective.

Necessary Procedures

Here, you'll find instructions for procedures that require a lab computer to be completed. From installing operating systems to modifying configuration defaults, the information in these sections addresses the hands-on requirements for the MCSE exams.

NOTE   Not every objective has procedures associated with it. For such objectives, the "Necessary Procedures" section has been left out.

Exam Essentials

In this section, we've put together a concise list of the most crucial topics of subject areas that you'll need to comprehend fully prior to taking the MCSE exam. This section can help you identify those topics that might require more study on your part.

Key Terms and Concepts

Here, we've compiled a mini-glossary of the most important terms and concepts related to the specific objective. You'll understand what all those technical words mean within the context of the related subject matter.

Sample Questions

For each objective, we've included a selection of questions similar to those you'll encounter on the actual MCSE exam. Answers and explanations are provided so that you can gain some insight into the exam-taking process.

SEE ALSO For a more comprehensive collection of exam review questions, check out the *MCSE Test Success* series, also published by Sybex.

How Do You Become an MCSE?

Attaining Microsoft Certified Systems Engineer (MCSE) status is a challenge. The exams cover a wide range of topics, and require dedicated study and expertise. This is, however, why the MCSE certificate is so valuable. If achieving the MCSE status were too easy, the market would be quickly flooded by MCSEs and the certification would become meaningless. Microsoft, keenly aware of this fact, has taken steps to ensure that the certification means that its holder is truly knowledgeable and skilled.

To become an MCSE, you must pass four core requirements and two electives.

Client Requirement

70-073: Implementing and Supporting Windows NT Workstation 4.0

or

70-064: Implementing and Supporting Microsoft Windows 95

Networking Requirement

70-058: Networking Essentials

Windows NT Server 4.0 Requirement

70-067: Implementing and Supporting Windows NT Server 4.0

Windows NT Server 4.0 in the Enterprise Requirement

70-068: Implementing and Supporting Windows NT Server 4.0 in the Enterprise

Electives

Some of the more popular electives include:

70-059: Internetworking Microsoft TCP/IP on Microsoft Windows NT 4.0

70-087: Implementing and Supporting Microsoft Internet Information Server 4.0

70-081: Implementing and Supporting Microsoft Exchange Server 5.5

70-026: System Administration for Microsoft SQL Server 6.5

70-027: Implementing a Database Design on Microsoft SQL Server 6.5

70-088: Implementing and Supporting Microsoft Proxy Server 2.0

70-079: Implementing and Supporting Microsoft Internet Explorer 4.0 by Using the Internet Explorer Administration Kit

---

TIP This book is part of a series of *MCSE Exam Notes* books, published by Network Press (Sybex), that covers four core requirements and your choice of several electives—the entire MCSE track!

Where Do You Take the Exams?

You may take the exams at any of more than 800 Sylvan Prometric Authorized Testing Centers around the world. For the location of a testing center near you, call (800)755-EXAM (755-3926). Outside the United States and Canada, contact your local Sylvan Prometric Registration Center. You can also register for an exam with Sylvan Prometric via the Internet. The Sylvan Web site can be reached through the Microsoft Training and Certification site, or at http://www.slspro.com/msreg/microsoft.asp.

To register for a Microsoft Certified Professional exam:

1. Determine the number of the exam that you want to take.

2. Register with Sylvan Prometric. At this point, you will be asked for advance payment for the exam. At the time of this writing, the exams are $100 each. Exams must be taken within one year of payment. You can schedule exams up to six weeks in advance or as late as one working day prior to the date of the exam. You can cancel or reschedule your exam if you contact Sylvan Prometric at least two working days prior to the exam. Same-day registration is available in some locations, although this is subject to space availability. Where same-day registration is available, you must register a minimum of two hours before exam time.

3. After you receive a registration and payment confirmation letter from Sylvan Prometric, call a nearby Sylvan Prometric Testing Center to schedule your exam.

When you schedule the exam, you'll be provided with instructions regarding appointment and cancellation procedures and ID requirements, and information about the testing center location.

What Does the NT Server 4.0 in the Enterprise Exam Measure?

The people who write the exams for Microsoft want to make sure that you are a well-rounded network administrator. The MCSE designation is kind of a Liberal Arts degree in Networking—you need to know something about multiple topics.

That philosophy shows in the Server-Enterprise exam and in the way the questions are worded. As you study, try to think like an exam writer. What would you write questions about?

- Is there special terminology that Microsoft uses?

- Are there tips presented on things such as troubleshooting?

- Is there a specific way of doing something, stressed over and over?

- Is there something about the subject that is very specific, such as minimum requirements or command-line switches?

The NT Server-Enterprise exam measures your ability to configure, implement, and maintain a Windows NT network in a large environment. Most of the exam will focus on technologies that are most appropriate on a large network—TCP/IP-related issues, network services such as DHCP and WINS, and integration with other operating systems.

When studying for this examination, think big! Look at each topic from the perspective of an administrator responsible for thousands of computers. Examine each objective and try to find the advantage of such a system for each technology discussed. If you can explain how each tool would benefit the administrator of a large network, you are halfway there. Once you know why a technology would be implemented, it is easier to master the necessary procedures to make it happen.

How Does Microsoft Develop the Exam Questions?

Microsoft's exam development process consists of eight mandatory phases. The process takes an average of seven months and contains more than 150 specific steps. The phases of Microsoft Certified Professional exam development are listed here.

Phase 1: Job Analysis

Phase 1 is an analysis of all the tasks that make up the specific job function based on tasks performed by people who are currently performing the job function. This phase also identifies the knowledge, skills, and abilities that relate specifically to the certification for that performance area.

Phase 2: Objective Domain Definition

The results of the job analysis provide the framework used to develop exam objectives. The development of objectives involves translating the job function tasks into a comprehensive set of more specific and measurable knowledge, skills, and abilities. The resulting list of objectives, or the objective domain, is the basis for the development of both the certification exams and the training materials.

NOTE The outline of all *Exam Notes* books is based upon the official exam objectives lists published by Microsoft. Objectives are subject to change without notification. We advise that you check the Microsoft Training and Certification Web site (www.microsoft.com\train_cert\) for the most current objectives list.

Phase 3: Blueprint Survey

The final objective domain is transformed into a blueprint survey in which contributors—technology professionals who are performing the applicable job function—are asked to rate each objective. Based on the contributors' input, the objectives are prioritized and weighted. The actual exam items are written according to the prioritized objectives. The blueprint survey phase helps determine which objectives to measure, as well as the appropriate number and types of items to include on the exam.

Phase 4: Item Development

A pool of items is developed to measure the blueprinted objective domain. The number and types of items to be written are based on the results of the blueprint survey. During this phase, items are reviewed and revised to ensure that they are as follows:

- Technically accurate

- Clear, unambiguous, and plausible

- Not biased toward any population, subgroup, or culture

- Not misleading or tricky

- Testing at the correct level of Bloom's Taxonomy

- Testing for useful knowledge, not obscure or trivial facts

Items that meet these criteria are included in the initial item pool.

Phase 5: Alpha Review and Item Revision

During this phase, a panel of technical and job function experts reviews each item for technical accuracy, then answers each item, reaching consensus on all technical issues. Once the items have been verified as technically accurate, they are edited to ensure that they are expressed in the clearest language possible.

Phase 6: Beta Exam

The reviewed and edited items are collected into a beta exam pool. During the beta exam, each participant has the opportunity to respond to all the items in this beta exam pool. Based on the responses of all beta participants, Microsoft performs a statistical analysis to verify the validity of the exam items and to determine which items will be used in the certification exam. Once the analysis has been completed, the items are distributed into multiple parallel forms, or versions, of the final certification exam.

Phase 7: Item Selection and Cut-Score Setting

The results of the beta exam are analyzed to determine which items should be included in the certification exam based on many factors, including item difficulty and relevance. Generally, the desired items are answered correctly by 25 to 90 percent of the beta exam candidates. This helps ensure that the exam consists of a variety of difficulty levels, from somewhat easy to extremely difficult.

Also during this phase, a panel of job function experts determines the cut score (minimum passing score) for the exam. The cut score differs from exam to exam because it is based on an item-by-item determination of the percentage of candidates who would be expected to answer the item correctly. The experts determine the cut score in a group session to increase the reliability.

Phase 8: Live Exam

Once all the other phases are complete, the exam is ready. Microsoft Certified Professional exams are administered by Sylvan Prometric.

Tips for Taking Your NT Server 4.0 in the Enterprise Exam

Here are some general tips for taking your exam successfully:

- Arrive early at the exam center so that you can relax and review your study materials, particularly tables and lists of exam-related information.

- Read the questions carefully. Don't be tempted to jump to an early conclusion. Make sure you know *exactly* what the question is asking.

- Don't leave any unanswered questions—they count against you.

- When answering multiple-choice questions that you're not sure about, use a process of elimination to get rid of the obviously incorrect questions first. This will improve your odds if you need to make an educated guess.

- Because the hard questions will eat up the most time, save them for last. You can move forward and backward through the exam.

- This exam has many exhibits (pictures). It can be difficult, if not impossible, to view both the questions and the exhibit simulation on the 14- and 15-inch screens usually found at the testing centers. Call around to each center to find out whether they have 17-inch monitors available. If they don't, perhaps you can arrange to bring in your own. Failing this, some people have found it useful to quickly draw the diagram on the scratch paper provided by the testing center and use the monitor to view just the question.

- Many participants run out of time before they are able to complete the test. If you are unsure of the answer to a question, you may want to choose one of the answers, mark the question, and go on—an unanswered question does not help you. Once your time is up, you cannot go on to another question. However, you can remain on the current question indefinitely when the time runs out. Therefore, when you are almost out of time, go to a question you feel you can figure out—given enough time—and work until you feel you have it (or the night security guard boots you out!).

- You are allowed to use the Windows calculator during your exam. However, it may be better to memorize a table of the subnet addresses and write it down on the scratch paper supplied by the testing center before you start the exam.

Once you have completed an exam, you will be given immediate, online notification of your pass or fail status. You will also receive a printed Examination Score Report indicating your pass or fail status and your exam results by section. (The exam administrator will give you the printed score report.) Exam scores are automatically forwarded to Microsoft within five working days after you take the exam, so you do not need to send your score to Microsoft. If you pass the exam, you will receive confirmation from Microsoft, typically within two to four weeks.

Contact Information

To find out more about Microsoft Education and Certification materials and programs, register with Sylvan Prometric, or receive other useful information, check the following resources. Outside the United States or Canada, contact your local Microsoft office or Sylvan Prometric Testing Center.

Microsoft Certified Professional Program—(800)636-7544

Call the MCPP number for information about the Microsoft Certified Professional program and exams, and to order the latest Microsoft Roadmap to Education and Certification.

Sylvan Prometric Testing Centers—(800)755-EXAM

To register for a Microsoft Certified Professional exam at any of more than 800 Sylvan Prometric Testing Centers around the world, or to order this *Exam Notes* book, call the Sylvan Prometric Testing Center number.

Microsoft Certification Development Team— http://www.microsoft.com/Train_Cert/mcp/examinfo/certsd.htm

Contact the Microsoft Certification Development Team through their Web site to volunteer for participation in one or more exam development phases or to report a problem with an exam. Address written correspondence to:

Certification Development Team
Microsoft Education and Certification
One Microsoft Way
Redmond, WA 98052

Microsoft TechNet Technical Information Network— (800)344-2121

This is an excellent resource for support professionals and system administrators. Outside the United States and Canada, call your local Microsoft subsidiary for information.

How to Contact the Authors

Gary Govanus can be reached at ggovanus@psconsulting.com.

Bob King can be reached at bking@royal-tech.com.

How to Contact the Publisher

Sybex welcomes reader feedback on all of their titles. Visit the Sybex Web site at www.sybex.com for book updates and additional certification information. You'll also find online forms to submit comments or suggestions regarding this or any other Sybex book.

CHAPTER

1

Planning

Microsoft Exam Objectives Covered in This Chapter:

▶ **Plan the implementation of a directory services architecture. Considerations include:** *(pages 4 – 24)*
- Selecting the appropriate domain model
- Supporting a single logon account
- Allowing users to access resources in different domains

▶ **Plan the disk drive configuration for various requirements. Requirements include choosing a fault-tolerance method.** *(pages 25 – 42)*

▶ **Choose a protocol for various situations. Protocols include:** *(pages 42 – 57)*
- TCP/IP
- TCP/IP with DHCP and WINS
- NWLink IPX/SPX Compatible Transport
- Data Link Control (DLC)
- AppleTalk

The information covered in this chapter revolves around decisions that you need to make *before* the physical implementation of Windows NT or a migration from another operating system. Much of this information is theoretical, which is the hardest material to study because it is always open to interpretation. Don't get discouraged, though—you just have to remember Microsoft's interpretations!

Before you can start installing servers, you need to define what services the network will be required to provide. This list will be different in every environment, but here are a few common business network needs:

- Centralized management of user accounts

- Centralized storage and backup of business-critical data

- A shared print environment

- Controlled access to resources

In addition to the requirements, you will probably have a list of desired services. This list can be as varied as the number of businesses using networks. Perhaps you will want to provide:

- A shared customer contact list

- E-mail, both internal and Internet

- Control over user desktop configurations

- A corporate Web site on the Internet

- Remote network access

Then, some services will not be feasible given your budget. Perhaps future plans will include:

- A corporate intranet to distribute internal information

- Electronic commerce on the corporate Web site

- High-speed network and Internet access

Every item on these lists can, and probably will, affect your network. Many of these services can produce overhead on both your servers and your network. Proper planning can help to reduce any negative impact on your environment.

Each of the objectives covered in this chapter concerns specific sets of decisions that you must make when planning a network. If you make the right decisions, you end up with a network that is efficient, fault tolerant, and easy to administrate. (You can serve a lot of pizza!) If you make the wrong decisions, you end up with a network that is none of these things. (People take their business down the street!) The information presented in this chapter is critical in your real-world applications—no matter the size of the environment in which you work. Remember that proper planning will save a tremendous amount of time and effort in the future—and given the mission-critical importance of modern information technology systems, proper planning can save the business. More than one company has failed due to a poorly implemented network.

The MCSE exam emphasizes the first objective—planning a directory services architecture. Questions on this objective will involve your ability to pick the best design given a set of specifications.

The next two objectives are assumed to be prerequisite knowledge gained either through another course or through practical experience. Few questions will be directly aimed at these two objectives, but the terms and technologies will be used in questions and answers on other topics.

Plan the implementation of a directory services architecture. Considerations include:

- Selecting the appropriate domain model
- Supporting a single logon account
- Allowing users to access resources in different domains

When designing an NT environment, the system administrator has two goals:

1. Simplify administration—this is especially important in an enterprise environment.

2. Simplify access for the users.

As an administrator, you would like to be able to manage your entire network from a single location, have a single account for each user, provide fault tolerance for your account information, integrate the other network operating systems into your NT structure, and ease the administration of the critical applications on which your users depend.

At the same time, you want to allow users to log on at any machine, have only one account and password to remember, and be able to access appropriate resources no matter where they are located in your environment.

With a little planning, you can accomplish all of these goals and end up with a system that is both easy to administrate and easy to use.

NOTE The MCSE exam tests quite heavily on the information presented in this section. Think of this from Microsoft's perspective—if you know how to properly design an NT domain structure and provide necessary services, networks based upon NT will perform and look their best.

Critical Information

Microsoft defines a *domain* as a "logical grouping of users and computers organized for administrative purposes." (*Microsoft Student Guide Course 689*, p. 23) Unfortunately, Microsoft also uses this phrase to define the term *workgroup*. (*Microsoft Student Guide Course 922*, p. 35) The major difference between a workgroup and a domain is where users are authenticated for the resources they are trying to access. In a workgroup, user accounts are defined locally on the machine that holds the resource. In a domain, user accounts are defined and managed in a central database—this database, called the security accounts manager (SAM), is managed by NT's directory services. So, a more accurate definition of an NT domain would be *an administrative grouping of users and computers, defined and managed through a single database.*

NOTE All NT-based computers (both Server and Workstation) have a SAM that defines permissions to local resources. The distinction made here is that in a domain, all members also share a common SAM—this shared SAM provides a central point of management.

The SAM is a secure database that contains information about the users, computers, global groups, and local groups defined in a domain. Each of these items is called an *object* in the database. The maximum number of objects that can be organized in a single SAM is 40,000. The SAM is stored on an NT server, which plays the role of domain controller for your network. A *domain controller* is an NT server that contains the domain SAM or accounts database. Domain controllers are responsible for the authentication of users—in other words, the logon process. There are two types of domain controllers—primary domain controllers (PDCs) and backup domain controllers (BDCs). The differences between the two types will be defined in Chapter 2, "Installation and Configuration."

Although the accounts database can support up to 40,000 objects, a system might be designed with multiple domains (accounts databases) for various reasons. These reasons include:

- Having more than 40,000 users, computers, and groups

- Wanting to group users or resources for management purposes

- Wanting to reduce the number of objects viewed in management tools (Do you *really* want to scroll through a list of 40,000 objects every time you need to manage an account?)

The act of splitting the users and resources into multiple domains is called *partitioning the database*. There are two main benefits to this type of design. First, you can delegate administration for each domain so that each department or location can manage its own resources. Second, you reduce the length of the list you have to scroll through to find a given object.

By default, each domain is a separate entity—domains do not share information, and resources from one domain are not made available to users defined in another domain. To allow users to access resources in another domain, you must establish a trust between the two domains. A *trust* can be defined as a one-way communications link between two domains. There are two domains involved in a trust—one that contains the user accounts that should have access to resources and another that contains those resources. The domain with the user accounts is called the *trusted* domain; the domain with the resources is called the *trusting* domain.

NOTE   It can be confusing to decide which domain should be the trusted domain and which should be the trusting domain. Remember that you never hear the phrase "trusted computer," but most companies do have "trusted employees." The domain where the employees are defined is always the trusted domain.

When you document your system, you should represent trusts with arrows. The arrows should point to the trusted domain. When one domain trusts another, this is known as a *one-way trust* (see Figure 1.1).

FIGURE 1.1: One-way trust

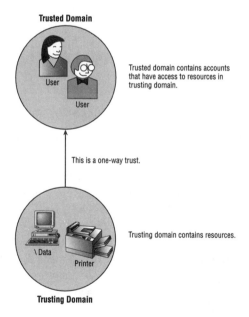

When both domains have users that need to access resources in the other domain, you will create a two-way trust. A *two-way trust* is just two one-way trusts set up in each direction (see Figure 1.2).

FIGURE 1.2: Two-way trust

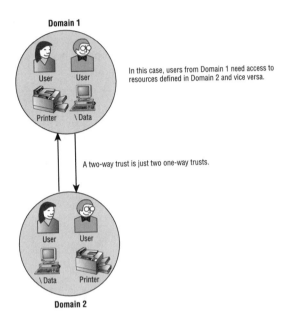

In this case, users from Domain 1 need access to resources defined in Domain 2 and vice versa.

A two-way trust is just two one-way trusts.

NT trusts are *nontransitive*—they are never inherited from one domain to another. If domain A trusts domain B, and domain B trusts domain C, this does not imply that domain A trusts domain C. You would have to create this trust manually. (This is a key point about trusts.)

TIP Suppose that you are going on vacation and you give your house keys to Harry, a friend from work. In this scenario, you have made Harry a trusted friend (and maybe you are a bit too trusting). When you get back from vacation, you find that Harry let his friends Tom and Dick use your keys. You'd probably be mad, right? You didn't expect that Tom, Dick, *and* Harry would have access to your house. Giving your keys to Harry was a nontransitive trust—you trusted Harry, not all his wild friends!

AGLP is an acronym that describes the fundamental process for granting permissions to resources across trusts—Accounts go into Global groups, which go into Local groups, which are granted Permissions.

The steps for granting these permissions are shown in Figure 1.3.

1. In the domain where the users are defined (Domain 1), either use an existing global group or create a new one, and make the appropriate users members of this group.

2. In the domain that contains the resource (Domain 2), create a local group with the necessary permissions.

3. Make the global group from Domain 1 a member of the local group in Domain 2.

This AGLP process is tested often on all of the Microsoft exams. You need to know it and be comfortable using it to succeed.

F I G U R E 1.3: AGLP

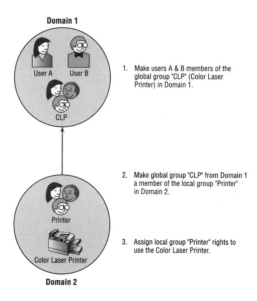

Domain 1

1. Make users A & B members of the global group "CLP" (Color Laser Printer) in Domain 1.

2. Make global group "CLP" from Domain 1 a member of the local group "Printer" in Domain 2.

3. Assign local group "Printer" rights to use the Color Laser Printer.

Domain 2

Selecting the Appropriate Domain Model

The way you design your NT environment can have a big impact on its performance. Microsoft emphasizes an understanding of the variables involved in planning, implementing, and maintaining an NT domain structure.

A *domain model* is a definition of how you will use directory services in your environment. There are four basic domain models— each has some definite advantages and disadvantages:

- Single
- Single master
- Multiple master
- Complete trust

Single Domain Model

The single domain model is the easiest to implement of the four models. All users and computers are defined in a single NT domain, as shown in Figure 1.4. This domain model is most appropriate when there are less than 40,000 users in close proximity to each other (no significant remote locations) and there is a need for central administration of the environment.

FIGURE 1.4: Single domain model

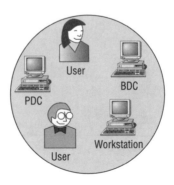

Since all resources are defined in a single domain SAM database, no trusts need to be established. Users have access to all resources to which they have been granted permissions. The advantages and disadvantages associated with the single domain model are listed in Table 1.1.

T A B L E 1.1: Advantages and Disadvantages of the Single Domain Model

Advantages	Disadvantages
Simple to implement and manage	Performance can degrade as the number of resources increases because the load on Security Manager increases
Central control of user accounts	All users are defined in the same database—no grouping by location or function
Central control of all resources	All resources are defined in the same database—no grouping by location or function
No trusts are necessary	Performance of browser service (not Web browser) will slow with large numbers of servers

Single Master Domain Model

A single master domain model consists of at least two domains. All user accounts are defined in a *master* domain. The other domains are used to manage physical resources, as shown in Figure 1.5. This design is most appropriate when you desire central control of user accounts, but departmental or geographic control of physical resources is the responsibility of a local administrator. This domain model is also appropriate when the number of objects (users and resources) defined in the SAM database exceeds the maximum (40,000). In this case, if you move the computer and other resource accounts to another domain, it would spread the object records over multiple domains. (Although, in a company of this size, you would probably start with the next model—the multiple master domain model.)

TIP If you think your company might grow into multiple locations or past the 40,000-object limit, start with the single master domain model. It offers more growth options than the single domain model.

FIGURE 1.5: Single master domain model

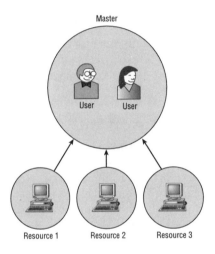

NOTE Each resource domain establishes a one-way trust with the master domain.

You use the AGLP process to assign users in the master domain permissions to the resources defined in the resource domains, as shown in Figure 1.6. Create a global group in the master domain with the appropriate members, then create a local group in the resource domain and assign it the necessary permissions. Next, make the global group a member of the local group.

The advantages and disadvantages associated with the single master domain model are listed in Table 1.2.

FIGURE 1.6: Groups in a single master domain model

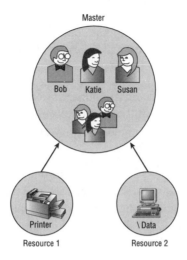

TABLE 1.2: Advantages and Disadvantages of the Single Master Domain Model

Advantages	Disadvantages
Best choice if resources need to be managed by different groups	As in a single domain, performance can degrade as the number of users defined in the master domain increases
User accounts are centrally located	Local groups must be defined in each resource domain
Resources are grouped logically (either by department or by geographic location)	The administrator of resource domains must trust the administrator of the master domain to set up global groups correctly
Global groups need to be created in only one domain	

Multiple Master Domain Model

The multiple master domain model is shown in Figure 1.7. This domain model is the most scalable of the four models. It looks much like the single master domain model, except that there is more than one domain where user accounts are defined. You might choose this model for various reasons:

- The accounts database is limited to a maximum of 40,000 objects (users, groups, and computer accounts). If your environment is large enough, you might be forced to partition the database just to stay within the limits.

- Your company's management strategy might lead to this model. If each location or department wants to manage its own user accounts, you might want to create separate domains for management purposes or divide user domains to match the corporate departmental structure.

- You might create multiple master domains for ease of administration—the accounts database *will* hold 40,000 accounts, but you will not like paging through that large list to find items.

- In a WAN (wide area network) environment, you might make multiple domains to reduce the amount of network traffic that crosses the wide area links.

FIGURE 1.7: Multiple master domain model

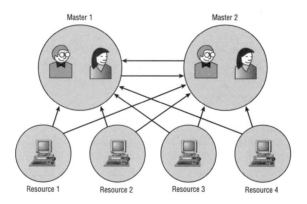

Master domains have two-way trusts between them; resource domains have a one-way trust to each master that contains users who might have to access their resources. You can determine the number of trusts in a multiple master structure by using the following formula: $M*(M-1) + (R*M)$, in which M is the number of master domains and R is the number of resource domains. (This formula assumes that each resource domain will have to trust each master domain.)

Assigning rights in a multiple master environment is a bit more confusing than in the preceding models. You still use the AGLP method, but you might have to create the global groups in each of the master domains, as shown in Figure 1.8.

FIGURE 1.8: Groups in a multiple master domain model

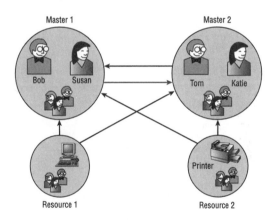

The advantages and disadvantages of the multiple master domain model are listed in Table 1.3.

TABLE 1.3: Advantages and Disadvantages of the Multiple Master Domain Model

Advantages	Disadvantages
Best model for a large environment with a central MIS department	Both local groups and global groups might have to be defined in multiple domains

TABLE 1.3: Advantages and Disadvantages of the Multiple Master Domain Model *(cont.)*

Advantages	Disadvantages
Scalable to a network of any size	Large number of trusts to manage
Each domain can have a separate administrator	User accounts are not all in one domain database

Complete Trust Domain Model

The complete trust domain model takes full advantage of directory services. In this model, each domain has both user accounts and resources, and each domain must trust all other domains. This model, as shown in Figure 1.9, is perfect for a company in which each department or geographic location wants to control both its physical resources and its user accounts.

FIGURE 1.9: Complete trust domain model

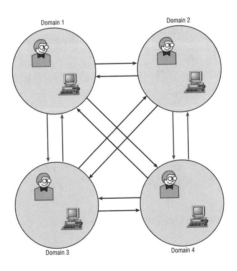

NOTE Most complete trust environments happen by accident. First, each department or location installs NT for their own use. Somewhere down the line, they realize that it would be nice if they could share resources. At that point, there are only two options—back up all data on all domain controllers and start from scratch with one of the other domain models, or implement a complete trust domain model and deal with the large number of trusts that must be managed.

TIP In a complete trust domain model, all domains trust all other domains. You can determine the number of trusts by using the following formula: $D*(D-1)$, in which D is the number of domains in the network.

Assigning rights in a complete trust environment can be extremely confusing. In this model, you must create both local groups and global groups in every domain, as shown in Figure 1.10.

FIGURE 1.10: Groups in a complete trust domain model

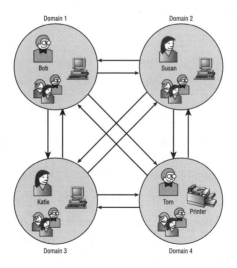

The advantages and disadvantages of the complete trust domain model are listed in Table 1.4.

T A B L E 1.4: Advantages and Disadvantages of the Complete Trust Domain Model

Advantages	Disadvantages
Works well for companies with decentralized MIS functions	Large number of trusts to manage
Scalable to any number of users	With more domains, there are more points of management
Each domain can have its own administrator	Each administrator must assume that all other administrators know what they are doing
Resources and user accounts are grouped into management units	

Supporting a Single Logon Account

In a traditional server-based network, each server maintains its own list of users who can access its resources. Since there are multiple lists of users (one for each server), users often have to remember multiple user account names and passwords, which is often confusing for the users. From an administrative perspective, defining users in multiple places adds complexity and redundant management.

Microsoft Windows NT allows a user to use a single user account to access resources on the entire network. A process called *pass-through authentication* makes it possible for users to log on from computers or domains in which they have no account. When a user sits down at a computer defined in a domain that trusts their home domain, they can choose their domain from a drop-down list.

The NT server in the computer's domain will then use the trust relationship to pass the authentication request in the user's home domain. If user Bob from DOMAIN 1 attempts to log on at a machine in DOMAIN 2, the logon process will use the procedure shown in Figure 1.11 and listed below.

FIGURE 1.11: Pass-through authentication

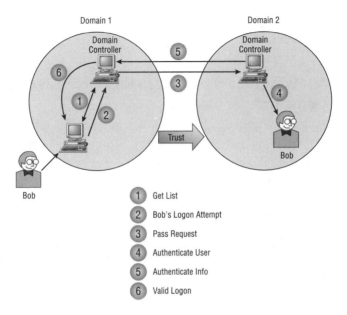

1. When the Windows NT Workstation machine boots, its NETLOG-ON service locates the primary domain controller in DOMAIN 1. As part of this process, the computer receives a list of all trusted domains to present on the logon screen.

2. When the user identifies himself as Bob from DOMAIN 2, the NETLOGON process passes the request to a domain controller in DOMAIN 1.

3. The domain controller in DOMAIN 1 recognizes that the request is for a user defined in a trusted domain, so it passes the request to a domain controller in DOMAIN 2.

4. The domain controller in DOMAIN 2 checks its accounts database to ensure that the user name is valid and the right password has been entered.

5. If the request to log on is valid, the domain controller in DOMAIN 2 passes the user's SID and group information to the domain controller in DOMAIN 1.

6. The domain controller in DOMAIN 1 trusts that the authentication was done properly, so it passes the information about user Bob back to the NT machine where Bob is trying to log on, completing the logon process.

Allowing Users to Access Resources in Different Domains

This exam objective refers to the process of using AGLP to grant users rights to resources defined in another domain. The most important thing to remember is that a user account can't cross the domain trust—only global groups can do this.

To grant a user rights to a resource in a trusting domain, create a global group in the user's home domain, which must be the trusted domain. Then, create a local group in the trusting domain. Grant the local group permission to the appropriate resource, and make the global group a member of the local group.

TIP Picture the trust as a highway between the two accounts—you can't use a highway to travel unless you have a vehicle. When you use a trust, the global group is the vehicle; user accounts are the passengers.

Necessary Procedures

Only one procedure is associated with the first exam objective. Be sure that you are *very* comfortable with the steps involved and the suggested order in which you should perform them.

Creating a Trust

Use the User Manager for Domains utility to create a trust between two domains. This is basically a two-step process—you must define the trust at both the trusted and the trusting domains. To set up the trust, you must be logged on as an administrative account in the domain. Although you can create either side of the trust first, it is better to establish the trusting relationship first and then move to the trusting domain to establish the trusted side of the relationship—the trust relationship will be established immediately. If you start at the trusted domain, there will be a 15-minute delay in establishing the trust relationship. Although 15 minutes is not excessive, it can seem like forever when you are staring at a computer screen.

1. In both domains, start the User Manager for Domains utility.

2. Choose Policies ➤ Trust Relationships.

3. At the trusted domain, add the name of the trusting domain to the Trusting Domains box.

4. At the trusting domain, add the name of the trusted domain to the Trusted Domains box. At the trusting domain, you should see a message telling you that the trust relationship was successfully established.

Exam Essentials

Expect to be tested heavily on the following points. Be sure that you know these points inside and out before taking the exam!

Be able to describe the difference between a domain and a workgroup. Both terms are used to describe a logical grouping of users and computers organized for administrative purposes. The major difference between the two terms is where the user accounts are created and managed. In a workgroup, user accounts are defined on each computer that is a member. In a domain environment, all accounts are created and managed in a single database.

Understand the function of the security accounts manager (SAM). The security accounts manager is a domain-wide database, stored on the primary domain controller (PDC) and copied to the backup domain controller(s) (BDC), that holds information about users, groups, and computers in an NT domain. The maximum recommended number of objects that should be defined in a single SAM is 40,000.

Define partitioning the database.   *Partitioning the database* is the process of creating more than one NT domain for a single environment. This might be done because the database has grown past the recommended maximum (40,000 objects or 40MB), or to group resources for ease of management.

Understand trust relationships.   A trust is established between two NT domains so that users in one domain can access resources in another. The domain with the user accounts is called the *trusted* domain; the domain with the resources is called the *trusting* domain. There are two types of trusts. A one-way trust indicates that one domain trusts another; a two-way trust indicates that each domain trusts the other. When you draw trust relationship diagrams, the arrow points from the trusting to the trusted domain.

Be able to explain the nontransitive nature of trust relationships. If domain A trusts domain B, and domain B trusts domain C, this does not mean that domain A trusts domain C. Trust extends only to the original domain.

Understand the concept of AGLP.   Accounts go into *Global* groups, which go into *Local* groups, which are granted *Permissions*. This is the fundamental process for assigning permissions across the trust relationship between two domains.

Know the four domain models.   The four domain models are single, single master, multiple master, and complete trust.

Understand the concept of pass-through authentication.   When a domain controller recognizes that a request is being made from an account defined in a trusted domain, the domain controller will pass the authentication request to a domain controller in that trusted domain. The first domain controller trusts that the second domain controller will perform the authentication process correctly.

Key Terms and Concepts

AGLP: Accounts go into *Global* groups, which go into *Local* groups, which are granted *Permissions*.

Complete trust domain model: An environment where users and resources are defined in multiple domains. Each domain trusts all other domains.

Domain: A logical grouping of users, groups, and computers, defined and managed through a central database.

Domain controller: A computer designated to hold the SAM.

Multiple master domain model: An environment where multiple domains manage only user accounts, with other resource domains defined by departmental or geographic boundaries.

Partitioning the database: Breaking down an existing domain SAM and creating more than one NT domain in a given environment to support organizational boundaries or domain limits.

Pass-through authentication: The process of authentication across a trust relationship.

Security accounts manager (SAM): The database containing information about users, groups, and computers defined in the NT operating system. The SAM used throughout the network is called the domain SAM, while the database contained by individual computers is called the local SAM.

Single domain model: An environment with only one domain.

Single master domain model: An environment where all user accounts are defined in a single NT domain, with all other resource domains defined by departmental or geographic limits.

Trust: A communication link between two domains that allows sharing of NT security data for permissions and accesses.

Sample Questions

1. Which of the following terms is defined by the phrase *a logical grouping of users and computers organized for administrative purposes?*

   A. Domain

   B. Workgroup

C. Department

D. Segment

Answer: A, B—Microsoft defines both workgroup and domain with the same phrase. To distinguish a domain from a workgroup, remember that a domain is defined and managed through a single database.

2. If users in Domain 1 need access to resources in Domain 2, which of the following trust relationships should be created?

   A. Domain 1 should trust Domain 2.

   B. Domain 2 should trust Domain 1.

   C. Both domains should trust each other.

   Answer: B—Trusts always refer to the users. Domain 2 should trust Domain 1's authentication of users.

3. Suppose that a company is made up of 80,000 users and groups; each user has their own NT workstation. Which domain model would you recommend?

   A. Single

   B. Single master

   C. Multiple master

   D. Complete trust

   Answer: C—You will see many questions of this type on the exam. As in this example, many of the questions won't give enough information to give a real-world answer. You will have to choose the answer that best fits the given information. In this example, you know that there will be at least 80,000 user accounts plus the associated groups. Since the SAM has a recommended maximum of 40,000 objects, you will need at least two domains for user accounts. This leaves either C or D as the possible answer. Most Microsoft answers do not favor the complete trust model—so you are left with C as the best answer.

Plan the disk drive configuration for various requirements. Requirements include choosing a fault-tolerance method.

You have numerous choices when planning the disk drive configuration for an NT server. You need to think about capacity, throughput, fault tolerance, and security. You also need to consider the physical aspects of the drive subsystem, choosing the appropriate type of disks and partitioning them correctly. When preparing for this objective, you must understand all of these concepts and be able to make design choices based upon the needs of a particular environment.

When you consider the disk subsystems on your servers, you need to consider capacity—how much data will you have to store? Throughput—how many users will need access to that data simultaneously? Fault tolerance—what is your method of recovery from a critical failure? And security—how do you secure that data, both physically (locked in a server room) and through your choice of operating systems?

Since the material covered in this section is not actually part of the Enterprise course, it is not heavily tested. Most of the exam questions that incorporate this material do so subtly. You might read a scenario that describes the needs of a company, and a fault-tolerant disk system might be presented as part of the solution. You will need to understand what is referred to in that case so that you can fully analyze the proposed solution.

NOTE Even though this is a "short" objective, there is a lot of information. Disk technology is an ever-growing arena. The information presented here (or in any written materials) represents the technology that was current at the time of writing. As a systems engineer, you will be responsible for keeping up to date on new advances in disk subsystems.

Critical Information

Many different types of disk systems are available in today's market—IDE, EIDE, SCSI, SCSI-2, Ultra-SCSI, Wide-SCSI, etc.—and the list grows every day. There are advantages and disadvantages in every choice. Your choice will usually be a compromise between budget, capacity, and speed. Examine your budget and buy the biggest, fastest system you can afford.

Since the disk subsystem is usually the slowest subsystem on a server, you shouldn't "buy for price." Upgrading later to a faster disk system can be expensive and time consuming. Since storage technology constantly changes, no book can explain all of the available options. However, here is a short list of the technologies that are commonly used on today's servers.

Controllers

There are numerous disk technologies on the market today, with more on the horizon. Table 1.5 lists some of the more common technologies used in servers, with their data transfer rates, advantages, and disadvantages.

T A B L E 1.5: Comparison of Disk Technologies

Type	Approximate Data Transfer Rate	Advantages	Disadvantages
IDE/EIDE	Up to 8.3MB per second (IDE) and 16.6MB per second (EIDE)	Included on most modern motherboards	Limit of two drives per controller

T A B L E 1.5: Comparison of Disk Technologies *(cont.)*

Type	Approximate Data Transfer Rate	Advantages	Disadvantages
IDE/EIDE (continued)		Easy to configure (just add drive to CMOS) Least expensive hardware	Traditional IDE drives were limited to 540MB; enhanced IDE has a work-around for larger drives, but not all BIOS will recognize large drives
SCSI	5MB per	Standard, mature technology Moderately expensive hardware	Must understand SCSI installation, termination, and IDs
FAST SCSI	10MB per second	Speed	Little more expensive
FAST-20 or ULTRA SCSI	20MB per second	More speed	More expensive
ULTRA SCSI-2	40MB per second	Most Speed	Most expensive next to RAID drives

Busmaster Controllers

Some controllers have an on-board processor designed to off-load processing from the CPU. The CPU passes a data or write request to the controller and can then continue with another task. The controller's processor handles the details of the request and interrupts the CPU only when the requested function has been completed. Busmastering is very common on high-end (SCSI) controllers, and is often used on servers.

Caching Controllers

Some controllers have their own memory. When the CPU needs to write data to disk, the data can be written into this memory. This process is extremely fast. The controller then writes the data to disk on its own. As in busmastering, the goal is to free up the CPU as quickly as possible.

WARNING   It is imperative to have a good UPS (uninterruptable power supply) on a server using a caching controller. Once the CPU has finished passing the data to the controller, it considers the data to have been written to disk. If power is lost before the data are flushed from the cache, no fault-tolerance system would be aware of the problem. This is usually not a big issue since most controllers have limits on how long data can sit in cache—but it's better to be safe than sorry.

Hardware-Controlled RAID (Redundant Array of Inexpensive Disks)

RAID technology is designed to add fault tolerance to a disk subsystem. In a RAID system, a duplicate of all data is stored on another disk (this is a simplification—RAID will be discussed in more detail later in the "Choosing a Fault-Tolerance Method" section). If one disk dies, the data can be rebuilt on the fly. Some controllers have RAID technologies built into the hardware.

Once you have chosen a type of disk subsystem and installed the hardware, you must configure those disks for NT. So, the discussion will now focus on partitioning your disks and choosing a file system.

Partitioning

Before a hard disk can be used by an operating system, the hard disk must be partitioned. When you partition a hard disk, you define the boundaries of a physical area on the disk. This area can then be formatted for use by an operating system such as Microsoft Windows NT.

You can use partitioning to organize your data by creating a "boot" partition that contains only NT system files, and another partition to hold your data. On a dual-boot computer, you can create separate partitions for each operating system so that each system file has its own physical space. An organized hard disk makes it easier to find your data.

Proper choices can make managing your disk space easy. Poor choices won't kill you, but could make upgrading difficult—you might end up with two operating systems that just won't get along on one partition.

On the physical level, a disk must be partitioned before an operating system can use its storage space. A partition is made up of unused space on the drive. The unused space will be used to form either a primary or an extended partition. You can create a maximum of four partitions on each disk.

A *primary partition* has the necessary configuration to be used by an operating system for the boot process. You can create up to four primary partitions on a single disk. This allows you to isolate the system files from multiple operating systems on a single drive. One of the primary partitions will be marked as active—this is the partition that will be booted from.

Once a partition is created, it must then be formatted. Formatting sets up the basic housekeeping or accounting system on the partition to allow files to be stored and retrieved successfully by the operating system. While several formats exist, the most popular is file allocation table (FAT). Almost every operating system can read FAT, including DOS, Windows 95, Windows NT, UNIX, and Macintosh.

In addition to FAT, advances in the file systems have developed more mature formats such as HPFS, FAT32, and NTFS. High performance file systems (HPFS) was developed for use with OS/2, and NT file system (NTFS) was developed for use with Windows NT. However, these file systems are not designed to be read by other operating systems such as DOS.

You can set up a computer to dual-boot NT and Windows 95. To accomplish this, the partition must be formatted with the FAT file system (which will be discussed later in the "Choosing a File

System" section). Note that NT cannot read a partition formatted with FAT32 (a file system available on Windows 95 SR2), so do not use this file system on machines on which you intend to dual-boot NT and Windows 95.

Primary partitions cannot be subdivided further. One way to get around the four-partition limit is to use an extended partition. There can be one extended partition on each disk (it *does* count against the four-partition limit). The *extended partition* can be subdivided into multiple logical disks, each of which will be given a drive letter by the system.

Like a primary partition, an extended partition is created from unused space on the drive. Since there can be only one extended partition, you usually create it last and use all of the remaining space on the drive. You can then divide it into logical drives for management purposes.

NT dynamically assigns drive letters to each partition using the procedure shown in Figure 1.12 and listed below.

1. Beginning with disk zero, the first primary partition on each drive is assigned a consecutive letter (starting with the letter C).

2. Beginning with disk zero, each logical drive is assigned a consecutive letter.

3. Beginning with disk zero, all other primary partitions are assigned a letter.

You can override these default assignments in the Disk Administration tool by choosing Tools ➤ Assign Drive Letter. This process will be illustrated in the "Necessary Procedures" section.

Understanding Partition Numbering and ARC Paths

Windows NT assigns each partition an identification number, as shown in Figure 1.13. NT uses the partition number in an ARC path (defined later in this section) to locate the needed area on a disk for read and write operations. For troubleshooting, you need to know how NT assigns partition numbers.

FIGURE 1.12: Assigning drive letters

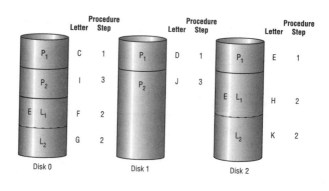

P_X = Primary Partition

E = Extended Partition

L_X = Logical Drive

FIGURE 1.13: Assigning partition numbers

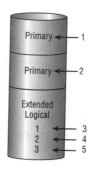

NT assigns a number to all primary partitions first, starting with the number *one,* and then assigns an ID to each logical drive in the extended partition (if one exists).

NT uses the partition numbers in an ARC (advanced RISC computing) path to find the partition. You must understand ARC paths, both for the exam and for real-world troubleshooting. An ARC path will look as follows:

multi/scsi(a)disk(b)rdisk(c)partition(d)

Each *a*, *b*, *c*, and *d* will have a value, as listed in Table 1.6.

T A B L E 1.6: ARC Path Components

Component	Definition
multi/scsi	Identifies the type of controller. If the controller is a SCSI device with the BIOS *not* enabled, this value will be *scsi*; for all others, it will be *multi*.
(a)	The ordinal value of the controller. As each controller initializes, it is given a value—the first will be given a value of *zero*, the next *one*, etc.
disk(b)	SCSI bus number; for *multi*, this value is always *zero*.
rdisk(c)	For non-SCSI disks, this will be the ordinal value of the disk. It is assigned in the same way as *(a)* above.
partition(d)	The ordinal value of the partition (as described above).

ARC paths will be discussed again in Chapter 6, "Troubleshooting."

Choosing a File System

NT supports three different file systems:

- FAT (file allocation table)
- NTFS (NT file system)
- CDFS (CD-ROM file system)

NOTE   Since CDFS is a specialized file system used for CD-ROMs, it will not be discussed here.

FAT File System

The FAT file system has been used since the earliest days of DOS computers. FAT has minimal overhead (less than 1MB) and is the most efficient file system for partitions smaller than 400MB. Since it is the only file system that DOS, Windows 95, and Windows NT have in common, the system partition must be a FAT partition on dual-boot machines. RISC-based computers will boot only from a FAT partition, so all RISC systems must have a small FAT partition to hold boot files.

On the downside, performance decreases as the number of files in a partition increases due to the way files are tracked. Another downside is that the FAT file system has no features to prevent file fragmentation, which can affect performance. As a security feature, Windows NT prevents a deleted file from being undeleted, but on a FAT partition (if the computer is booted to DOS), undelete tools might be able to recover deleted files. Also, there is no file- or directory-level security available on a FAT partition. The only security is that available through directory-level sharing supplied by the operating systems.

The version of the FAT file system included with Windows NT has been enhanced to support long filenames. Filenames adhere to the following criteria:

- Can be up to 255 characters (including the full path)

- Must start with a letter or number, and can include any characters except for quotation marks (" "), forward and backward slashes (/\), brackets ([]), semicolons (;), colons (:), equal signs (=), commas (,), carets (^), asterisks (*), and question marks (?)

- Can include multiple spaces

- Can include multiple periods, but the last period denotes the file suffix, which is similar to DOS 8.3 naming conventions (for example, .EXE, .COM)

- Preserve case, but are not case sensitive

TIP   As an aid to troubleshooting, many administrators create a FAT partition and place the NT boot files there. In the event of a problem, they can then boot to DOS and access the files on the partition, replacing corrupt files or using DOS-based disk diagnostic tools.

NTFS

NTFS is the file system specifically designed for use on a Windows NT–based computer. NTFS offers many advantages over the older FAT file system:

- File- and directory-level security.

- Larger file and partition sizes. Theoretically, both the maximum file and the maximum partition size is 16 exabytes. Functionally, with today's hardware, the limit is 2 terabytes.

- Built-in file compression.

- A recoverable file system. It uses a transaction log for disk activity. The log file can be used to redo or undo operations that failed.

- Bad-cluster remapping. If a write error occurs, the file system will move the data to another sector of the disk.

- Support for Macintosh files. (You must install Services for Macintosh.)

- Support for POSIX.1-compliant software.

- Reduced file fragmentation.

There are only two, small drawbacks to NTFS—since it has a fairly high overhead (approximately 50MB), floppy disks cannot be formatted with NTFS. Also, NTFS does not support removable media (when using removable media formatted with NTFS, you must restart the computer to change disks).

Managing Hard Disks

The next step in planning your disk drive configuration is to determine how those disks will act together to store your data. NT offers many configuration options—you must be able to determine which option is right for your environment.

Volume Sets

You can add together areas of free space on your hard disks to create one logical drive—thus creating a volume set. This process will be examined later in the "Necessary Procedures" section. Once created, this area must then be formatted with either FAT or NTFS. Once you have created the volume set, it will appear as one drive to the system. When using a volume set, NT will fill each segment, before starting to use the next.

You can also add space to an existing NTFS volume by choosing Extend Volume Set from the Partition menu in Disk Administrator. Once free space has been added to a volume set, you cannot take it back. The only way to reclaim that space is to delete the *entire* volume set (and thus any data stored there).

TIP If you need to extend a volume set formatted with the FAT file system, first convert it to NTFS using the CONVERT.EXE command-line tool. Remember that this is a one-way operation—once you have converted to NTFS, you cannot go back to FAT.

Stripe Sets

Like a volume set, a stripe set adds free space on two or more hard ~~BigRedExpress.com~~olume set, however, a stripe set must include space on at least 2 drives (up to a maximum of 32 drives). The areas created must be approximately the same size (if they are not, Disk Administrator will make the necessary adjustments).

When data are placed in a stripe set, the data are written evenly across all physical disks in 64KB "stripes." While a stripe set does not provide fault tolerance, it can improve I/O performance.

Choosing a Fault-Tolerance Method

Because of the critical nature of most data stored on servers, the disk subsystem must be fault tolerant. A *fault-tolerant disk system* can survive the death of a single hard drive, with the data still accessible. The fault-tolerant features of Windows NT are managed through the Disk Administrator tool.

NT provides fault tolerance through software-controlled implementation of redundant array of inexpensive disks (RAID). There are seven primary levels of RAID in the industry; NT Server can implement software versions of three RAID levels—0, 1, and 5. Level 0 (disk striping) is just the ability to create a volume set that spans multiple hard drives. Since this provides no fault tolerance, it will be ignored in this discussion.

Level 1 RAID is commonly referred to as disk mirroring. In a *mirror system,* there is a redundant copy of all data on the partition. With mirroring, if the primary disk dies, the system can switch over to the redundant disk—the users will not notice the hardware failure.

Disk duplexing is a subset of mirroring in which the disks are accessed through separate controllers. In mirroring, if the controller dies, there is no way to access the redundant disk. Since you have multiple controllers in a duplexed system, the server can survive a controller failure—the users will not notice a problem.

Level 5 RAID consists of disk striping (as discussed above) with the addition of a parity set. The *parity set* is a calculation of the contents of the data, placed on another disk in the set. If one disk dies, the RAID system can use the parity information to re-create the missing data on the fly.

Level 1 RAID (mirroring) is an efficient way to provide fault tolerance (especially if you upgrade it to duplexing). Since an entire copy of the data exists on another hard drive, the user will not notice any difference in performance in the event of a hardware failure. However, mirroring is more expensive than level 5 RAID—in mirroring, only 50 percent of the disk space is usable, since the other half is used to maintain redundancy. Mirroring is also the only way to make your system and boot partitions fault tolerant. These two partitions cannot be part of a volume set, stripe set, or stripe set with parity.

Level 5 RAID is very common in today's business environments. It actually increases I/O performance by splitting the work across the hard disks. It is also more cost effective than mirroring. In a level-5 implementation, the more disks involved in the stripe set, the lower the percentage of disk space used for the fault-tolerant information. In mirroring, one-half of the total disk space is used to provide fault tolerance. In a level-5 implementation with the minimum of three disks, only one-third of the space is used to hold the parity information (one-fourth with four disks, one-fifth with five disks, etc.). Level 5 RAID can support up to 32 disk partitions. Keep in mind, though, that level 5 RAID can survive the loss of only one disk. If you lose more than one disk, all the information on the disk array becomes inaccessible and useless.

NOTE Windows NT provides software-controlled RAID. Although this is an inexpensive way to achieve fault tolerance, it is not necessarily the correct choice. Some hardware has been specifically designed to provide RAID functions. In most cases, hardware-based RAID will be faster than software-based RAID.

Necessary Procedures

Most servers act as repositories of data that are accessed by end users. NT administrators must be able to configure and manage the disks on their servers. The procedures for this exam objective concern the skills necessary to manage the disk configuration of an NT server.

Reassigning Drive Letters

You reassign disk drive letters by using the Disk Administrator tool. Click the partition you want to reassign, choose Tools ≻ Assign Drive Letter, and change the letter.

Creating a Volume Set

In Disk Administrator, Ctrl-click all of the partitions that should be included and choose Partition ≻ Create Volume Set.

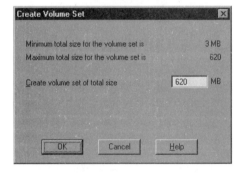

Creating a Stripe Set

In Disk Administrator, Ctrl-click all of the partitions (2–32) that should be included in the set. Remember that the segments must be approximately the same size (Disk Administrator will adjust the size for you if they are not). Choose Partition ≻ Create Stripe Set.

Creating a Mirror Set

In Disk Administrator, Ctrl-click the two partitions that will make up the set (they must be on different hard drives) and choose Fault Tolerance ≻ Establish Mirror.

Creating a Stripe Set with Parity

In Disk Administrator, Ctrl-click the partitions (3–32) that will make up the segments of the set. Remember that these must be approximately the same size (Disk Administrator will adjust the size as appropriate). Choose Fault Tolerance ➤ Create Stripe Set with Parity.

Exam Essentials

Of all the components that can fail on an NT server, the hard disks are the most likely to do so. NT administrators have to understand the options available to minimize the impact of disk failures on their users. Microsoft is quite aware of this, and tests accordingly. Before taking this exam, make sure you are comfortable with Microsoft's disk configuration options.

Know how NT assigns drive letters to partitions. NT will dynamically assign drive letters to each partition using the following procedure:

1. Beginning with disk zero, the first primary partition on each drive is assigned a consecutive letter (starting with the letter C).

2. Beginning with disk zero, each logical drive is assigned a consecutive letter.

3. Beginning with disk zero, all other primary partitions are assigned a letter.

Know how to read an ARC path. An ARC path will look as follows:

multi/scsi(a)disk(b)rdisk(c)partition(d)

Refer back to Table 1.6 for an explanation of an ARC path's components.

Know how to define a volume set. A *volume set* is a collection of partitions combined into one logical drive. The segments do not have to be the same size, and can exist on the same hard drive.

Know how to define a stripe set.   A *stripe set* is a collection of 2–32 partitions, from different hard drives, combined into one logical drive. The partitions must be approximately the same size. NT will write data to each of the drives in succession in 64KB stripes. This is also known as level 0 RAID.

Understand mirroring.   *Mirroring* is having an exact duplicate of a partition on another hard drive. This is level 1 RAID.

Understand duplexing.   *Duplexing* is mirroring, but the two drives must be connected to different controllers. This is another form of level 1 RAID.

Know how to define a stripe set with parity.   A *stripe set with parity* is a fault-tolerant disk system that uses 3–32 partitions in a stripe set. Data are written to each of the drives in succession in 64KB stripes. For each stripe, a calculation of parity information is processed and written to a different drive in the set. This allows the system to re-create the data using the parity information in the event that one of the drive partitions in the set fails.

Key Terms and Concepts

ARC path: A path to a particular partition, on a specific disk, on a computer.

FAT (file allocation table):   The file system used by many operating systems to organize and access data on a hard drive. DOS, Windows 95, and Windows NT operating systems can access the FAT file system.

Fault-tolerant disk system: A disk system with redundant data storage that enables it to continue to function in the event of hardware failure.

NTFS (NT file system):   A file system specifically designed for Windows NT. It was designed for larger hard drives and environments that need file- and directory-level security.

Partition: A physical section of a hard drive, set aside for the use of an operating system.

RAID (redundant array of inexpensive disks): An industry standard definition of fault-tolerant disk subsystems.

RAID level 0/stripe set: A disk system that allows a logical drive to span multiple hard drives.

RAID level 1/disk mirroring: A disk system that has a complete copy of a partition on a separate hard drive.

RAID level 5/disk striping with parity: A disk system that stripes data across multiple drives. In addition, a calculation is performed on each write, which creates parity information that can be used to re-create the data. This information is stored on another drive in the set, which allows the system to continue functioning if one of the drive partitions in the set fails.

Sample Questions

1. Which of the following file systems provides file- and directory-level security?

   A. FAT

   B. HPFS

   C. CDFS

   D. NTFS

   Answer: D

2. Which of the following disk configurations provides some level of fault tolerance?

   A. Volume set

   B. Stripe set

   C. Mirroring

   D. Duplexing

   E. Stripe set with parity

   Answer: C, D, E—Volume sets and stripe sets do not continue to provide services in the event of a disk failure.

3. When a disk fails in a stripe set with parity, you can expect which of the following things?

    A. Users will no longer have access to the data stored on the stripe set with parity.

    B. Users can continue to access the data stored on the stripe set with parity.

    C. Performance will not change.

    D. Performance will degrade.

Answer: B, D—The whole point of a stripe set with parity is to provide fault tolerance. If a disk fails, the system can re-create the data on the fly from the parity information. However, this will probably affect performance since the information must be re-created for each data access.

Choose a protocol for various situations. Protocols include:

- TCP/IP
- TCP/IP with DHCP and WINS
- NWLink IPX/SPX Compatible Transport
- Data Link Control (DLC)
- AppleTalk

In its simplest sense, *protocol* can be defined as a set of rules that govern behavior. Using this definition, one faces, and masters, complex protocols all the time. One of the most common protocols is the one that governs the use of automobiles. Without a set of rules, driving would be a dangerous undertaking (no pun intended).

This analogy can be applied to the protocols that govern the communication between computers. With computers, too, you are controlling traffic on an infrastructure—you need rules that govern right-of-way, how to handle congestion, what types of vehicles are allowed, speed limits, even how to let other drivers know what you are trying to accomplish. If you understand how communication protocols work, it will help you choose the protocols you want to implement in your environment.

You might think that this would be a no-brainer—use all the protocols so that everything can talk to everything else, right? Wrong! Implementing too many protocols on the network is probably the most common cause of slow performance. As a systems engineer, you need to understand when each protocol is appropriate and when it is not. You need to know how you can use a single protocol to provide as many services as possible, and you need to know how to choose that protocol for a given environment. Also, you need to know how to configure each protocol and implement it in the most efficient manner. In other words, you need to understand how computers talk to each other.

NOTE   The objectives in this section are designed to test your ability to choose the right protocols based upon the needs of the network.

A lot of different protocols will be presented. The most important one is probably TCP/IP, because it is the protocol of the Internet. Its strengths and weaknesses will be discussed, as well as two tools to help make implementation a little easier—DHCP and WINS. Microsoft always tests heavily on TCP/IP. This is the protocol of choice—it's one of the three default protocols available when you install NT server.

After the discussion of TCP/IP, "special case" protocols will be discussed. You will implement these protocols only if you specifically need them. Those needs will be defined. (Configuration will be discussed in the next chapter, "Installation and Configuration.")

Critical Information

Of the protocols covered in this objective, the most important one is TCP/IP. Microsoft has made a concerted effort over the last few years to position the NT operating system as Internet-capable. TCP/IP is a key piece of that positioning. Microsoft has also received a bad reputation for its products not integrating well with other operating systems. Microsoft is trying to change that reputation by stressing the various protocol options available in the NT environment.

TCP/IP

TCP/IP is a hot topic in today's networking world. If you pick up any of the industry magazines, you'll find at least one story about the installation, management, or new developments of the TCP/IP suite. TCP is regarded as the future of networking—you will need to understand it to work with the networks of today and tomorrow.

TCP/IP is really a suite of protocols, each piece of which provides a very specific service to the network. The name TCP/IP will be used to refer to the entire suite. If you understand what each piece does, it can greatly increase your ability to solve network-related problems. TCP/IP is also a protocol created, maintained, and advanced by committee. TCP/IP is based upon a complex set of RFCs (requests for comments)—documents that propose additions to the suite and changes to existing protocols. Just about anyone can submit an RFC. It then goes through a series of revisions, until it either gets pushed aside (this happens to most RFCs), gets made an optional piece of a TCP/IP environment, or gets added as part of the standard.

The best way to start when learning TCP/IP is to get a feel for the entire suite. Table 1.7 lists some of the more common protocols in the suite and their functions.

T A B L E 1.7: Common TCP/IP Protocols and Their Functions

Protocol	Function
TCP (transmission control protocol)	Used for connection-oriented, reliable transport of packets
UDP (user datagram protocol)	Used for connectionless, nonreliable transport of packets
IP (Internet protocol)	Provides addressing and routing functions
ICMP (Internet control message protocol)	Used for protocol-level management messages between hosts
ARP (address resolution protocol)	Used to obtain the hardware address of a host. "Resolves" a known IP address to a physical MAC (media access control) address
NetBT (NetBIOS over TCP/IP)	Used by NetBIOS applications to communicate over a TCP/IP-based network
SNMP (simple network management protocol)	An industry standard method of monitoring and configuring hardware or software over a TCP/IP-based network

Windows NT ships with a series of utilities that provide network services on a TCP/IP network. Table 1.8 lists the more commonly used (and tested upon) utilities and their functions.

T A B L E 1.8: Common TCP/IP Utilities and Their Functions

Utility	Function
PING (packet Internet groper)	Tests IP connections
FTP (file transfer protocol)	Bidirectional file transfer services. Requires user to log onto the host providing FTP services, even if anonymous

T A B L E 1.8: Common TCP/IP Utilities and Their Functions *(cont.)*

Utility	Function
TFTP (trivial file transfer protocol)	Bidirectional file transfer services. Usually used for UNIX system code files
Telnet	Terminal emulation to a host offering Telnet services
RCP (remote copy protocol)	File transfer services
RSH (remote shell)	Runs commands on a UNIX host
REXEC (remote execution)	Runs a process on a UNIX host
FINGER	Retrieves system information from the host running the finger service
Microsoft Internet Explorer	Browser software
ARP	Displays local ARP cache
IPCONFIG	Displays your current IP configuration
NBTSTAT	Displays cached information for connections using NetBIOS over IP
Netstat	Protocol statistics and connections
ROUTE	Works with the local routing table
Hostname	Displays the host name of your computer
Tracert (trace route)	Displays the route to a remote host

NOTE For this exam, you will not be expected to be an expert in many of these utilities, but you might be expected to know what functions they perform.

Now for the meat of this objective—how does one know if TCP/IP is the right choice? From Microsoft's perspective, that question really should be—why shouldn't one use TCP/IP? TCP/IP is one of the default protocols when you install NT Server, it is discussed in just about every Microsoft course, it is the default protocol used in the classroom for Microsoft-authorized courses, and it is tested upon in just about every MCSE exam. Why? The following bulleted list describes the benefits of TCP/IP.

- TCP/IP was specifically designed to allow diverse computing systems to communicate. No network operating system can hope to make it in the market unless it provides a common protocol that allows communication with existing systems. Most medium- or larger-sized systems are made up of a mixture of hardware and operating systems, and it is not economically feasible to migrate *everything* to NT at once.

- TCP/IP was specifically designed for a routed network. It is the most routable protocol in use today. If you plan on connecting through any type of WAN link, TCP/IP will give you the best performance, the most control, and the least congestion.

- TCP/IP has SNMP (simple network management protocol). This is the industry standard protocol for use in managing routers, bridges, gateways, and all the other components that make up a network. Just about every network-management software package can use the SNMP protocol, and there is no indication that this will change. The bottom line—if you want to manage your network, TCP/IP will be your protocol of choice.

- TCP/IP is the protocol of the Internet. If you plan on connecting to the Internet, creating a Web site, or using e-mail, you will be using TCP/IP.

- A whole slew of tools is available to make TCP/IP more manageable—not only for managing pieces of your network, but for managing the protocol itself. These tools include DHCP (dynamic host configuration protocol), WINS (Windows Internet name service), DNS (domain name service), and others. These tools take the headache out of installing and configuring TCP/IP hosts (more on these tools later in this section).

TCP/IP with DHCP and WINS

As mentioned earlier, numerous tools are available to help manage the TCP/IP protocols. Two of the most commonly implemented tools are DHCP and WINS. Each of these tools is designed to alleviate some of the more common headaches encountered in a TCP/IP network.

DHCP (Dynamic Host Configuration Protocol)

To really appreciate the value of DHCP, you must understand a little more about how TCP/IP works. In an IP network, each host has a unique identifier called an IP address. This address must be unique when compared to all other hosts that are attached to any network with which the local host can communicate. (Stop and think about this—if you are connected to the Internet, your computer must have an address that is different from the addresses of millions of other hosts that can attach to the Internet.)

A discussion of IP addressing is beyond the scope of this book. This knowledge is tested on the exam for the MCSE course "Intranetworking with Microsoft TCP/IP on Microsoft Windows NT 4.0"— thankfully, you won't need to be an expert for the Enterprise test. You do need to know that a unique IP address must be configured on every device that communicates (using TCP/IP) on your network. Along with the IP address, numerous other parameters might also need to be configured. The traditional method for configuring an IP host was to walk to the device, sit down, and start typing. While this was OK for small companies, it had some big drawbacks on most networks.

Traditional IP Headaches

Here is a list of some traditional IP headaches:

- Configuring each host takes time—and lots of it! Each host was configured by hand, which meant that either someone from the IS department went to each device in turn or you trained your users. Neither solution is an efficient use of time and resources.

- Configuration by hand means mistakes! It does not matter how well you type—if you are configuring 500 machines, you are bound to make at least a couple of mistakes. At best, duplicate or invalid addresses will affect only the host where the mistake was made; at worst, they can affect communication across your network.

- Change is problematic. There is a very strict and complicated set of rules for addressing in an IP network. Networks will grow, and sometimes you have to change your addressing scheme. This means changing the configuration at *all* hosts.

- If you add a new IP-based service, you may need to add or change a configuration parameter at each host.

- If you physically move a device within your environment, you may need to change its IP configuration. Usually, when you move a machine, the last thing on your mind is its configuration (you are thinking about what a pain users are, you are griping about a management team that can't leave well enough alone, or you have a list of more important things that you should be doing). Even worse—users occasionally take it upon themselves to move a device without letting you know. In this case, you have addressing problems and don't even know what has changed.

Why DHCP?   Using traditional methods to manage an IP network was a hassle, but it was necessary. DHCP was designed to overcome some of these hassles. The theory behind DHCP is fairly simple— DHCP is a protocol specifically designed to configure IP hosts as they attach to the network. DHCP runs as a service on an NT server. This service manages a pool of IP addresses and configuration parameters. When a DHCP client boots, one of the first things it does is try to find a DHCP server. If it finds one, the DHCP sends it all of the TCP/IP configuration information necessary to function on the network. From a management perspective, this means you have only one place to manage your TCP/IP environment. You assign addresses appropriately, make changes, and add configuration parameters to the "pool"—these changes are reflected every time a client boots on your network.

WINS (Windows Internet Name Service)   Another tool designed to ease the management of a Windows-based network that uses the TCP/IP protocol is WINS. Once again, to really appreciate WINS, you have to delve a little deeper into how IP and NetBIOS work. (NetBIOS is the upper-level protocol that Windows-based networks use to communicate.) WINS adds two basic services to your network—NetBIOS name registration and name resolution.

Name registration   In a NetBIOS-based network (any Windows network), each computer is given a unique name—the NetBIOS name. Since NetBIOS uses this name to communicate between machines, these names *must* be unique. In a traditional NetBIOS network, each machine sends a NetBIOS broadcast that announces its name as it boots. If another host already exists with that name, it will send a message to the new client saying that the name is in use. If it doesn't get a message back, the client assumes that the name is available.

This process works OK on a single-segment network. Unfortunately, most routers do not pass NetBIOS broadcast traffic. This means that there is no mechanism to prevent two computers from having the same name if they are on different network segments. Duplicate names *will* cause communication errors somewhere down the line!

While routers can be set up to pass these broadcasts, there is a more elegant and effective solution—the Windows Internet naming service (WINS). In a WINS environment, each client is configured with the IP address of the WINS server. When the client boots, it sends a message to this server—a request to use a name. The WINS server keeps a database of all the NetBIOS names that are in use—if the name is *not* already in use, it returns an acknowledgement; if the name *is* already in use, it returns a denial. If the name is approved, the WINS server places a record for that client (made up of its NetBIOS name and IP address) in its database.

WINS clients send a name release to the WINS server when they are properly turned off. This allows the WINS server to update its database so that it contains only names for computers that are currently available on the network.

Name resolution Users shouldn't be forced to remember complicated IP addresses for all of the machines with which they need to
communicate. Unfortunately, acquiring this address is mandatory
before communication can happen. You should give your computers
names that are easy to remember so that users can use a "friendly"
name to represent a computer.

First, the NetBIOS name (the name you gave the computer when
you installed NT) must be resolved into an IP address. Traditionally,
this is done by broadcasting a request on the network. Basically, the
computer shouts on the wire, "Hey, I'm looking for a computer
named XYZ." If computer XYZ receives the request, it will send a
message back that contains its IP address. There are two problems
with this technique. First, broadcast traffic must be analyzed by
every computer on the network, adding overhead to machines that
are not involved in the communication. Second, most routers are
configured *not* to pass broadcast traffic, so your request will be ful-
filled only if you are attempting to communicate with a device on
your own network segment.

To get around the broadcast problem, you could create a text file
named LMHOSTS on every computer. This text file would contain
the NetBIOS name and IP address of every computer with which
you are going to communicate. What a hassle! Every time you add a
new computer to your network, you will have to update the
LMHOSTS file on all other computers in your network.

If you have implemented WINS, though, you already have a database that contains the names and IP addresses of all computers
available on the network. In a WINS environment, when your computer wants to communicate with another computer, it sends a
name-resolution request to the WINS server. This request contains
the NetBIOS name of the machine to which you wish to connect.
The WINS server looks through its database. If it finds a matching
NetBIOS name, it returns the IP address of that machine.

Why WINS? WINS saves time and traffic on your network, therefore helping to keep it efficient. Without WINS, many of the procedures for establishing a connection with another machine are based

upon broadcast traffic. Broadcast traffic is the bane of systems engineers. When a packet is broadcast, all computers that receive it must stop what they are doing and waste time reading the packet to determine if they should respond. In a WINS environment, all of this traffic is directed to the WINS server. It is the only computer that will analyze these packets, while all others continue processing without interruption.

NWLink IPX/SPX Compatible Transport

Now that you have a firm grasp of TCP/IP, you can turn your attention to the other protocols supported by NT. These protocols can be called "special case" protocols, because in most cases you will implement them when the situation demands it, but not as your main protocol for communication.

NWLink is Microsoft's implementation of the IPX/SPX protocol suite used by Novell's NetWare products. On most NT networks, you will implement NWLink only if you need to communicate with a NetWare server. As far as the protocol suite goes, IPX/SPX has some advantages and disadvantages of which you will need to be aware. For that reason, NWLink is not installed by default on an NT machine, Server, or Workstation.

IPX/SPX is easy to implement and manage. There are no complex addressing schemes. Each computer gets its unique identifier from its network interface card. This means that you do not have to configure any unique parameters at each computer for communication to occur. Further advantages include:

- IPX/SPX supports routing between networks.

- IPX/SPX allows you to easily connect your NT environment to your NetWare environment. You can slowly integrate NT servers into your network, without having to replace your existing resources.

NOTE Installing NWLink is only the first step in integration. The rest of the process will be discussed in Chapter 4, "Connectivity."

Although there is no address configuration at each computer, you do have to give unique identification values to each network segment. Unlike TCP/IP, there is no addressing scheme to these addresses. The LAN administrator comes up with a segment-numbering plan and implements it. Other disadvantages include:

- Until recently, there was no way to register your IPX network addresses. This made it difficult to connect to any kind of central network or shared wiring scheme.

- IPX/SPX is not used on the Internet. If you intend to connect to the Internet, you must use TCP/IP.

- IPX/SPX does not support SNMP.

- IPX/SPX uses more broadcast-based traffic to organize the network. Although the process is automatic, it increases the traffic on your network.

NOTE   On the exam, you will implement NWLink only if you need to communicate with Novell NetWare-based file servers.

Data Link Control (DLC)

You need to know even less about DLC than about NWLink. The DLC protocol is mostly used to communicate with printers that are directly attached to the network, or to access SNA (system network architecture)-based mainframes. It can also be used to communicate with some Hewlett Packard network printers, but those are usually legacy hardware installations.

AppleTalk

AppleTalk is the transport protocol developed by Apple for Macintosh networks. The NT implementation is designed to allow your Macintosh clients to access your NT servers for file and print services. Since NT servers are fully AppleShare compliant, they need to be able to communicate with Macintosh clients. Most modern Macintosh clients have TCP/IP connectivity, so that is preferentially used to ensure maximum access to network resources.

NOTE Although AppleTalk allows your Macs to connect, Services for Macintosh must be installed and configured on your server to allow any real functionality.

All Macintosh computers can use AppleTalk to communicate on a network. However, only Macintosh computers can use AppleTalk to communicate. You will still have to configure another protocol for your Windows 95 and NT clients.

Exam Essentials

There is no network without connectivity, and there is no connectivity without properly installed and configured protocols. This statement implies that understanding the various protocols that can be used on an NT network is critical to the success of any MCSE in the field. Microsoft is aware of this and tests accordingly.

Know the advantages of TCP/IP. TCP/IP was designed to allow diverse clients to communicate. Every major operating system can use the TCP/IP protocol suite. TCP/IP was designed to be a routable protocol, has many mature tools available for management, includes SNMP, and is the protocol of the Internet.

Understand the major protocols that comprise the TCP/IP suite. These protocols include TCP (transmission control protocol), UDP (user datagram protocol), IP (Internet protocol), ICMP (Internet control message protocol), ARP (address resolution protocol), NetBT (NetBIOS over TCP/IP), and SNMP (simple network management protocol).

Know the tools commonly used on a TCP/IP network. These tools include PING (packet Internet groper), FTP (file transfer protocol), TFTP (trivial file transfer protocol), Telnet, RCP (remote copy protocol), RSH (remote shell), REXEC (remote execution), FINGER, Microsoft Internet Explorer, ARP, IPCONFIG, NBTSTAT, Netstat, ROUTE, Hostname, and Tracert (trace route).

Understand why DHCP is used.   On a traditional TCP/IP-based network, each host must be configured with a unique IP address and other TCP/IP-based parameters. By using a DHCP server, you can avoid this manual process. DHCP was designed to configure IP clients dynamically from a central server.

Understand why WINS is used.   Traditional NetBIOS networks use broadcast traffic to ensure that computer names are unique and to find the IP address of each host with which they must communicate. A WINS server provides two services:

1. It builds and controls a database of registered names on the network, thus preventing duplication.

2. Clients can access this database to resolve a NetBIOS name into an IP address.

Since the clients are configured with the IP address of the WINS server, any WINS traffic will be directed to it via broadcast. Unlike broadcast packets, these directed packets can cross routers, thus ensuring communication across a routed network.

Know when to install NWLink on an NT server.   You use the NWLink protocol if your NT server must communicate with a Novell NetWare server.

Understand the advantages and disadvantages of NWLink. NWLink is easy to implement and manage, supports routed networks, and allows easy connection to NetWare servers. However, each network segment must have a unique address, most network addresses are not registered with a managing service (which can make it difficult to connect to a shared wiring system), NWLink is not used on the Internet, it does not support SNMP, and it uses more broadcast traffic to organize the network.

Know when to implement DLC.   You use DLC to connect to certain older HP line printers or mainframe environments.

Know when to use AppleTalk.   You use AppleTalk when there are Macintosh computers on your network that must communicate with an NT server and cannot support TCP/IP protocols.

Key Terms and Concepts

AppleTalk: The native protocol of Macintosh computer networks.

Data link control (DLC):   A protocol usually associated with HP line printers or mainframes.

Dynamic host configuration protocol (DHCP):   A service that configures TCP/IP clients automatically as they attach to the network.

LMHOSTS: A text file, stored on each client, used to store NetBIOS names and their associated IP addresses.

Name registration: An action taken by the client as it joins the network. The NetBIOS client queries the WINS server to determine if its name is unique.

Name resolution: Before two NetBIOS computers can communicate, they must acquire each other's IP addresses. Name resolution is the process of asking a WINS server for the IP address of a particular NetBIOS name.

NWLink: Microsoft's implementation of the IPX/SPX protocol suite.

Simple network management protocol (SNMP):   One of the protocols in the TCP/IP suite. This protocol was designed to allow remote monitoring and management of resources, and is commonly used by network management tools.

TCP/IP: A suite of protocols designed to provide diverse computing environments with the ability to communicate.

Windows Internet name service (WINS):   A service used to build a database of NetBIOS clients and their IP addresses. This database is used to prevent duplicate names on the network and resolve names into IP addresses.

Sample Questions

1. Which of the following protocols must be used to communicate over the Internet?

   A. TCP/IP

   B. NWLink IPX/SPX Compatible Transport

   C. Data Link Control

   D. NetBEUI

   E. AppleTalk

   Answer: A

2. Which of the following protocols must be used to communicate with a Novell NetWare server?

   A. TCP/IP

   B. NWLink IPX/SPX Compatible Transport

   C. Data Link Control

   D. NetBEUI

   E. AppleTalk

   Answer: B

3. DHCP is used to perform which of the following tasks?

   A. Assign IP addresses to clients

   B. Dynamically upgrade client software

   C. Configure NetBEUI parameters

   Answer: A

CHAPTER

2

Installation and Configuration

Microsoft Exam Objectives Covered in This Chapter:

Install Windows NT Server to perform various server roles. Server roles include: *(pages 62 – 72)*

- Primary domain controller
- Backup domain controller
- Member server

Configure protocols and protocol bindings. Protocols include: *(pages 72 – 88)*

- TCP/IP
- TCP/IP with DHCP and WINS
- NWLink IPX/SPX Compatible Transport
- DLC
- AppleTalk

Configure Windows NT Server core services. Services include: *(pages 88 – 99)*

- Directory Replicator
- Computer Browser

Configure hard disks to meet various requirements. Requirements include: *(pages 100 – 108)*

- Providing redundancy
- Improving performance

Configure printers. Tasks include: *(pages 108 – 124)*

- Adding and configuring a printer
- Implementing a printer pool
- Setting print priorities

Configure a Windows NT Server computer for various types of client computers. Client computer types include: *(pages 125 – 129)*

- Windows NT Workstation
- Windows 95
- Macintosh

Now that you have planned your network—chosen the domain model, designed a disk subsystem, and chosen a protocol—the next step is to implement your plan. In this chapter, the installation and configuration of an NT server in a multiple server or domain environment will be thoroughly discussed. If you make the proper choices during the installation of NT, it will make working with that server easier in the future. At best, if you make a wrong choice, you will have to work a few extra hours. At worst, you will have to reinstall the operating system.

If you sit down at the computer knowing what to expect and what choices you need to make, NT installation will take very little time and go smoothly, and that server will be ready for use as soon as you are done.

Before starting the installation process, you will want to ask yourself a number of questions:

- What type of server will this be: primary domain controller (PDC), backup domain controller (BDC), or member server?

- What protocols are you using? What IP address and subnet should you use?

- Does this machine have to talk to any other types of systems, such as a NetWare server?

- What type of network interface card did you buy? And what drivers does it need?

- If you see two drives in the box, should you mirror them?

- What types of clients need to access this server?

Install Windows NT Server to perform various server roles. Server roles include:

- Primary domain controller
- Backup domain controller
- Member server

When you install an NT server, you should have a clear idea of the services that it will provide to your network clients. An NT server can provide numerous services—from DHCP and WINS to acting as a domain controller and your e-mail server. Each of these services will add overhead to a server. This overhead will be characterized in Chapter 5, "Monitoring and Optimization." For now, the discussion will be limited to the first service-related decision you have to make during the installation—whether a server should be a domain controller. In Chapter 1, a domain controller was defined as a server that holds a copy of the domain accounts database (SAM). However, as you'll see in this section, that definition is not complete.

Critical Information

One of the first things that you do when planning a network is determine the role each server will perform. This decision will influence your purchase plans, network design, and long-term management.

Primary and Backup Domain Controllers

Primary and backup domain controllers are similar—they both hold a copy of the SAM and are used for authentication during the logon process. Since they are alike in their duties, their hardware needs are similar. Before their function is examined, hardware will be discussed.

Necessary Hardware

The process of choosing hardware for a domain controller is not as easy as it would seem. Sure, you *could* just buy the best computer that you can afford—but how do you know whether that will be enough? Before you buy your server, you need to know the load.

Load is mainly determined on a domain controller by the size of the SAM. The bigger the SAM, the bigger the load. A big SAM indicates a large number of users, and the more users there are, the more logons the server will have to authenticate and the more changes there will be to the database. Before you can determine the minimum requirements for a domain controller, you need to approximate the size of the SAM it will support.

If you took the Microsoft-authorized Course 689, "Supporting Microsoft Windows NT 4.0 Enterprise Technologies," you have a piece of software to help you. From your class CD-ROM, install the Job Aid and follow the directions. If not, you'll have to use math.

The number of objects you define determines the size of the SAM. Each object represents a record in the database; each type of object has a record of a different size. Table 2.1 describes the sizes of the various records in the SAM.

T A B L E 2.1: Objects in the SAM

Object Class	Size
User account	1KB
Computer account	.5KB
Global group account	512 bytes plus 12 bytes for every member
Local group account	512 bytes plus 36 bytes for every member

You need to estimate the number of user and computer accounts that you will create. This *should* be easy—determine how many users and NT-based servers and workstations are in your company.

Next, you need to estimate the number of groups that you will create. Analyze the resources you will share, then come up with a plan for sharing each resource. This will tell you approximately how many groups you will need to create. Once you have the number of groups, estimate how many users will be members of each group. Take the numbers and do a little math.

Once you've calculated the size of the database, use the information in Table 2.2 to determine the minimum hardware needed to support it.

WARNING These numbers were obtained from Microsoft's TechNet Technical Information Network (Article Q130914). They are probably a little low for most installations, because Microsoft assumes that the server will be dedicated to the task of acting as a domain controller—in other words, that you will not use the server to provide any other network services.

T A B L E 2.2: Hardware Requirements Based upon SAM Size

Number of Users	SAM Size (MB)	CPU Needed	RAM Needed (MB)
3,000	5	486DX/33	16
7,500	10	486DX/66	32
10,000	15	Pentium, MIPS, or Alpha	48
15,000	20	Pentium, MIPS, or Alpha	64
30–40,000	40	Pentium, MIPS, or Alpha	128

When planning your domain, you should compare the estimated size of the SAM with the hardware you will have available as a server. If the hardware won't support the SAM, buy a more robust server.

The only other option is to split the domain into multiple domains, until the hardware *will* support the SAM, which can make for a long-term administrative headache.

Now that you have chosen your hardware, the functions of domain controllers can be discussed. The primary responsibility of domain controllers is user authentication. Since domain controllers are the only computers that hold the accounts database, all users must access them when logging onto the network. When the user logs onto the network, their name and password are compared to information in the SAM. If the name and password match an existing account, the domain controller creates the SID (system identification) for that user. The SID contains the identification and the access control elements of the user and any groups of which the user is a member. This information will be used when the user tries to access a resource, so copies of the accounts database must be synchronized on a regular basis. If it isn't, information about the user might not be current at the domain controller to which the user attaches during the logon process.

Synchronizing Primary and Backup Domain Controllers

The primary domain controller holds the main copy of the accounts database. All changes to the SAM must be made on the primary domain controller (PDC), which then updates the copies stored on the backup domain controllers (BDC). This is known as a *single master model*, because all changes are made to the master copy and then synchronized with all other copies. The process of synchronization is fairly simple. Every time a backup domain controller comes online, one of the first things it does is try to find the primary domain controller (PDC) to verify that its user accounts database is up to date. The PDC keeps a log of all changes to the database. Each change that has been made is given a version ID—think of this as a counter. When the PDC updates a BDC, it records the highest version ID (counter) on the updated records. The next time the PDC checks for changes, it compares the highest version ID of the last synchronization with the version IDs in the change log. If anything in the change log has a higher value than the last recorded update of the BDC, that change has not been synchronized on the BDC. The PDC will then synchronize the changes on the BDC.

By default, the PDC checks the BDC version IDs against the change log every five minutes. This time period is referred to as the pulse. There are two types of updates—partial and complete. In a partial update, only the changed information is synchronized. In a complete update, the entire database is sent to the BDC. From an optimization perspective, it is preferable to do a partial update rather than send the entire database.

A complete update might occur for various reasons:

- Every time a new BDC is brought online.

- When the change log fills up (it has a specific size), the PDC starts writing over the oldest change records. If there are enough changes in a pulse, the last known version ID for a BDC will no longer be in the change log. In this case, the PDC can no longer be sure of exactly which changes have been synchronized and which have not. At this point, a complete update must occur.

- When an error occurs during a partial update.

- When the administrator forces a complete update. (Use Server Manager to accomplish this task.)

This synchronization traffic can have an impact on where you physically place domain controllers on the network backbone. If you place a backup domain controller on the other side of a WAN link, the synchronization traffic will have to cross that link—this could affect the link's ability to support other types of traffic. On the other hand, if you don't place a BDC across the wire, all logon traffic will have to cross the link to find a domain controller for authentication.

Microsoft expects you to understand the trade-off between synchronization traffic and logon traffic. For faster synchronization, put all domain controllers in a central location. For faster logons, put the domain controllers near the users so that logons can be done locally.

WARNING Most consultants consider synchronization traffic to be a reasonable cost of business. You don't optimize for background traffic—you optimize for your users. If you force users to cross a WAN link every time they log on, it is not a good design. The logon process will take too long, and if the link is down, users cannot log onto local resources. Distributed design adds significant redundancy and insulates your network somewhat from data-pipeline outages that can be beyond your control.

Most of the time, you will distribute domain controllers across your network so that users don't have to cross any slow links to log on, which means that the synchronization traffic *will* have to cross those links. If you are short on bandwidth, you can change a couple of registry parameters to control the amount and frequency of traffic generated.

Synchronization Parameters in the Registry

There are two ways to control synchronization traffic—controlling how often it happens and/or controlling how much traffic is generated. Both of these methods are accomplished through a parameter called the ReplicationGovernor. This parameter is set to a percentage. By default, it is set to 100 percent, which means that the PDC can take up to 100 percent of the available bandwidth and buffer 128KB of data at a time. This can greatly affect a slow link where users are also competing for a limited amount of bandwidth. If you set the ReplicationGovernor to 50 percent, the NetLogon service can buffer only 50 percent as much data (64KB) for each transmission and can have synchronization messages on the network only 50 percent of the time. This will spread out the traffic over twice as much time.

WARNING If you set this value too low, it can prevent synchronization from completing. It can also make more complete updates (rather than partials) occur because it takes longer for changes to be synchronized.

You can also change the timing of the pulse. By default, the PDC checks for changes every five minutes. You can increase this time by increasing the pulse parameter—to a maximum value of 48 hours. (Once again, though, if you check for changes less frequently, it is more likely that you will be forced to do a complete update.)

To increase the odds of being able to do partial updates, increase the size of the change log by changing the ChangeLogSize parameter. By default, the change log is 64KB, which is enough room to record approximately 2,000 changes. You should make changes to the pulse and the ChangeLogSize in parallel.

Member Server

A *member server* is any NT server that was not installed as a domain controller. Unlike domain controllers, member servers are not involved in the management of the domain accounts database, which means that the processing power and memory will be more fully utilized by functions other than domain administration. You might install a server as a member server for three reasons:

- You already have enough domain controllers for your environment. Microsoft recommends that you have at least one backup domain controller for fault tolerance. After that, though, they recommend one backup domain controller for every 2,000 users. If you have 5,000 users and 10 servers, Microsoft would recommend one PDC (mandatory for each domain) and three backup domain controllers, for a total of four domain controllers.

- A server performs a function that is so processor or memory intensive that no resources are left for the overhead of acting as a domain controller. Perhaps the server will act as an SQL or Exchange server. In this case, you might choose to limit any other services that it provides.

- Member servers can be moved from domain to domain. Domain controllers, on the other hand, cannot be moved from the domain into which they were installed. If a server might be moved from domain to domain, it would be better to install it as a member server.

Exam Essentials

As discussed in Chapter 1, planning is critical if you want to create an NT-based network that is manageable. You must understand the role of your NT servers. This objective concerns the various roles that NT servers can take in your network. For this exam, you must be comfortable with the various services that an NT server can provide.

Understand domain controllers.   A domain controller is an NT server that holds the domain security accounts manager (SAM) database. Because it holds the database, the server can perform authentication functions during the logon process.

Know the difference between a primary domain controller (PDC) and a backup domain controller (BDC).   The PDC holds the master copy of the domain accounts database. All changes and additions to the database must be made to this copy first. The PDC then synchronizes those changes to all of the BDCs in the domain. BDCs hold a copy of the domain accounts database. They receive all changes made to the master copy from the PDC on a regular basis.

Understand member servers.   A member server is any NT server that was not installed as a domain controller. Member servers cannot be used to authenticate a user to the domain. Unlike domain controllers, member servers can be moved from one domain to another.

Understand the process for determining the hardware needed at a domain controller.   First, estimate the size of the SAM. Then, check Table 2.2 to determine the hardware that will be necessary for a SAM of that size. If your hardware will not support the SAM, upgrade as needed. Otherwise, partition the database until you reach an estimated size that your hardware will support.

Understand the synchronization process between the PDC and a BDC.   Every five minutes (the default pulse value), the PDC checks its SAM for changes. It compares the version ID for the last changes sent to the BDC with the version ID of changes in the change log. It will synchronize all changes in the change log that have version IDs greater than that of the last change updated to the BDC.

Understand how the ReplicationGovernor works. The ReplicationGovernor is a registry setting that controls the synchronization process between domain controllers. It controls how often the synchronization process will occur and how much data can be transferred. By default, it is set to 100 percent, which means that 128KB of data can be buffered for updates and the PDC can utilize 100 percent of the available bandwidth to accomplish this task. If you change the value to 50 percent, the PDC can buffer only 64KB for transfer and can have synchronization messages active only 50 percent of the time. If you set this value too low, the BDCs may never fully synchronize.

Key Terms and Concepts

Backup domain controller (BDC): An NT server that performs authentication functions using a copy of the domain accounts database.

Change log: A log of the changes made to the domain accounts database. Used to determine which records need to be updated on the BDCs.

Domain controller: An NT server that holds a copy of the domain accounts database.

Primary domain controller (PDC): An NT server that performs authentication functions using the master copy of the domain accounts database.

ReplicationGovernor: A registry setting that controls the frequency of synchronization and the amount of data transferred.

Synchronization: The PDC holds the master copy of the SAM. When changes are made to the database, the process of synchronization updates the copies stored on the BDCs.

Version ID: Each change in the change log is given a version ID (counter). The PDC compares the version ID of the last change replicated to the BDC with the version ID of changes in the log file. Changes with higher values need to be replicated.

Sample Questions

1. When the change log fills up, which of the following things will occur?

A. A new log will be created.

B. Records will be overwritten.

C. A complete update will occur in the next pulse.

D. An administrative alert will be sent to members of the administrators group.

Answer: B, C—The change log records transactions to the domain SAM. If it fills up between synchronization pulses, the oldest records will be overwritten. Since this means that certain changes might not have been synchronized to the BDCs, a complete update will occur.

2. If you are placing domain controllers to facilitate the logon process, which of the following statements would be correct?

A. Place all domain controllers on the same side of a WAN link.

B. Place domain controllers near the users that will need them.

C. The placement of domain controllers will have no effect on the logon process.

Answer: B—Users must access a domain controller each time they log onto the network. If all domain controllers are across a WAN link (from the users), authentication traffic will have to cross that WAN link every time a user logs on.

3. To update a member server to a domain controller, what would you do?

A. Use the PROMOTE.EXE command-line utility.

B. Reinstall Windows NT, choosing to make the server a domain controller during the installation process.

C. Use Server Manager.

D. Install the domain controller service in the Network control panel.

Answer: B—There is no convenient way to promote a member server to a domain controller. The only method would be to back up all data, install NT Server, and then restore your data from the backup.

Configure protocols and protocol binding. Protocols include:

- TCP/IP
- TCP/IP with DHCP and WINS
- NWLink IPX/SPX Compatible Transport
- DLC
- AppleTalk

In this section, the installation and configuration of the protocols discussed in Chapter 1 will be examined. For each protocol, the tools used for installation and the configuration parameters available will be discussed.

Critical Information

Unfortunately, you will probably encounter a number of questions on the exam in which the answers are a list of menu choices. This is why you will see a lot of lists and screen captures in this chapter.

TPC/IP

Numerous configuration options are available with the TCP/IP protocol. Fortunately, only a few are absolutely necessary for communication. The first choice you will have to make is whether this machine should get its IP configuration from a DHCP server. In most cases, you will want to manually configure the IP information at NT servers just in case the DHCP server goes offline.

WARNING If you configure your servers as DHCP clients, you could be asking for a big problem. Suppose that a storm knocks out power at your office. When the power comes back on, all of your servers will power up and boot. (Of course, if you have a proper UPS, this wouldn't be an issue.) When they boot, they will look for the DHCP server to configure them. If that server either didn't boot properly or booted slow, your other servers won't get IP addresses. However, don't take this to mean that DHCP isn't the right tool for client workstations.

You can set three IP addressing parameters: the IP address, the subnet mask, and the default gateway.

If this server is to be a DHCP client, click Obtain IP Address from DHCP Server on the Properties page for the TCP/IP protocol; if not, you need to configure the parameters described in Table 2.3.

TABLE 2.3: IP Parameters

Parameter	Description
IP address	A 32-bit unique identifier for each host on an IP network. The four-octet address is made up of two parts—a network address and a host or node address.
Subnet mask	Used to identify which portion of the IP address represents the network and which portion represents the host. Most IP networks are divided into subnets to help control traffic on the wire.
Default gateway	Identifies a router address to send all packets that are not local (the destination is not on the local subnet).

SEE ALSO For more information on subnetting, see the Sybex book *MCSE: TCP/IP Study Guide, Third Edition,* by Todd Lammle.

If your environment includes WINS servers, your server needs the IP address of your WINS servers.

If you use DNS (domain name service) on your network, you will need to configure the DNS information for this server. DNS will be discussed in Chapter 4, "Connectivity."

TCP/IP with DHCP and WINS

The configuration of DHCP and WINS clients was examined above. Now, setting up the DHCP and WINS server services will be discussed.

DHCP

Once you have added the DHCP service to a server, you will find a new tool in the Administrative Tools group—DHCP Manager. Although a complete discussion of the configuration of a DHCP server is beyond the scope of this exam, you will need to know a couple of the basics. These basics will be discussed in the "Necessary Procedures" section.

WINS

WINS is also installed as a service on your server. Once it is installed, you will find a new menu item in your Administrative Tools group—WINS Manager. There isn't a lot to configure at a WINS server. If the service is turned on and your clients are configured with the correct IP address, WINS builds the database without much trouble.

WINS provides two basic services to your network—name registration and name resolution. When a WINS client initializes, it contacts that WINS server, announcing itself and its name. The WINS server checks its database to ensure that the name is unique on the network. If not, the WINS server will send back a negative acknowledgement—the client will display a message saying that the name is already in use on the network. If the name is not already in use, WINS will add the name and IP address of the client to its database.

When a WINS client needs to access another computer on the network, it will contact the WINS server, asking for the IP address of the destination computer. The WINS server will search its database for a computer with the name requested and return the IP address if available.

The only configuration information that you need to be aware of is the partner relationship between multiple WINS servers. If a company has multiple sites, it won't want its clients to have to cross the WAN link every time they need to communicate with a local host. In this case, you would set up a WINS server on each side of the link. Each WINS server would build a database of the local computers. You can then configure the two WINS servers to trade their databases back and forth so that each has a complete list of the computers in your network. The process of trading the databases is called WINS replication.

There are two kinds of partnerships—push and pull. In a push relationship, the WINS server waits until a certain number of changes have been made to the database. When this number has been reached, the WINS server will alert all of its partners that replication needs to occur. In a pull relationship, each server asks its partners for changes at scheduled intervals.

NOTE This has been a very quick discussion of configuring DHCP and WINS on an NT server. While it should be enough for the Enterprise exam, it is not the entire story. For more information, check out the Sybex book, *Mastering TCP/IP for NT Server 4*, by Todd Lammle and Mark Minasi.

NWLink IPX/SPX Compatible Transport

As discussed in Chapter 1, NWLink is usually used to communicate with Novell NetWare environments. You will need to configure only two parameters: internal network number and frame type.

The internal network number is used to identify servers on an IPX/SPX network. In the case of NT, you might set this if your server is running a program that can be directly accessed by clients. (In an NT environment, this would probably be SQL Server or Microsoft SNA Server.) In other words, the program can be accessed *without* logging onto the NT domain. This allows Novell clients to access the service without loading Microsoft Windows client software. The internal network number is a hexadecimal value that must be unique across your entire IPX/SPX network.

The frame type defines how IPX/SPX packets will be formed for transmission on the physical wiring of the network. Each packet transmitted on the network has a series of headers attached to the data. These headers identify items such as the sender of the packet, its intended recipient, a checksum (calculation against the contents that can be re-created at the destination to see whether the packet has been corrupted in transit), or other information defined by the protocol. The definition of how these headers are organized is called the frame type. Many frame types are defined to be used in an IPX/SPX network.

The nice thing about NT is that it will pick a packet off the network and determine its frame type for you. To configure this, click Auto Frame Type Detection on the Properties page for the NWLink protocol. Unfortunately, NT will detect only one packet type in the automatic mode. So, if you are using multiple frame types on your network, you will have to manually configure them. On the same page, click the Add button and pick the frame type(s) in use from the drop-down list.

That's it for configuring the NWLink protocol. Of course, it is only half the story. To actually communicate with a NetWare server from a Windows NT domain client, other services must be installed and configured. These will be discussed in Chapter 4, "Connectivity."

DLC

There are no configuration options available with this protocol. To install this protocol, open the Network control panel and select the Protocols tab. Click the Add button.

AppleTalk

The AppleTalk protocol is installed as part of the Services for Macintosh service. The configuration of this environment will be discussed later in this chapter.

Protocol Bindings

In the most generic sense, to *bind* is to link components at different levels to enable communication. The architecture of NT is made up of various layers—each layer provides a certain type of service. Some of these services will need to communicate with the services on another layer. The process of binding enables this communication. In the discussion of protocols, binding referred to establishing a communication channel between the network adapter card driver and a protocol.

On a simple server, you don't need to worry too much about protocol bindings. By default, each protocol you install will be bound to all network adapters installed in the computer. In a more complex environment, though, you can control the use of the binding of protocols to increase security or performance.

Increasing Security

Binding enables communication between the adapter's driver and a protocol. If you do *not* bind a protocol to an adapter, that card cannot communicate using that protocol. You can use binding to control traffic on your network and provide increased security.

To increase security, first consider your environment. Which protocols are needed, and where are they needed? Suppose that you work for the following company:

> King Technologies, LLC, is a small company made up of less than 10 employees. The owner of the company has decided that the company should be represented on the Internet. You have been assigned the task of implementing a Web server and ensuring security. After discussing the project, you decide that:

- You want to ensure that no traffic from the Internet can make it to your internal Web.

- None of your employees need to access the Internet at this time.

- You will host the Web server on your own machine so that you have total control.

After analyzing your needs, you determine that you really don't need TCP/IP on your internal network. You will use NetBEUI instead, because it is fast and easy to configure. Your server will have two network adapters installed—one attached to the internal network, one with access to the Internet. You can use the protocol bindings to ensure security by disabling the TCP/IP binding to the adapter attached to your internal network. This configuration would ensure that no TCP/IP traffic can be routed from the Internet to your internal network.

Increasing Performance

In the Network applet on the Binding tab, you can manage the protocol bindings. The protocols are bound to both server and workstation services. The order in the list of bindings affects the efficiency of network communication. When an NT-based computer attempts to communicate with another device on the network, it will try to communicate using the protocols in the binding list—in the order that they are listed. If you have multiple protocols in the list, make sure that the most commonly used protocol is listed first.

As an example, assume that you have a TCP/IP-based network. Because of a few legacy NetWare servers, you added the NWLink protocol to your NT servers. If NWLink is listed first in your binding list, all communication attempts will try to use IPX/SPX first, and switch to TCP/IP only after IPX fails. You can decrease connection time to most hosts by moving TCP/IP to the head of the list.

Necessary Procedures

The MCSE exams are designed to determine a candidate's ability to perform administrative tasks associated with an NT network. Protocol management is a big part of those tasks. Be comfortable with the various procedures listed for this objective before you take the exam.

Installing a Protocol

You install all of the protocols discussed in this chapter from the same location. To install a protocol, do as follows:

1. Right-click the Network Neighborhood icon on your desktop and choose Properties (or open the Network control panel).

2. Click the Protocols tab.

3. Click the Add button. You will see the following list:

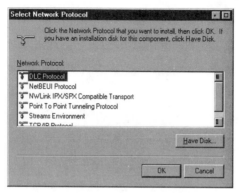

Installing a Service

The network services discussed in this section are installed in a similar manner:

1. Right-click the Network Neighborhood icon on your desktop and choose Properties (or open the Network control panel).

2. Click the Services tab.

3. Click the Add button. You will see the following list:

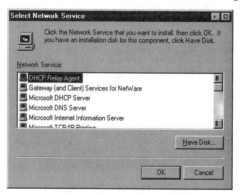

Setting the IP Addressing Information

You can configure the following addressing parameters: IP address, subnet mask, and default gateway.

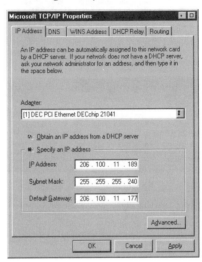

Setting the WINS Server Address

Access the configuration screen by clicking the WINS Address tab on the protocol's Properties page. Add the primary (and secondary) WINS server IP addresses.

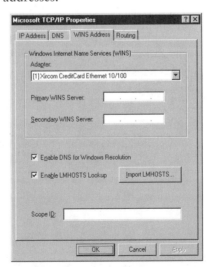

Setting the DNS Client Information

Enter the host name for this computer (in most cases, it will be the same as the NetBIOS name) and the IP addresses of your DNS servers.

Configuring DHCP as a Server

There are two main configuration tasks associated with setting up the DHCP server. Both are accomplished through DHCP Manager. The first task is to create a scope. The scope is the pool (or pools) of IP addresses that this server will hand out to clients. For each subnet on which this server might provide addresses, you will need to create a different scope if a DHCP relay agent is not available to pass broadcast DHCP messages across the subnet boundary.

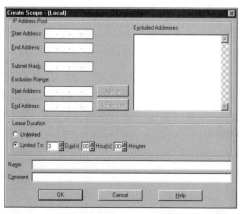

When configuring the scope, you will need to provide the information listed in Table 2.4.

T A B L E 2.4: DHCP Scope Parameters

Parameter	Description
Start and end address	The contiguous range of IP addresses that this scope hands out to clients.
Subnet mask	Identifies which portion of the IP addresses represents the network address. Subnet masking is often considered the most confusing part of configuring an IP network.
Exclusion range (start, end)	If some addresses within the defined range should not be given to clients, you can exclude those addresses here.
Lease duration	DHCP clients "lease" an IP address from the DHCP server for a defined period of time. When a client is given an IP address, the DHCP marks that address as in use. If the client machine is removed from the network, the address will be marked as available when the lease time runs out.
Name	A descriptive name for administrative purposes.

The second task in configuring DHCP services is to decide which additional TCP/IP configuration parameters should be associated with each scope. In addition to the minimum IP address and subnet mask , you might need to set many parameters on your clients—everything from a default gateway to the address of your WINS servers.

To add a parameter to a scope, scroll down the list on the left, pick the parameter, and click the Add button. Then, with that parameter highlighted in the Active Options list, click the Value button and set the value(s).

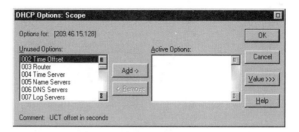

Configuring a DHCP Relay Agent

You will need to be aware of one more DHCP for this exam—the DHCP relay agent. When a DHCP client asks for and receives its IP configuration, all traffic in the process is broadcast based. As you'll remember from Chapter 1, most routers are configured to block broadcast traffic. This presents a problem when using DHCP on a routed network—the clients are not able to reach the DHCP server if it is not on their own subnet. To overcome this limitation, you can configure an NT server as a DHCP relay agent. The agent is configured with the IP address of your DHCP server.

The DHCP relay agent "listens" for the broadcast traffic generated when a client tries to find a DHCP server. The agent passes this request along to the DHCP server. Because the agent is on another subnet, it must have a static IP address (you must manually configure the address). Since it has been manually configured *and* knows the IP address of a DHCP server, it can use directed calls to cross the router.

Configuring NWLink

Open the Network control panel. On the Protocols tab, highlight NWLink IPX/SPX Compatible Transport and click the Properties button. Unless you need to change the default values, leave the Internal Network Number set to 00000000 and Auto Frame Type Detection selected.

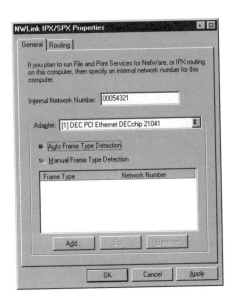

Exam Essentials

While you are not expected to be an expert in each of the protocols listed in this objective, you are required to be comfortable with them.

Know the three main TCP/IP parameters and what they represent. The parameters are as follows:

IP address—A 32-bit unique identifier for each host on an IP network. The address is made up of two parts—a network address and a host address.

Subnet mask—Used to identify which portion of the IP address represents the network and which portion represents the host. Most IP networks are divided into subnets to help control traffic on the wire.

Default gateway—Identifies a router to send all packets that are not local (the destination is not on the local subnet).

Know what is entailed in setting up a DHCP scope. Two main tasks are involved in configuring a DHCP scope—entering the beginning and ending IP addresses with the subnet mask in the range that the DHCP server will manage; and configuring any additional parameters that should be configured on each client.

Know the function of a DHCP relay agent. Since most routers are configured to not pass broadcast traffic, and DHCP traffic is broadcast based, DHCP clients cannot usually receive their IP addresses from a DHCP server on a different subnet. The DHCP relay agent passes requests on behalf of these clients using directed traffic.

Understand the purpose of the partner relationship between two WINS servers. A WINS server is used to register all NetBIOS names on the network, and in all name resolution requests. If your network spans a WAN link, all of this traffic will cross that slow, expensive connection. To control this traffic, you can create a WINS server on each side of the link. Each will be responsible for the requests of clients on their own side. To ensure that all client names are unique, you can configure these two WINS servers to trade their databases on a regular basis so that no duplicate names will exist on the network and clients can resolve the names of hosts across the wide area link.

Understand the two types of WINS partnerships—push and pull. In a push relationship, each WINS server will inform its partner of changes after a set number of changes have been made to its WINS database. In a pull relationship, each WINS server will request changes from its partners on a regular schedule.

Understand what the IPX network number is used for. The IPX network number uniquely identifies a server on an IPX/SPX network.

Understand what a frame type is. A frame type is a definition of how the data within a packet should be organized.

Understand the uses for the DLC protocol. The DLC protocol is commonly used to communicate with printers directly attached to the network, and with mainframe computers.

Know when to use the AppleTalk protocol.   There is very little exam material regarding the configuration of AppleTalk. Just know that it is the protocol used to communicate with Macintosh computers. A NT server can use this protocol, but only if the Macintosh is using an Ethernet or similar common physical network interface.

Understand how to use protocol bindings to increase security. You can increase security by using a different protocol on each side of a router. By not binding each protocol to both network interface boards, traffic cannot be routed between them.

Understand how to use protocol bindings to increase performance.   When a packet is received, NDIS (network driver interface specification) passes that packet to each protocol until one of them accepts it. By placing the most efficient or frequently used protocols early in the list, you can reduce the amount of time involved in processing each packet.

Key Terms and Concepts

Binding: To link components at different layers of the operating system so that they can communicate. More specifically, to link the NDIS NIC driver to a communication protocol.

Default gateway: The IP address of the device to which a client will send packets destined for a host on another IP subnet.

DHCP relay agent: A computer designated to pass DCHP requests to a DHCP server across a router.

Domain name service (DNS):   A TCP/IP service used to resolve an IP address from a host name.

Dynamic host configuration protocol (DHCP):   A service used to configure IP clients as they attach to the network.

Frame type: The definition of the industry standard way to organize data and headers within a packet. On an IPX network, two computers cannot communicate unless they are using the same frame type.

IP address: A unique identifier for each host on an IP network.

Scope: A definition of the IP addresses and other configuration parameters that the DHCP server should send to clients as they initialize.

Subnet mask: An IP parameter that identifies which portion of the IP address represents the network address.

Windows Internet name service (WINS):   An NT service designed to register NetBIOS names to ensure that they are unique, and to resolve NetBIOS names into IP addresses.

WINS partner relationship: A pair of WINS servers configured to trade their databases so that each server has a list of resources on the entire network.

Sample Questions

1. Which of the following TCP/IP configuration parameters are mandatory for clients on a routed network?

   A. IP address

   B. Subnet mask

   C. Default gateway

   D. DNS server address

   Answer: A, B, C—The DNS server address would be important for the process of finding resources using fully qualified domain names, but is not critical to the functioning of TCP/IP.

2. Which of the following items describes the purpose of a subnet mask?

   A. To mask out unwanted hosts from your Network Neighborhood

   B. To prevent communication between a list of hosts

C. To define which portion of the IP address represents a network and which represent a host

D. To define a NetBIOS scope ID

Answer: C—The subnet mask defines the number of bits that represent the network ID portion of an IP address.

3. Which of the following parameters should be configured for the IPX/SPX protocol?

A. Frame type

B. Packet size

C. Network number

D. NetWare server name

Answer: A, C—The frame type defines how packets are formed—what headers will be included and in what order they will appear in each packet. The network number identifies the network segment.

Configure Windows NT Server core services. Services include:

- Directory Replicator
- Computer Browser

NT can be configured to work on a small scale, but it is also flexible enough to expand to an enterprise. Microsoft knows that you don't want to work any harder than necessary, so they have provided core services to alleviate some of the pain of routine and mundane tasks. Windows NT Server core services are as follows:

Directory Replicator—Provides the ability to automatically move logon scripts, policies, folders, and files from one server to another.

Computer Browser Services—Makes it possible to see network resources from the Network Neighborhood utility. Computer Browser Services establishes the hierarchy of how search tasks are divided and which domain controller will fill which role.

NOTE If you are operating a small network with a single domain, containing one or two servers, this objective will not have much impact on your world. As you study for the MCSE exam, however, you will need to understand this material.

Critical Information

It is time to figure out what information is passed from one server to another, how many applications you have on the network and where the licenses are kept, and how many of your domain controllers are overworked. It is now up to you to configure (tweak) the network. You can assign the server that will keep track of information and replicate it. The replicating server can service several other servers. Not every server needs to receive the same information—you can be selective. Backup domain controllers can either participate in the browser election process or wait for the results to determine their place in life.

Directory Replicator

Directory replication is a method of copying files and folders containing commonly used information from one NT server to another. This can also be referred to as an update. The most common items that need to be replicated are logon scripts, system policies, and information commonly shared across the network. In addition, you can use replication for load balancing by choosing which information to send to a server at a certain time of day or night.

Directory replication has several components. You must have an export server, an import computer, and export and import directories.

Export server—This is the single point of administration for the shared files, but a network can have as many exporters as they have servers. Changes you make to this server will be replicated throughout the system, as you designate. The export server must be running NT Server.

Import computer—You can't export without something willing to import. The import computer can be running NT Server, NT Workstation, or Microsoft LAN Manager OS/2 servers. These machines receive the information from the export servers. An import computer can receive updates from more than one export server, just like an export server can export to multiple import servers.

Export and import directories—How does the export server know what to export to each import computer? This is done through a series of folders and subfolders that each of the computers knows about and agrees on. For example, by default, information to be exported will be placed in subfolders of the \Winnt\System32\ Repl\Export folder. As a system administrator, you will create subfolders and files under this folder for each group of files that need to be exported.

Each import computer will have a directory that corresponds to the export server's export directory. For example, suppose that your network is the backbone of a company that is growing rapidly. It is necessary to export and import information to servers at each of the regional offices. Take a look at the directory structure below. The system will be configured to export/import this spreadsheet.

On the export server, you have the following directory:

    \Winnt\System32\Repl\Export\INF

On the import computer, you have the following directory:

    \Winnt\System32\Repl\Import\INF

TIP If you want to set a default import and export path, use Server Manager. These folders must be manually configured. Files stored directly under the export directory will not be exported.

Now that the folders are in place, here is a broad overview of how the system works:

- Information that needs to be passed to other servers is saved to the Export folder on Server-1. The replication service on Server-1 checks occasionally to determine whether there is anything that needs to be replicated. When it finds new information, it sends an update notice to all the computers or domains that are configured to import from the INF folder.

- Once the import computer has received the update notice, it checks the export server's directory structure.

- The import computer will now copy any new or changed files to its import directory. In addition, it will do some house cleaning—it will delete any files or subfolders that are no longer present in the export directory.

Computer Browser

You will definitely need to know about browser service. This service allows workstation and server computers to use Network Neighborhood to see other resources.

At this point, you know that when you add a computer to a domain, people can use Network Neighborhood or Explorer to browse for shares or services that are offered to the network. What keeps track of where all those computers are located and how to find the services that are offered? Computer Browser Services provides this service. There are five types of browsers:

Domain master browser—The computer on your desk is part of a massive computer network. Your WAN could have hundreds or thousands of servers, services, and shares available to users. What keeps track of all that information? The primary domain controller (PDC) is not just for authentication and management. It has several other responsibilities, including maintaining a master list of services available for the entire domain. That makes it the domain master browser. The PDC delegates some of its chores. The first delegation goes to the master browser.

Master browser—In any network, there is at least one workgroup. If you have a larger network, you may have several workgroups. If you have several network cards in your file server and are using the TCP/IP protocol, you will have several subnets in your network. Each of these workgroups or subnets must have a master browser. If there is another NT server on the subnet or in the workgroup, when that server comes up, it will check in with the master browser and tell it what services the newcomer has to offer. When you open your Network Neighborhood, the new server and its services will magically appear. What does the master browser do with the list of all services available in its workgroups or on its subnet? It passes that list up to the domain master browser so that the domain master browser knows where everything is in the domain.

Backup browser—The backup browser acts as a kind of backstop for the master browser. The master browser is always trying to keep track of all the services on the subnet or in the workgroup. While the master browser is gathering and sorting all of that information, the backup browser answers all of the "where is" requests floating around the network. The backup browser gets its list from the master browser.

Potential browser—The potential browser is otherwise known as the browser wanna-be. This computer just hangs out while waiting to become a browser.

Nonbrowser—The name says it all. This computer cannot act as a browser. Actually, it is probably too busy doing other things to be bothered with answering browser requests.

How does a master browser get to be a master browser while a potential browser waits around with all of its potential going to waste? Computer networking is really much more democratic than you may have thought—the systems can call for an election.

For example, suppose that you boot your workstation and go into Network Neighborhood looking for the Joke Repository share. Your computer first looks to the master browser and asks for a list of backup browsers. Once your computer has the list of backup browsers, it will ask the backup browser for the location of the share. If the master browser fails, a browser election is held. The election is somewhat weighted. For example, if a computer is running NT Server, it gets more votes than a computer running NT Workstation. If a computer is just running Windows 95—you get the picture.

Now that all of the computers with NT Server have checked in, there is still a deadlock—NT 4 is higher than NT 3.51, so it gets more votes. If there is still a tie, the backup browser will get a higher vote than the potential browser.

You can rig the election by tweaking the HKEY_Local_Machine\ System\CurrentControlSet\Services\Browser\Parameter setting. If you set the parameter to Yes, the system will always try to become a browser. If you set the parameter to No, the system will sit on the sidelines and watch the elections go by. If you set the parameter to Auto (the default), it ensures that the server is at least a potential browser.

Necessary Procedures

This objective covers a lot of really useful material, even if it were not on the exam. The fact that most of this material is covered on the exam makes this section even more critical.

Configuring the Replication Service

Before you start configuring directory replication, review the basics:

- You need something to share.

- You must configure the replication service.

- You must configure an export server.

- You must configure an import server.

- Information stored in the \Winnt\System32\Repl\Export root folder will not be exported. You must manually create subfolders to share information.

To configure directory replication:

1. The replication service needs a user account. This account is set up just like any other user account—using User Manager for Domains. The account must meet the following criteria:

   - All logon hours are allowed.

   - The User Must Change Password at Next Logon checkbox must be cleared.

   - The user must be a member of Backup Operators and the Replicator group for the domain.

   - The Password Never Expires checkbox must be selected.

2. Open the Services control panel. Click Directory Replicator Service to open the Directory Replicator Service window.

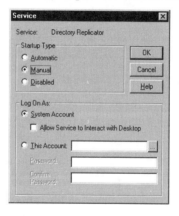

3. The Directory Replicator Service window is used to configure Directory Replicator to start automatically and to log on using the account you just created. You will have to enter the password and a confirmation for the password.

Configuring the Export Server

To configure the export server:

1. Create the folders that will be replicated. These folders must be created in the folder \Winnt\System32\Repl\Export.

2. Start Server Manager by selecting Start ➤ Programs ➤ Administrative Tools ➤ Server Manager.

3. Highlight the Export Server and press Enter.

4. Choose Replication.

5. Select Export Directories and click Manage.

6. Click Add.

7. Type in the name of the subdirectory and click OK to call up the Manage Exported Directories window.

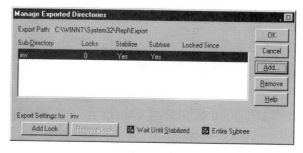

You will notice several checkboxes at the bottom of the window and selections to add or remove a lock.

- Add Lock prevents the directory from being exported.

- Wait Until Stabilized makes the file remain in the subdirectory for a set period of time before being exported.

After clicking OK, you can choose to which computers you want to export these files:

1. Select Add (located under To List:).

2. Highlight and select the computers to which you want the information copied.

3. Click OK.

4. Click OK again—replication services will start.

Configuring the Import Computer

To configure the import computer:

1. Open the Services control panel. Configure the Directory Replicator to start automatically and log on using the account you just created.

2. From Server Manager, configure the import computer to import files from other computers or domains.

To manage the import process:

1. Start Server Manager.

2. Highlight the import computer and press Enter.

3. Choose Replication, which will bring up the Directory Replication window.

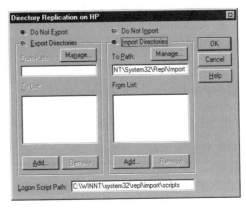

4. Select Import Directories and click Manage.

5. Click Add.

6. Type in the name of the subdirectory and click OK.

After clicking OK, you can choose the computers from which you want to import:

1. Click the Add button under From List:.

2. Highlight and select the computers from which you want the information copied.

3. If you click Manage, it will allow you to enter specific subdirectories from which you will be importing. You will also be given information on whether the subdirectory is locked, the status of the master file, when the last update has been received, and how long the folder has been locked. You can also use the Manage screen to lock the receiving folder.

4. Click OK.

5. Click OK again—replication services will start.

All information that is placed in these subfolders will be replicated to other servers. Policies and logon scripts will be covered in more detail later in the book.

Configuring a Computer to Participate in Browser Elections

To configure a computer to participate in the browser elections, you must modify the \HKEY_LOCAL_MACHINE\SYSTEM\ CurrentControlSet\Services\Browser\Parameters\MaintainServer-List parameter:

1. Start \WINNT\System32\Regedt32.EXE.

2. Select the HKEY_LOCAL_MACHINE hive.

3. Double-click SYSTEM.

4. Double-click CurrentControlSet.

5. Double-click Services.

6. Double-click Browser.

7. Double-click Parameters.

8. Click MaintainServerList. At this point, you can enter three values: Yes, No, or Auto.

   ▪ Yes—Computer will be a master or backup browser.

   ▪ No—Computer will not be a browser.

   ▪ Auto—Computer can be a master, backup, or potential browser.

If your computer is on a network that does not have a PDC (such as a workgroup), you can force a computer to be the master browser by changing the key \HKEY_LOCAL_MACHINE\SYSTEM\ CurrentControlSet\Services\Browser\Parameters\IsDomainMaster to True. It is set to False by default, even on a PDC.

Exam Essentials

Exam writers really like parts of this section. You will see questions on licensing modes and the different types of browsers.

Know the default directory path. Anytime there are mandatory directory structures involved, it is a good idea to memorize them. In this case, remember the \WINNT\System32\Repl\Export and \WINNT\ System32\Repl\Import directories.

Know where to put information to be replicated. You must manually create subfolders on both the export server and the import server before any replication can take place.

Know the difference between a domain master browser, master browser, and backup browser. The domain master browser is always the PDC. It maintains the domain master list. Each workgroup or subnet must have a master browser. It gathers information on services for the domain or subnet, gives the list to the PDC to include in the domain master list, and passes the list to the backup browser. The backup browser answers all the browsing inquiries and gets the browser list from the master browser.

Key Terms and Concepts

Backup browser: Answers all the browsing inquiries and gets the browser list from the master browser.

Domain master browser: Always the PDC. Maintains the domain master list.

Hive: A part of the registry made up of keys, subkeys, and values. A hive is stored in its own file \\WINNT\System32\Config.

Logon scripts: Batch files, executables, or another form of command structure attached to a user account to configure the environment after logon.

Master browser: Each workgroup or subnet must have one. Gathers information on services for the domain or subnet, gives the list to the PDC to include in the domain master list, and passes the list to the backup browser.

System policy files: Another way of controlling the user's work environment or system configuration.

Sample Questions

1. WINS provides what kind of name resolution?

A. DNS name to IP address

B. IP address to DNS name

C. NetBIOS name to IP address

D. IP address to NetBIOS name

Answer: C—WINS resolves NetBIOS computer names to IP addresses, even if the computers are not on the same subnet.

2. The types of browser computers include:

A. Domain master browser

B. Backup browser

C. Potential browser

D. BDC browser

Answer: A, B, C—Computers can be a domain master browser, backup browser, or potential browser.

Configure hard disks to meet various requirements. Requirements include:

- Providing redundancy
- Improving performance

In Chapter 1, disk technologies were discussed, including partitioning, choosing a file system, and configuring your disks on an NT server. In this chapter, the procedures for setting up disks and the best configurations for different types of environments will be examined.

Critical Information

When the time comes to configure the hard drives on your NT-based computer, you will have to make a few choices. There are two bottom-line considerations:

- Redundancy
- Performance

One of the important functions of most servers is central storage of data. If your environment demands instant access to the information on your server, you will have to purchase hardware that can meet those needs. Before buying hardware, you will have to compare the various technologies to find a disk system that will meet the needs of your users and still fit within your budget.

Although performance is an important consideration, reliability is even more important. NT includes various fault-tolerant disk configurations that you can implement to make your system more reliable. Most of these solutions include a type of redundant storage. When used in this context, *redundant* refers to a disk system that can withstand a disk failure without interfering with the users' access to data. This is accomplished by storing data (or information about those data) in two locations. If the first location fails, the second can fill in until you have corrected the problem.

Providing Redundancy

Because of the number of options available, it can sometimes be hard to keep track of what you can and cannot do on an NT computer. Microsoft expects all MCSEs to know the differences between the various disk options. On the exam, you will probably see a few questions about which configuration would be best in a given situation.

NT provides fault tolerance though software-controlled RAID. There are many levels of RAID in the industry—NT supports RAID levels 0, 1, and 5. Level 0 is the ability to create a volume set that spans multiple hard drives. Since this provides no fault tolerance, it can be ignored in this discussion.

The various disk options available are as follows:

- Volume set—Combining areas of free space on one or more drives into one logical drive. Data are written to each disk until the allocated portion is full before moving to the next disk in the set.

- Stripe set—Combining free areas on two or more drives into one logical drive. Data are written in 64KB stripes across all disks in the set.

- Mirroring—Creating a duplicate of all data on a redundant disk. If the primary disk fails, the system will use the mirrored disk.

- Duplexing—A subset of mirroring with the two disks attached to different controllers. Provides fault tolerance in the event of a controller failure.

- Stripe set with parity—A stripe set with the addition of a parity calculation on each write. The parity information is written on a different disk than the one that holds the actual data. If one disk in the set fails, the system can re-create the data on the fly from the parity information.

NOTE This knowledge is heavily tested. If you are unclear on any of the available configurations, review Chapter 1 before continuing.

Of the five options, only mirroring, duplexing, and stripe set with parity offer any fault tolerance. Without fault tolerance, the loss of a single hard drive will cause the loss of data and potential downtime. With a fault-tolerant disk system, the loss of a disk does not cause a loss of services.

The Importance of a Fault-Tolerant Disk System

Often, the Accounting department is hesitant to purchase the extra hardware necessary for a fault-tolerant disk system. Never lose this argument. Add up the number of people who would not be able to perform their duties in the event of a network problem. Next, estimate an average hourly wage for these people. Multiply the number of people times the average wage—this is the hourly cost of downtime.

The next step is to call the vendor you purchase equipment from and ask them how long it would take to deliver a hard drive of the same size as the one currently in your server. Multiply the hourly cost of downtime by the time it would take to acquire and install the drive.

Now you know what a dead disk will cost your company. If the Accounting department is still not convinced, remind them that this estimate does *not* include the cost of reentering any data that might have been input since the last backup or data that might be lost in the process.

Next, you need to decide on the form of fault tolerance that best fits your environment. Table 2.5 compares mirroring with stripe set with parity.

T A B L E 2.5:   Mirroring Compared with Stripe Set with Parity

Mirroring	Stripe Set with Parity
50 percent of the disk space is used to provide fault tolerance.	33 percent of the disk space is used to provide fault tolerance in a three-disk set (25 percent in a four-disk set, 20 percent in a five-disk set, etc.).
Can decrease write performance. This is not the case in a duplexed system.	Can increase I/O performance.
Can hold the NT system or boot partitions.	Cannot hold the NT system or boot partitions.

A stripe set with parity is usually your best bet, because it provides better performance at a lower cost. Remember, though, that the NT system and boot partitions cannot be part of a stripe set with parity. Many companies set up a duplexed set for the system and boot partition, and a stripe set with parity for all other data. This provides a completely fault-tolerant disk environment.

For the exam, you must be able to calculate the size of a stripe set or stripe set with parity given a description of the disks. When you take the exam, read the questions carefully to determine what is being asked. Here is an example:

Suppose that you are implementing a stripe set with parity across four disks. Three of the disks have 500MB of free space; the other has 400MB. Two questions might be asked:

- In Disk Administrator, what is the total size of the stripe set with parity? Remember that the areas of free space must be approximately the same size. The smallest free space is 400MB. The stripe set would be made up of four 400MB segments—for a total of 1600MB.

- What is the total amount of useable space in this stripe set? The size of each segment has been determined. Because of the parity information, the total *useable* space will be one-divided-by-*x* times less than the total (*x* equals the number of disks in the set). In this case, the total useable space would be one-quarter less than the total, or 1200MB.

Improving Performance

After you protect your data by building a fault-tolerant disk system, the next consideration is performance. Purchasing fast hardware is the first step. Disk technologies were discussed in Chapter 1, so it is assumed that you bought high-quality, fast hardware. You can do a few other things to increase the performance of your disk subsystem.

Spreading the Load

When you get ready to install applications and data on your server, stop to think about the physical layout of your disks. Your disk subsystem is the path to your applications and data. If you have multiple controllers in your machine, you have multiple paths for traffic. Use that to your advantage. If you are installing two disk-intensive applications, split them between drives on separate controllers. Another option is to buy the fastest RAID level 5 hardware equipment you can afford. The bottom line here is to use all of your resources equally—don't overwork any single component.

Moving or Splitting the Paging File

One function is disk intensive on almost every busy NT server—the use of the paging file. NT uses a process called demand paging to swap information from memory to a file named PAGEFILE.SYS. Unfortunately, NT does not use a very sophisticated method to determine which disk will hold this file. The paging file will be placed on the partition with the most free space when you install NT. At that point, you haven't installed any applications or placed any data on the server. If you have multiple disks and plan to install a disk-intensive program on the server, you will probably place it on the largest disk. Guess which disk has the most free space when PAGEFILE.SYS is created?

After the installation of NT, you can move the paging file or even create multiple smaller paging files across separate disks. On many servers, if you move the paging file to a disk that is less busy, it will noticeably increase performance. Remember that the physical disk(s) that contains the system and boot partition is always busy. Microsoft recommends that you move the paging file off these disks if possible.

Necessary Procedures

Microsoft is proud of its fault-tolerant disk configuration solutions. You should know how to implement them for the exam.

Creating a Mirror Set

Use Disk Administrator to create mirror set. Highlight two partitions of equal size (on two different disks) and choose Fault Tolerance ➢ Establish Mirror.

Creating a Stripe Set with Parity

In Disk Administrator, Ctrl-click the partitions that will make up the segments of the set. Remember that they must be approximately the same size (Disk Administrator will adjust the size as appropriate). Choose Fault Tolerance ➢ Create Stripe Set with Parity.

Exam Essentials

The importance of the disk subsystem was stressed in earlier objectives. The number of times that this subject is covered should indicate its importance.

Know the three fault-tolerant disk configurations offered by Microsoft Windows NT. They are mirroring, duplexing, and stripe set with parity.

Be able to compare mirroring with a stripe set with parity. Review Table 2.5.

Be able to calculate the total size of a stripe set with parity.
Remember that all segments must be the same size. Take the
smallest segment available and multiply its size by the number of
disks in the set.

Be able to calculate the useable size of a stripe set with parity.
Of the total space, the size of one segment will be used to hold parity
information. Subtract the size of one segment from the total space to
find the total useable space.

Know the two methods for improving disk performance. Split
the workload over multiple disks and controllers, and move the
paging file to a less-busy disk.

**Explain what you can do with the paging file to improve system
performance.** Microsoft recommends that you don't place the
paging file on the system or boot partitions. Try to place the paging
file on your least-busy physical disk. You can also split the paging file
between disks to spread the workload over more devices.

Key Terms and Concepts

Duplexing: A subset of mirroring in which each disk is attached
to a different controller.

Fault tolerance: When a system is designed to survive the failure
of one of its components.

Mirroring: A disk configuration in which two disks hold the
same data.

Stripe set: When areas of free space on two or more drives are
combined into one logical drive. Data will be written to each disk
in turn in 64KB stripes.

Stripe set with parity: A set of three or more disks to which data
are written in turn in 64KB stripes. For each stripe, a parity calculation is performed—the results are stored on another disk in the set.

Volume set: When areas of free space are combined into a logical
drive. Each segment will be filled with data before anything is
written to the next segment.

Sample Questions

1. How many partitions can exist on a hard disk?

    A. 1

    B. 2

    C. 4

    D. There is no limit.

Answer: C—Each hard drive can have a maximum of four partitions, one of which can be an extended partition.

2. On a system with two hard drives, drive 0 has one primary partition and one extended partition with three logical drives; drive 1 has two primary partitions and one extended partition with two logical drives. What would be the assigned drive letters for drive 1?

    A. g, h, i, j

    B. d, e, i, j

    C. d, j, h, i

    D. c, d, e, f

Answer: C—Drive letters are assigned in the following order: Starting with drive 0, the first primary partition on each drive is assigned a consecutive letter (starting with the letter C); starting with drive 0, each logical drive is assign a consecutive letter; starting with drive 0, all other primary partitions are assigned a letter.

NOTE For these kinds of questions, use your scribble pad. Draw out the drives with all partitions and logical drives, and then follow the rules.

---

3. Which of the following ARC paths would point to the second partition of drive 1 in the question above? (Assuming IDE disks.)

    A. multi(0)disk(0)rdisk(2)partition(2)

    B. multi(0)disk(1)rdisk(0)partition(2)

C. scsi(0)disk(1)rdisk(0)partition(2)

D. multi(0)disk(1)rdisk(0)partition(1)

Answer: A—Each component of the ARC path represents a piece of the path to a partition. If this is confusing, review the material for this objective.

Configure printers. Tasks include:

- Adding and configuring a printer
- Implementing a printer pool
- Setting print priorities

What is the name of the device that actually puts the ink/ toner to paper? In the real world, you go out and buy an XYZ laser *printer*. In MicroSpeak, the object you load paper into is called a *printing device*. However, don't let the name change fool you—a printing device is still connected to a computer by way of a parallel or serial cable. Printing devices can also be connected directly to the network or through an infrared port.

If a printing device is the object that puts ink to paper, what is a printer? A *printer* is the software interface that takes the information from your application and redirects it to a printing device.

Another term that requires definition is print driver. A *print driver* is the piece of software that translates application information into the printer-specific commands that are passed to the actual print device. The printing objective receives *lots* of attention on the exam. This objective and the objective on configuring hard disks to meet various requirements are probably the hardest hit. You have been warned—read carefully.

Critical Information

In the NT print architecture, the application that you use to generate the output does not care about the kind of printer you are using. It just sends the job off to the printer and the print job magically appears. This magic is made up of many processes that work together to give your users the desired results.

Adding and Configuring a Printer

Printing is an ever-evolving process. You will constantly add or upgrade printers to make sure that your users have access to the appropriate resource. For example, you don't want to provide the CEO's administrative assistant with a high-speed dot matrix printer to send out the boss' correspondence, when a laser printer would do a better job.

Printer configuration has many aspects, depending on the driver that is supplied with the printer. Usually, you will be able to configure paper size, input trays, duplexing, fonts, and paper layout. You can also specify default settings for specialty printers. To understand the complexities of printing, you must understand the entire printing process—from the selection of Print to the final output.

To make this workflow more understandable, suppose that you need to print a copy of last week's expense report. You open the file in Excel, click Print, and your workstation goes to work. It first attaches to the printer device to which you will print. This is more complicated than it seems. For example, the workstation client can obtain a software print driver from the server, which means the print driver does not have to be stored locally (on the workstation) or updated at the workstation if a new driver comes out. It can be upgraded at the print server—the print server will update everything else.

Excel has no idea what kind of printer your report will go to, nor does it care. It simply creates an application print request and passes that request to the graphics device interface (GDI). The GDI is the first of several "translation" pieces. The GDI takes the application print request and translates it into device driver interface (DDI) calls.

Next, the print request begins to move from the generic to the specific. The DDI calls apply specific printing characteristics to the document. Notice that the term used was *printing* characteristics, not *printer* characteristics—the job has not gotten far enough to worry about a specific printer. When the DDI gets done with the file, it can now be called a print job. There are two types of print jobs:

Raw print job—A set of commands that the printer will understand to produce the final product.

Journal file print job—A list of DDI calls that can be used to come up with a raw print job. This is used when the printer is directly attached to the workstation printing the job.

The print job still isn't printer specific. Now that the DDI calls have been stored in the print job, the print driver comes into play. It takes these generic calls and turns them into printer-specific commands.

The print job is basically complete. It just needs to find its way to the right printer. So, the printer router takes over. It looks at the print job and figures out the best way to get it to its destination printer. The printer router does not look for the actual printer—it looks for the print spooler. The print spooler (also called a provider) is the holding area where the job waits until the printing device is ready to print the job. When the printing device is ready, a print monitor takes the job from the print spooler and feeds it to the printing device.

NOTE The print monitor is actually three DLL files. One handles local printing devices through the parallel and serial ports. This is the LOCALMON.DLL. The HPMON.DLL sends jobs to HP printers hooked directly to the network rather than to a computer. The LPRMON.DLL (LPR stands for line printer) sends jobs to Unix print daemons.

Printing devices come in several categories:

- Network printing device—A printing device hooked directly to the network cable.

- Local printing device—To be local, the printing device must be hooked directly to the server computer.

- Remote printing device—Any printing device hooked to another computer on the network.

In this book, connecting a network printing device to the system will not be discussed. If you are configuring a network printing device, you are using a third-party printing solution. Follow the manufacturer's installation instructions.

Implementing a Printer Pool

Every network administrator reaches the time in their professional life when the amount of paper to be generated by a specific department is greater than the capacity of a single print device. A decision must be made—upgrade to a bigger, faster print device, or just add another print device of the same type to take up the slack. If you decide to add another printer of the same type, you can create a printer pool to double your output. With a printer pool, one printer controls multiple printing devices. This is beneficial to the administrator, because print jobs are spread across multiple printers, balancing the load and decreasing the time an end user must wait for their output. A particular printing device will not sit around without printing, while jobs are stacking up for another device.

While this concept sounds appealing, there are some catches. First, the printing devices in the printer pool must be the same type—they must use the same driver. For the sake of logistics, it is also a good idea to have all of the devices located in the same area, because the print job will be given to the next available printer in the pool. Users get really finicky when they show up to collect a print job at one printer and the job has printed to a printer on the other side of the room.

Setting Print Priorities

To set a print priority, you must first configure two printers for the printing device in question. One of the printers is granted a higher priority. When two print jobs hit the printers at the same time, the printer with the higher priority will print and the other job will wait.

NOTE   Print priorities are set from 1 to 99. A printer with a priority of 99 has a higher priority than a printer with a priority of 1. Higher numbers print first.

Necessary Procedures

There is much to do in this objective. You will install several different kinds of printers and printing devices, create a printer pool, and set up print priorities.

Creating a Local Printer

Here, you are creating a local *printer*. Before you can send tasks to a local *print device*, you have to configure a local printer.

To create the local printer:

1. Log on as an administrator on the computer.

2. Choose Start ➤ Settings ➤ Printers.

3. Double-click the Add Printer icon.

4. Because you are creating a local printer, check the My Computer radio button. Click Next.

5. Choose the port to which the printer will be attached. Click Next.

6. You will see two lists. The one on the left allows you to select the manufacturer of your printer. The one on the right lets you pick the model of your printer. Make your choices and click Next.

7. Give your printer a name. If it will be the default printer (the one you usually print to), select the Yes checkbox; otherwise, select No. Click Next.

8. If you want to share the printer, enter a share name. What if you want the printer to be shared by something other than a Windows product? Hold down the Ctrl key and click all of those other operating systems with which you want to work. Then, click Next to continue.

9. The Wizard will let you print a test page. This is usually a good idea, because it helps in troubleshooting. If there is a problem, it is good to find it early.

10. Make sure that you have your NT Server installation CD-ROM handy. NT may ask for it to copy some files.

11. If you look closely at the Printer window, you should notice a new icon for your printer. You can use the icon to make changes to the printer.

12. Click OK to exit the Install a Printer Wizard.

Configuring a Local Printing Device

Now that the printing device is installed, it is time to configure it. Configuration is done from the Printers control panel. Choose the printer you want to configure, highlight it, right-click, and select Properties.

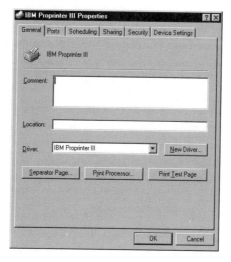

As you can see, there is plenty to play with on this page. The properties shown here are a function of the particular print driver, so your Properties page may not look like the one shown.

General Tab

Under the General tab, you will see the New Driver button. If you click it, the first screen will warn you that changing the drivers may change the Properties screen. If you agree to the warning, the system reopens the Add Printer Wizard to the driver's page. Make your selection here, or use the Have Disk function.

Back to the General tab. If you click Separator Page, it will allow you to put a page between each document or switch printing modes from PCL to PostScript. You can create a document for this purpose and browse to it. Once you have found the document you want, click OK. This option is important in the following situations:

- In a busy office where many people share the same printer. The separator page will let your end users know when they have grabbed someone else's document.

- If you are using a laser printer that can handle both PostScript and PCL languages, but cannot automatically sense the change. This was the case in early versions of the HP III SI. Most printers that can use both PCL and PostScript can automatically sense—the printing device recognizes the PostScript header and switches to PostScript mode automatically.

The Print Processor button allows you to choose the way you want jobs processed. The print processor is the rendering piece of the printing puzzle—it is where the print job is completed before being sent to the print monitor. NT provides two generic processors, with selections for each.

- Windows print processor:

    - RAW—Set of instructions that will result in a printed document.

    - RAW (FF Appended)—Puts a form feed at the end of the job, if one is not already there.

- RAW (FF Auto)—Automatically puts a form feed at the end of a print job.

- NT EMF 1.003—When you print a document that contains a read-only embedded font not listed as an installed font in the Fonts folder, Windows NT uses a substitute font if the printer is set to use NT EMF 1.003 mode. Windows NT prints the font correctly in RAW mode.

- Text—Prints documents in Text mode.

- Macintosh print processor:

  - Handles jobs sent from a Macintosh workstation to a non-PostScript printer attached to an NT computer. In other words, this processor translates PostScript code into something the designated printer can understand.

The last selection on the General tab is self-explanatory—Print Test Page. This is a great place to start troubleshooting.

Ports Tab

While looking at the Ports tab, you will notice all of the standard ports that any good computer should have. There is LPT1 to LPT3 for your parallel printing devices, COM1 to COM4 for serial printing devices, and the FILE selection so that you can print to a file rather than a real printing device. If this does not give you enough choices, you can always add your own port by clicking the Add Port button. If you click Add Port, you can add specialty ports, such as a digital network port, DLC ports, TCP/IP ports, or a local port. When you configure the port, it will set the Transmission Retry parameter. The Transmission Retry parameter sets the amount of time the user must wait before NT reports that the printer is not available. This setting not only affects the specific printer, but all printers using the same driver.

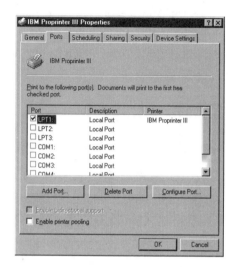

Don't overlook the two checkboxes at the bottom of the screen. The top checkbox allows you to enable or disable bidirectional support. The bottom checkbox allows you to enable printer pooling.

NOTE A printer pool is defined as multiple print devices of the exact same type that work together. For example, you may have six HP LaserJet 5Ps combined into a printer pool to provide printing services for the Word Processing area of your company.

Scheduling Tab

On the Scheduling tab, you determine when this printing device will be available to actually print. You can choose to have the printing device always available, or you can specify certain hours when the print device will be available. You can also use this tab to specify a priority to jobs going to the printing device.

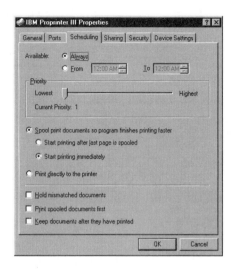

NOTE The default priority is set to Lowest.

Once you decide whether this device will have a special schedule or priority, you can decide how you want it to handle print jobs. It can spool documents so that the program finishes faster or print directly to the printer. If you choose to spool documents, you can make the system wait to start printing until the last page is spooled, or you can start printing immediately.

The checkboxes at the bottom of the screen are as follows:

Hold Mismatched Documents—Suppose that the Accounting department has only one printer. That printer can be used to print both checks and memos. You have mismatched documents when checks and memos are sent to the printer at the same time. In this case, the printer will expect you to manually change the paper.

Print Spooled Documents First—This option groups the documents together by type. In the case mentioned above, all checks would be printed, and then all memos would be printed.

Keep Documents After They Have Printed—When a job moves through the printing process and is finally outputted on the printing device, the print job is deleted. Usually, this is not a problem, because you have a copy of the document stored somewhere on the system. However, some applications will generate a report, send it to the printer, and then delete the report. This option allows you to keep the print job in the spooler until you are sure it has printed correctly, and then you must manually delete it.

Sharing Tab

The next tab available on the Properties screen is the Sharing tab. It is a fallback to the Sharing tab from the Install Wizard. Here, you can select the drivers that you want the printer to make available. You can choose from a variety of alternate drivers, depending on the operating systems your clients are running.

Security Tab

The Security tab will allow you to manage who can use the printer. By clicking Permissions, you can grant users the right to use or manage the printer, or take away their right to even see the printer.

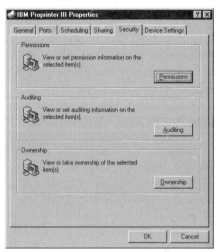

From the Security tab, you can select from Permissions, Auditing, and Ownership.

Permissions—This button is for user permissions. User permissions define who can print to this printer and who can manage the documents submitted to this printer. By default:

- Administrators have full control.

- The creator or owner of the document has the permission to manage documents.

- Everyone can print.

- Print operators have full control.

- Server operators have full control.

Auditing—This button allows the administrator to track the success or failure of various print functions.

Ownership—This button allows a user to take ownership of a printer.

Device Settings Tab

The final tab is the Device Settings tab. This tab is driver/printing device specific. It lets you define which paper tray will be used for which form, how much memory is installed in the printer, if there are any font cartridges installed, and what soft fonts are accessible.

Installing a Remote Printer

A remote printer is a printing device that is attached to another computer on the network. It is not physically attached to your NT server. When the print job is sent to the remote printer, the job is first sent to the remote printer, where it is spooled for the printer.

A remote printer leads a double life. Not only is it shared with other computers, but it is still a local printing device. You begin the installation process by going to the computer that the printing device will be attached to and configuring the printer as a local printer for that computer. Once that is done, you can share the printer with others. After that, for everyone you have just shared the printer with, it is a remote printer.

For your users to share the printer, do as follows at the workstation that needs access to the printer:

1. Choose Start ➤ Settings ➤ Printers.

2. Click Add Printer. This will begin the Add Printer Wizard.

3. Choose Network Printer instead of Local Printer.

4. Browse the network to find the appropriate printer.

5. Select the printer you want and click OK in the Connect to Printer dialog box. You may be asked to install a print driver if one is not available from your operating system.

6. You will be asked whether this printing device will be your default printer. This is your call—it is a Yes or No decision.

7. Click Finish.

Implementing a Printer Pool

To create a printer pool:

1. Open the Printers control panel.

2. Highlight the printer that will be part of the pool and right-click.

3. Select Properties and then choose the Ports tab.

4. Check the Enable Printer Pooling option.

5. Select the ports that also have printing devices of the same type attached to them.

- If the printing devices are attached to physical ports (LPT2 and LPT3 as well as LPT1), select those ports.

- If the printing devices are remote printers, connected through an LPR port, select each network printer port. Use this selection if you are using TCP/IP printing.

6. Select OK.

Setting Print Priorities

Once you have put the pieces together, you can change the priority of one printer to a higher setting:

1. Create two printers connected to the same printing device.

2. In the Printers control panel, highlight the printer that will receive the higher priority, right-click, and choose Properties. Select the Scheduling tab.

3. Change the priority to the highest setting.

NOTE   The default priority setting is Lowest. So, when you simply change the priority on one printing device, it accomplishes the task as outlined.

---

4. Click OK.

Exam Essentials

Printing is hit hard on the exam—each of the three subobjectives will be addressed.

Know how to install print drivers.   If a print driver needs to be updated, update it only on the print server. Once that has been accomplished, the driver will be passed to all workstations using the printing device.

Know which print drivers to install.   Windows 95, NT 3.51, and NT 4 approach printing differently. If you have a mix of workstation operating systems, including OS/2, you will have to install the drivers for each OS.

Know about the use of a separator page.   A separator page can be used to switch printing devices between PostScript and PCL modes. If you look in the \Winnt\System32 folder, you will see a file called PCL.SEP provided for this purpose.

Know how to share a printer. Printer sharing can be accomplished during the printer installation process or from the individual printer's Properties page. If you share the printer, it makes it available to other network users.

Know how to create a "hidden" shared printer that will be shared between several coworkers, but not with everyone in the office. To do this, put $ in the share name.

Know how to attach to a shared printer. If you are using a Windows NT-or Windows 95-based application, this is not a difficult task. You can map a UNC path to the printer. If you are trying to print from a DOS-based application, you need to map a physical port to the network printer.

Know how to manage printer security for operating systems other than Windows NT. If you are working from a Windows 95 workstation, you can load and run Windows NT Server Tools for Windows 95, which gives you the User Manager for Domains and Server Manager utilities. However, neither of these tools will allow you to manage printer permissions. A little known fact is that the Server Tools utilities also change Windows Explorer—you can manage file permissions and printer permissions from Explorer.

Know scheduling. For large print jobs, you can create and configure a printer to be available during after-hours. All large jobs must be sent to this printer. When print jobs are sent to this printer during the day, they will be stored in the print spooler.

Know how to create a printer pool. All printers in the printer pool must be connected to the same print server. All printers should be identical or use the same print driver. To add a new printer to an existing printer pool, enter the port for the new print device. Printers in the pool share the same printer name and print driver.

Know how a printer pool is used. A printer pool is used to balance the load of printing across several printers. This provides increased redundancy and a more responsive printing environment.

Know why print priorities are used. Print priorities are used to give one printer quicker access to the printing device than another printer. A priority of 99 is a higher priority than a priority of 1—the higher the number, the higher the priority.

Know how to configure print priorities. Configure two printers for the same printing device. Give one printer a higher priority by choosing the Scheduling tab on the Properties page and setting the priority to High. Print jobs will be handled from the high-priority printer before print jobs are handled from the low-priority printer.

Key Terms and Concepts

Local printer: A printer that sends the print jobs it receives to disk. It then processes the jobs and forwards them to a printing device.

LPR printer port: A printer port configured to use TCP/IP print properties.

Network-attached printing device: A physical device that connects parallel or serial printing devices to the network, or a printing device that has an internal network interface card.

Print priorities: Provide the scheduling opportunities for one set of print jobs to print routinely before another.

Print server: A computer that shares its printers with network clients.

Printer: A software device to which applications send print jobs. A Windows NT printer matches a name with a printer driver, an output port, and various configuration settings. (Often referred to in other operating systems, such as Novell, as a *queue*.)

Printer pool: A collection of similar printers attached to the same print server. The printers must use the same printer driver. Ideally, the printers will be in the same physical location.

Printing device: The device that physically produces printed output.

Queue: A holding area for print jobs received by a print server but not yet sent to the target printing device.

Remote printer: A printer that does not save the print jobs it receives to disk. Instead, it redirects its jobs directly to a print server.

TIP For more information on printing, check out *MCSE: NT Server 4 Study Guide, Second Edition,* by Matthew Strebe and Charles Perkins with James Chellis, published by Sybex. It is a great resource.

Sample Questions

1. In the world of NT, what is an HP Laserjet 5P?

   A. A printer

   B. A print device

   C. A print server

   D. A print spooler

Answer: B—When taking a Microsoft exam, read each question carefully. In printing, an HP Laserjet 5P is a print device. A printer is a software tool that operates at the client or workstation.

2. In the NT printing subsystem, what is a printer?

   A. Hardware

   B. Software

   C. Hardware and software

   D. Virtual

Answer: B—A printer is a software device that operates at the start of the printing process.

3. What is a queue?

   A. A line to a movie in London

   B. A physical connection between a print device and a computer

   C. A print job in waiting

   D. A holding area for print jobs

Answer: D—A queue is a holding area for print jobs.

Configure a Windows NT Server computer for various types of client computers. Client computer types include:

- Windows NT Workstation
- Windows 95
- Macintosh

Now that the network is configured, you can tweak the configuration to make the server more accessible to various client types. If you work in a mixed environment (and most people do), this section can help alleviate the complaint that the network is slow on a given day. When you take the exam, if you know the information in this section, it will put your mind at ease when you see questions that start out as follows: "You have a network comprised of 45 Windows 95 clients, 100 Windows NT Workstation machines, and 37 Windows-based systems..."

Critical Information

In Chapter 1, there was a section devoted to protocols. In that section, you were shown how to configure your server to communicate with different clients utilizing different protocols. Depending on the client computers that your network is servicing, it is important to provide the right protocol. As you saw in Chapter 1, some of the protocols supported by NT Server are NetBEUI, TCP/IP, IPX/SPX, DLC, and AppleTalk (also DHCP, WINS, and DNS, but these are really services). Not all of the clients that you attach to the network will have the flexibility to connect using each of these protocols. Table 2.6 lists the protocols or services that can be used with various operating systems.

T A B L E 2.6: Operating System Protocols and Services

Client	NetBEUI	NWLink IPX/SPX	TCP/IP	DLC	DHCP	WINS	DNS	AppleTalk
MS-DOS	Yes	Yes	Yes	Yes				
LAN MAN for DOS	Yes	Yes	Yes	Yes				
LAN MAN for OS/2	Yes		Yes					
Windows 95	Yes	Yes	Yes		Yes	Yes	Yes	
Macintosh								Yes
NT Workstation	Yes	Yes	Yes	Yes	Yes	Yes	Yes	

Once you have configured the server to support the protocols, you can enhance client operation by changing the binding order on client machines—it is the client that chooses the protocol it will use to "talk" with the server. If you place the more frequently used protocols at the top of the binding order, performance will increase.

Necessary Procedures

Working with binding order at the workstation machine may affect how quickly it communicates over the network.

Changing the Binding Order of Protocols

To change the binding order of protocols for a client machine using Windows NT Workstation:

1. Highlight Network Neighborhood.

2. Right-click and select Properties.

3. On the Network screen, select the Bindings tab.

4. Expand Workstation.

5. Highlight the chosen protocol and use the Move Up or Move Down button.

Exam Essentials

There isn't much in this section, but the material is tested.

Know how binding order affects system performance. Make sure that the most frequently used protocols are at the top of the binding order.

Key Terms and Concepts

AppleTalk: The set of network protocols on which AppleTalk network architecture is based. When you set up Services for Macintosh, it installs the AppleTalk protocol stack on a computer running Windows NT Server so that Macintosh clients can connect to it.

DLC (data link control): An older network transport protocol that allows PCs to connect to IBM mainframes and some HP printers.

DNS (domain name system): Sometimes referred to as the BIND service in BSD UNIX. Offers a static, hierarchical name service for TCP/IP hosts. The network administrator configures the DNS with a list of host names and IP addresses, allowing users of workstations configured to query the DNS to specify remote systems by host names rather than IP addresses. DNS domains should not be confused with Windows NT networking domains.

NetBEUI: A network protocol usually used in small, department-sized local area networks of 1 to 200 clients.

NetBIOS (network basic input/output system): An application program interface (API) that can be used by application programs on a local area network. NetBIOS provides application programs with a uniform set of commands for requesting the lower-level services required to conduct sessions between nodes on a network and transmit information back and forth. Can be driven on NetBEUI or TCP/IP transport protocols.

NWLink IPX/SPX compatible transport: A standard network protocol that supports routing and can support NetWare client-server applications, in which NetWare-aware sockets-based applications communicate with IPX\SPX sockets-based applications.

Protocol: A set of rules and conventions for sending information over a network. These rules govern the content, format, timing, sequencing, and error control of messages exchanged among network devices.

TCP/IP (transmission control protocol/Internet protocol): A set of networking protocols that provides communications across interconnected networks made up of computers with diverse hardware architectures and various operating systems. TCP/IP includes standards for how computers communicate and conventions for connecting networks and routing traffic.

WINS (Windows Internet name service): A network service for Microsoft networks that provides Windows computers with Internet addresses for specified NetBIOS names, facilitating browsing and intercommunications over TCP/IP networks.

Sample Questions

1. You notice that the NT workstation you are using communicates slowly on the network. What can you do to speed up communications?

   A. Change the Ethernet card to a Token Ring card

   B. Change the Token Ring card to an Ethernet card

   C. Change the binding order of the protocols

   D. Add another network card to the workstation

   Answer: C—Changing the binding order at the workstation may affect the speed of communications on the network. NT workstation uses the different protocols in the order they were bound.

CHAPTER

3

Managing Resources

Microsoft Exam Objectives Covered in This Chapter:

▶ **Manage user and group accounts. Considerations include:** *(pages 134 – 152)*
- Managing Windows NT user accounts
- Managing Windows NT user rights
- Managing Windows NT groups
- Administering account policies
- Auditing changes to the user account database

▶ **Create and manage policies and profiles for various situations. Policies and profiles include:** *(pages 152 – 162)*
- Local user profiles
- Roaming user profiles
- System policies

▶ **Administer remote servers from various types of client computers. Client computer types include:** *(pages 163 – 167)*
- Windows 95
- Windows NT Workstation

▶ **Manage disk resources. Tasks include:** *(pages 168 – 190)*
- Creating and sharing resources
- Implementing permissions and security
- Establishing file auditing

O ne of the best definitions of a network is having two or more people with information to share, a communication medium to send the information, and rules to govern the communication. The whole reason for having a computer network is sharing—sharing information, sharing resources, and sharing applications. That very broad overview is great for discussions over your favorite frosty, cold beverage, but it tends to get complicated really quickly when the amount of people with something to share grows to 50, 100, 1000, or more. It is especially complicated when *you* have to provide others with the opportunity to share files and peripherals throughout the entire company. It can be a daunting task. However, it doesn't have to be that way. As you study this chapter, you will find ways to cut that task down to size.

The first objective involves how to create user accounts, and then how to group those accounts together and control them. What rights does a particular group or individual need to gain access to a network resource? Is there a way to set up a basic set of rights for each user when the account is created? Is there a way to monitor the network to see that the users are not abusing the rights you have given them? These are the questions that will be answered with the first objective.

While the first objective groups users together and handles them *en masse*, the second objective starts to give the user some human characteristics. Now, the user is a person who actually uses this specific computer. The user is not only someone who works on the network, but roams from office to office, desk to desk, and still needs to access the same resources in the same way, no matter where they are. System policies let the administrator control the way users "see" their desktops. The third objective pertains to remote server administration. If you are administering a network of 500 people or more, that network will almost certainly contain more than one server computer. Those servers may not be in the same building or the same state as your desk. However, you still have to make changes to the servers, even if you can't sit down in front of the monitor and move the server's local mouse. There are utilities that will allow you to administer an NT server remotely from a Windows 95 workstation or a Windows NT workstation. The tools are similar. By the end of the section, you will know which utilities you can use based on the operating system installed on your next desktop or laptop.

The fourth objective on managing disk resources is not a rehash of Chapter 2. It shows how to manage the information stored on the disks. In this section, some of the subtle touches that you must be aware of when making rights and policies decisions will be examined. This section also delves into security. Impressive chapter, isn't it? Lots of exam questions will be asked about the material covered in this chapter—be sure to pay close attention to the concepts of local groups and global groups. Questions on groups will haunt you during the NT Server test, the NT Enterprise test, and beyond.

Manage user and group accounts. Considerations include:

- Managing Windows NT user accounts
- Managing Windows NT user rights
- Managing Windows NT groups
- Administering account policies
- Auditing changes to the user account database

To break down this objective, remember one of the commandments of LAN administration—do unto many. Anytime you can group users together as one entity, it will make your life much easier.

Critical Information

As you try to see the "big picture" of your network, you look around at all those users, running all those applications, printing to all those printers, and you have to wonder how you can manage all of that. The more you look, the more you realize these people can be grouped by the tasks they perform and the resources they require.

Managing Windows NT User Accounts

The more users you group together, the less work for the administrator or Information Services team. Who wants to work harder? The NT domain model provides security for the files and resources on your network. This security is implemented by assigning permissions to four types of objects: the local user, the global user, the global group, and the local group. Are you wondering how each is used?

NOTE Make sure you pay close attention to this discussion, because you need to know what can go where. Questions about which users can go in which groups and which default user can do what will keep showing up in exam after exam.

Let's start the discussion small—with the user. With Windows NT, there are two kinds of users, local users and global users. Each has separate roles to fill. In addition, NT creates a set of default users that you can use as templates or role models.

Local User Account

Sometimes, naming can be tricky. This is one of those times. A local user account is created on an NT computer via an NT domain, and its purpose is to serve a single user on just that server. That user account can enable access for local users in addition to those from other NT domains. For example, assume that you have a diverse network made up of NT servers and Windows 95 clients. A user who primarily logs on and uses the services of the NT network could have direct server login authentication provided through a local user account—without a local account, they would not.

NOTE Local accounts can access services only from within the NT server (or workstation) where they reside, since they are in the local (via domain) SAM. They are created in the individual computer SAM by using the User Manager utility as opposed to the User Manager for Domains utility.

Global User Account

Because global user accounts are the most commonly created, they are generally referred to as just "user accounts." A global user account differs from a local account in that it can provide permissions to access resources in any domain, beginning with the domain in which it was created. As long as there is a trust relationship between domains, these accounts can utilize resources in any trusting domains.

Global user accounts can receive these permissions either individually or through membership in a group. A global user account is created with User Manager for Domains.

As mentioned, two default user types are created with the NT installation:

- Administrator—user account for administering the computer and/or domain

- Guest—user account for providing guest access to the computer and/or domain

A local user account is designed for the user who will log onto the computer itself. A global user is someone who is allowed to log on and access resources from the domain. Local accounts are created using User Manager if the NT computer is designed as a part of a peer-to-peer network or standalone system. Local users can be implemented regardless of whether the server is being used in an NT domain environment. Otherwise, global users are created using User Manager for Domains.

User accounts can be created two ways—you can create a new user account or you can copy an existing user account. No matter which way you choose to create the account, you can still make changes in three key areas—user account information, group membership information, and user account profile information.

The New User dialog box is shown in Figure 3.1.

The procedures for creating each account type will be discussed in the "Necessary Procedures" section of this objective.

What do you do with the users once they have been created?

Managing Windows NT User Rights

Now that the users have been created, you have to give them permission to do something. If you remember the beginning of this chapter, it was mentioned that the assignment of rights and permissions is a democratic thing—the majority rules. If you can do unto many, you probably won't have to do unto the individual.

F I G U R E 3.1: New User dialog box

Usually, you will plan for your groups first. In most cases, rights and permissions can be assigned at the group level, leaving user accounts to be assigned to global groups.

Even if you have laid out a security plan in which all rights and permissions are assigned to groups, there are still some universal settings you may want to set for all users, such as using the corporate logo as wallpaper or making sure the network hookup is just the way you want it. You can make these edits on the User Environment Profile screen. Microsoft's TechNet defines a *user profile* as follows:

> Configuration information that can be retained on a user-by-user basis, and is saved in user profiles. This information includes all the per-user settings of the Windows NT environment, such as the desktop arrangement, personal program groups and the program items in those groups, screen colors, screen savers, network connections, printer connections, mouse settings, window size and position, and more. When a user logs on, the user's profile is loaded and the user's Windows NT environment is configured according to that profile.

The User Environment Profile screen is shown in Figure 3.2.

FIGURE 3.2: User Environment Profile

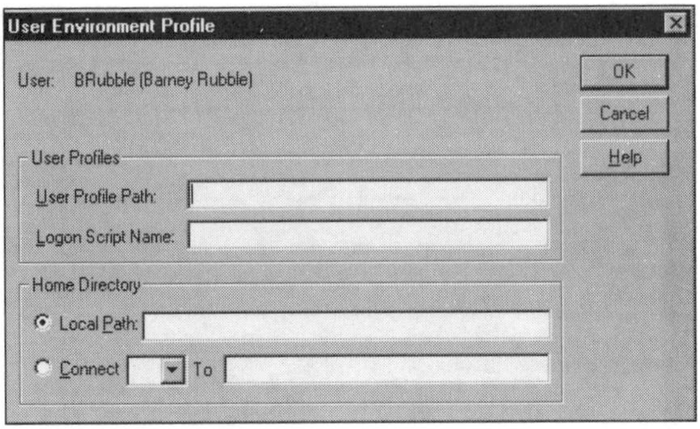

This screen allows you to point to where you have stored the user profile and the name of the logon script that the user should execute. You can give a user a path to their home directory, where they can store all that really private user stuff. This directory can be on any server or share.

User profiles contain those settings and configuration options specific to the user—installed applications, desktop icons, color options, and so forth. This profile is built from system policy information (for example, those things that a user has access to and those things that a user can and cannot change), the default user profile, and permitted, saved changes that a user makes to customize their desktop.

Remember that mandatory profiles can be created by changing the profile suffix from .DAT to .MAN. This resets profile settings to the mandatory values each time a user logs on. While it saves time and prevents users from mangling their desktop settings on a permanent basis, the downside to this implementation is that if the domain controllers are unavailable, users cannot log on, even with cached profile information.

NOTE User profiles deal with a specific user. User policies deal with all users of a domain.

How do you tell which groups a user is a part of? The Group Memberships screen (see Figure 3.3) shows you which groups a user is a member of and to which groups a user can be added.

F I G U R E 3.3: Group Memberships

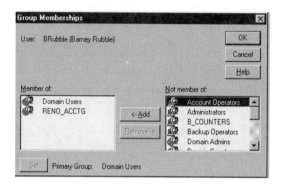

Although the Group Memberships screen shows you where you add a user to a group, you still don't know how and why groups interact.

Managing Windows NT Groups

Windows NT uses a very sophisticated group model that consists of local groups and global groups. At its simplest, in a multiple-domain environment, you create users and global groups in the domain. Users get placed in global groups. Local groups are created on individual NT computers to give access to resources of that server or workstation. Global groups are made a part of local groups, and the users can access the resources.

Global Groups

Global groups are simply users from the same domain grouped together. Global groups can contain only user accounts from their domain—they cannot contain other groups.

While a global group can contain only users in its domain, it is not limited to receiving permissions from only that domain. Global groups can be granted permissions to access resources in other domains. Global groups are created only on NT servers functioning as domain controllers using User Manager for Domains.

Local Groups

Unlike global groups, which can receive authentications from outside their domain boundaries, local groups can receive permissions only on the computer in which they were created. Local groups are created to grant permission to resources or allow users to perform specific tasks. Local groups can be made up of local user accounts, users from within their domain, users from trusted domains, and global group accounts both from their domain and from any trusted domains.

Default Groups

The types of groups described above are those that you can create. NT has taken some of the work out of planning for groups by creating some default groups to do various management tasks:

- Domain Users—global group containing all domain users except the user Guest

- Domain Guests—global group giving limited access and containing the user Guest

- Domain Admins—global group that allows administrator permissions to the entire domain

- Guests—local group for server guests containing the global group Domain Guests

- Print Operators—local group for the members that are assigned to administer domain printers

- Replicator—local group for the accounts that support directory and file replication in the domain

- Server Operators—local group for the members that can administer domain servers

- Users—local group for ordinary users. Contains the global group Domain Users by logging on locally and conducts sharing, hard drive, and backup operations

- Backup Operators—local group for backing up and restoring the server regardless of directory and file permissions

- Administrators—local group that has full control over the server. Includes the Administrator local user account and the Domain Admins global group

- Account Operators—local group that can access both the server's local SAM and domain SAM (if the server is a domain controller)

NOTE   Always remember that in the Microsoft-selected model of group management, users are always put in global groups. Global groups are added to local groups. Local groups are always assigned access permissions. Users are never put in local groups.

Administering Account Policies

There are other ways of improving the security settings of a user account. One way is to alter the default account policies. This is another section under-emphasized by the exam writers, but is very important for the network administrator.

- *Account policies* are the defaults that the administrator sets to handle various security issues.

Account policies are handled through User Manager for Domains. System policies are administered through the System Policy Editor.

Account Policies

Account policies set broad policies for all the users of your domain. To access the Account Policies page, start User Manager for Domains and choose Policies ≻ Account (see Figure 3.4).

FIGURE 3.4: Account Policy options

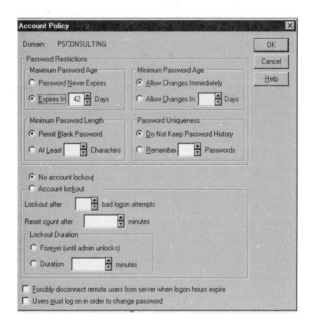

Setting default user security is key to this utility. However, setting user security is a two-edged sword. The network and data are more secure, but your end users will probably whine about the changes. The Account Policy page offers the following selections:

- Maximum Password Age—for password restrictions, the administrator can set the Maximum Password Age. If you work in an environment where security is not an issue, you may choose Password Never Expires. If security is an issue, there is a setting that forces passwords to be changed every so many days. Keep in mind as you view this figure that the default is set to 42 days. While decreasing the amount of time a password is active may make great sense from a security point of view, the chances that your users will understand why they have to change their passwords so often are slim to none.

- Minimum Password Age—this forces a user to keep a password for at least a certain period of time. By default, users can change their passwords immediately.

- Minimum Password Length—how long must a password be? If no changes are made, blank passwords are permitted. If you increase the minimum password length, your users will have to start thinking before typing. Most experts say that six to eight characters is about the right length, but Microsoft doesn't have a particular policy.

- Password Uniqueness—you have heard the stories of the user who kept the same password for years and years. By the time the user left the company, everyone knew his or her password. This is almost as bad as having no password at all. Password Uniqueness, which is turned off by default, will remember a number of passwords, forcing the user to come up with something new every time the password must be changed, even if changing only capitalization (recall that passwords are case sensitive). You get to choose the length of the history list.

- Account Lockout—this is an attempt to prevent hackers from attempting to access your network over and over again. If Account Lockout is enabled and someone tries to log onto a valid user account unsuccessfully so many times, the account will be locked and the user will not be able to log onto the system. You can set the number of bad logon attempts, reset the count after so many minutes, and set the lockout duration. Once the account is locked, the hacker doesn't know if it is locked for 10 minutes or an hour and 10 minutes. At that point, there are probably easier networks to attack.

- Forcibly Disconnect Remote Users from Server When Logon Hours Expire—if you select this checkbox, it will cause users who are working when the allowed time expires to be kicked off the system. If this option is not selected, the remote server user can continue to use the system, but cannot open any new sessions.

- Users Must Log On in Order to Change Password—this selection makes your users change their passwords before they expire. If the password expires, the end user will have to contact the administrator, and the administrator will have to reset the password.

At this point, you know the types of users and groups. You know how each user and group interacts with the others. You know the Microsoft-approved method of putting users in global groups and putting global groups in local groups. You know all about the default types of users and groups and how to standardize some of the user settings. There is also a way to check on the changes that are made to the user database. It is called auditing.

Auditing Changes to the User Account Database

NT allows you to audit what is happening to user accounts and who is making changes or performing certain tasks. Don't get bogged down with auditing, but if you know how to use it, it can come in handy. It can certainly help answer an exam question or two.

Setting an audit policy can help spot security breaches. By default, auditing is turned off. You can change the audit policy through User Manager for Domains by choosing Policies ➤ Auditing. Take a good, close look at Figure 3.5.

F I G U R E 3.5: Audit Policy screen

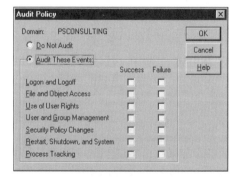

You have a limited amount of options for auditing. Remember that if you turn on auditing, it may help you track down a security breach. However, it will also put a serious load on your server, perhaps slowing response time.

As you can see from the options on the Audit Policy screen, you can audit the success or failure of seven common network events. The information is stored in a security log. You can view the log by using the Event Viewer.

Necessary Procedures

This objective encompasses several routine management procedures that need to be addressed.

Creating a Global User Account

To create a global user account, fire up User Manager for Domains and open the New User dialog box:

1. Click Start.

2. Select Programs.

3. Select Administrative Tools.

4. Click User Manager for Domains. The New User dialog box appears. (See Figure 3.1 earlier in the chapter.)

NOTE   You can also create a new user by using the Administrative Wizard, or by starting User Manager for Domains and choosing User ➤ New User.

Using the New User dialog box, you can enter the basics to create a new user. Start with a unique user name. In many cases, Username will differ from the next field—Full Name. Depending on corporate standards, the user name might be GGovanus and the full name might be Gary Govanus.

- Description—an optional field for location, title, or any indentifying information.

- Password—can be up to 14 characters and is case sensitive. You can force the new user to change the password at the next logon.

TIP Some applications or services require a special account to start the service. If this is the case, enable the checkboxes for User Cannot Change Password and Password Never Expires.

- Account Disabled—disables the user account. If you want an account to be available when a user returns from a short leave, you can disable the account. The account will be inactive until the user returns from leave. This is also a good way to store user accounts that may be set up as templates, without them being illegally used.
- Groups button—gives the administrator the ability to add users to global and/or local groups.
- Profile button—activates the User Environment Profile screen, specifying where the user profile is stored, the name of the login script, and where the user's home directory is located. (See Figure 3.2 earlier in the chapter.)

NOTE See the next objective for an in-depth discussion of user profiles.

- Hours button—you can force your users off your network by setting the hours during which they can access the network.

TIP Using the Hours button is an especially handy trick when you are trying to get a clean backup with as few open files as possible.

- Logon To button—specifies which workstations a user may log onto. The default is All. If this is selected, a maximum of eight workstations can be assigned.

- Account button—allows you to expire an account and specify the account type. The account types are Global Account for a regular user in the domain and Local Account for a user from an untrusted domain. (See Figure 3.1 earlier in the chapter.)

- Dialin button—allows the user to access the server using remote access service (RAS).

NOTE Remote access service will be discussed further in Chapter 4.

Creating a User Template

One of the ways to create a large number of users with the same requirements is to create a user template or model user. The user template is configured exactly the way you want your new users configured, except this account has the Account Disabled field enabled. When it is time to create the new account, you simply copy the model and provide the information necessary to make the account unique. The following fields can be copied:

- Description
- Groups
- Profiles
- Hours
- Logon To
- Account
- Dialin

The mandatory fields include:

- Username
- Full Name
- The Account Disabled checkbox is always cleared when an account is created by copying a template. The User Must Change Password at Next Logon checkbox is set.

To create and use a template:

1. If you are logged on as an administrator, go into User Manager for Domains and create a model user with all the properties that will be the defaults for the new group of users. Be sure to select the Account Disabled checkbox. Consider using an account name that represents the fact that this account is a template, such as Finance Template. Add the user.

2. Highlight the user you have just created and press F8 to copy the user. Notice that the Username and Full Name fields are blank, and that the Account Disabled checkbox has been cleared.

Deleting User Accounts

To delete a user account:

1. Log on as an administrator.

2. Start User Manager for Domains.

3. Select the user account to be deleted.

4. Either choose User and Delete or simply press the delete key.

5. Agree to the screen asking if you really want to delete the user.

6. Choose Yes to actually delete the user.

7. Close User Manager for Domains.

Renaming Users

When you change the name of the account, nothing else about the account changes. To change the user name of an account:

1. Log on as an administrator or a similar superior being.

2. Start User Manager for Domains.

3. Select the user to be renamed from the User account list.

4. Choose User ➤ Rename.

5. Change the Username and click OK.

Exam Essentials

The information in this section is so important that you will see questions on it in exam after exam. If you get it right the first time, the rest is easy. Know placement!

Know the relationship between global groups, local groups, and users. Global groups exist at the domain level and can be added to local groups if the local group exists on a server that is a member of a domain that trusts the global group's domain. Local groups can be created on any Windows NT workstation or server within the domain. Global groups are limited to containing user accounts from the domain. Local groups can consist of users from the domain, global groups from the domain, or global groups from a trusted domain. Global groups are used to organize users; local groups are used to grant rights and permissions to resources.

Know what can be done to a user account. User accounts can be renamed. If you have a user who is leaving the company and their replacement needs access to the same information, simply rename the account and change the password. This process is completed using the User Manager for Domains utility. The default Administrator and Guest accounts can be renamed, but not deleted.

Know what happens when you delete a user account. Once a user account has been deleted, the only way to re-create the account is to start over. Accounts are not re-created using the exact same user name again.

Know which groups have the right to log onto an NT server locally by default. The system-created accounts are Server Operators, Account Operators, Backup Operators, and Print Operators. By default, they have the right to log onto an NT server locally.

Know the privileges granted by default to the various groups. Backup Operators can back up files to tape and restore files from tape only when logged on locally.

Know how logon hour restrictions affect users. If a user is allowed to log on from 7:00 A.M. to 6:00 P.M., what happens to the user when 6:00 P.M. arrives? If there are no system policies set, the user will be allowed to continue the session, but will *not* be allowed to establish new connections.

Know what happens when a user's logon time has expired with the Forcibly Disconnect selection enabled and with the Forcibly Disconnect selection cleared. With the Forcibly Disconnect selection enabled, the user will be disconnected from all connections and then logged off. With the Forcibly Disconnect selection cleared, the user will be allowed to continue with the current connection, but cannot establish any new connections.

Know how to expire an account and how to reactivate it. To instantly expire the account, start User Manager for Domains, double-click the user, choose Account, select the End Of button, and fill in the date for the account to expire. This is similar to disabling it. To reactivate the account, start User Manager for Domains, double-click the user, choose Account, and either select the Never button or advance the date in the End Of field to a date in the future.

Know how to create user accounts using a template. Start User Managers for Domains, highlight the template account, and press F8 to copy the account and provide a new user name, full name, and password.

Know how to set an audit policy. Setting an audit policy can be a useful tool for troubleshooting security problems. If you audit the failure of logon and logoff attempts, it may show that hackers are attempting to gain entry to the network. The audit log is viewed using the Event Viewer.

Key Terms and Concepts

Account policy: Settings governing password restrictions, ages, and account lockouts.

Auditing: Keeping track of certain successful or failed key events on the network computers.

Disabling an account: Temporarily suspending access. The account can be reactivated at a later time. This is done manually and cannot be automated.

Expiring an account: Used for temporary or seasonal workers. You provide a date for when the account expires. After that date, the account cannot be accessed without administrator intervention.

Global account: A normal user account in an NT domain. Most network user accounts are global accounts.

Global group: A group that can be used in its own domain's member servers and workstations, and those of trusting domains. In all those places, it can be granted rights and permissions, and can become a member of local groups. However, it can contain only user accounts from its own domain.

Local account: A user account provided on a computer for a user who does not have or does not wish to log into a global account.

Local group: A group that can be granted permissions and rights only for its own resources. However, it can contain user accounts and global groups both from its own domain and from trusted domains.

Permissions: Windows NT security settings you place on a shared resource that determine which users can use the resource and how they can use it.

Policy: Default settings for a variety of NT objects.

Rights: Define a user's access to a computer or domain and the actions that a user can perform on the computer or domain. User rights permit actions such as logging onto a computer or network, adding or deleting users in a workstation or domain, and so forth.

Trusted relationship between domains: A link between domains that enables pass-through authentication, in which a trusting domain honors the logon authentication of a trusted domain. With trust relationships, a user who has a user account in one domain can potentially access the entire network.

Sample Questions

1. The basic Microsoft understanding of groups is as follows:

A. Local groups can be placed in global groups.

B. Global groups should be placed in local groups.

C. Never use local groups; always use global groups.

D. Never use global groups; always use local groups.

Answer: B—Microsoft recommends that you place all users in global groups and make global groups members of local groups.

2. Which of the following statements is true?

A. Global groups can contain members from multiple domains.

B. Global groups must contain members from multiple domains.

C. Local groups can contain members from multiple domains.

D. Local groups must contain members from multiple domains.

Answer: C—Global groups can contain only members from their own domains. Local groups can contain global groups from different domains; therefore, local groups can contain members from different domains.

Create and manage policies and profiles for various situations. Policies and profiles include:

- Local user profiles
- Roaming user profiles
- System policies

Control is a wonderful thing, especially when you are a network administrator. People on your network can do so many things to make your life more challenging. Just the thought of it can keep a person up at night.

Fortunately, there are ways around the problem. NT provides you with tools called policies and profiles that allow you to maintain some semblance of order and control over the workstations on your network. As you can see from the objective, there are local user profiles, roaming user profiles, and system policies—which entail control over the local user, control over the user who roams from system to system, and control over hardware profiles.

Critical Information

What kinds of things do you need to control? Often, the mundane, routine things. The Chief Executive Officer was roaming through the office and saw someone with wallpaper that was customized in a manner not appropriate to corporate life. The CEO reflected on this and decided that all users in the company will hereby use a custom-designed wallpaper showing the corporate logo. You control wallpaper choices through profiles and policies.

Local User Profiles

Local user profiles store information on how a user has configured their computing environment. This isn't really flashy stuff; it is more everyday information such as:

- Have you ever wondered where the information is stored that lets 32-bit applications know the last few documents you accessed? It's in the profile.

- How does the computer know to reattach all those connections to all those shares and printers? It's in the profile.

- How does the computer remember where you put all the bookmarks in Help? It's in the profile.

The subdirectory on every Windows NT machine that contains the user profile information is \WINNT\Profiles. Under that folder, there is a subfolder named for each user. Those subfolders contain a file called NTUSER.DAT. This file contains all the registry entries. There are also folders for Application Data, the Desktop, Favorites, Personal, Start Menu, and other information that pertains to a specific user.

When a user logs onto a system for the first time, the system knows there is no local user profile, so it goes out to the network to look for a roaming user profile. If there is no roaming user profile, NT creates a local user profile subdirectory for the user in the \WINNT\Profiles directory. NT then needs to provide the user with some of the basics, so it gets the information from the \WINNT\ Profiles\Default user directory.

At this point, the user has the default profile settings. Any changes that the user makes will be stored in the local user profile for the new user. The next time the user logs onto the local machine, the user is presented with the system just the way it was left.

There are occasions when you do not want a user to be able to change the desktop. How do you keep that from happening? Easy, just configure the system the way you want it for the tech-weenie-wannabe and save the settings by logging out. Go back into the system as another user and change the name of the NTUSER.DAT file to NTUSER.MAN. When you add that little extension—.MAN—it changes the file to a mandatory profile. The user can change the desktop in a variety of fashions, but none of the changes will be retained.

Roaming User Profiles

With a roaming user profile, a profile is created and centrally stored. When a user logs onto a workstation on the network, the workstation checks for a roaming user profile, finds it, and *voila*—the desktop looks just the same, no matter where the user logs on from.

What happens if there are a local user profile and a roaming user profile, and the local user profile is more recent? NT is nothing if not polite; it will ask which profile you want to use. Otherwise, it will just go with the roaming user profile.

When the user logs off, the new profile is saved (if it is not mandatory or the user has not logged on as guest), and any changes that have been made are saved for posterity.

Now that you know how to standardize your desktop, be sure to share the wealth. Other people on the network roam, too, so you may want to give them the flexibility of a roaming profile.

TIP   The path to the roaming user profile is specified using User Manager for Domains.

System Policies

System policies are created with the System Policy Editor. Using system policies, you will be able to maintain machine configurations and user policies from one machine.

The System Policy Editor operates in either Registry mode or System Policy mode. Since the objective mentions system policies rather than Registry mode, apparently the exam writers think system policies are more significant.

Registry mode allows you to edit all sorts of interesting things. Take a look at Figure 3.6.

F I G U R E 3.6: Local Computer Properties

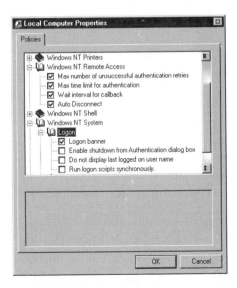

Several things jump out at you while looking at this screen:

- You can specify which applications to run at startup.

- You can create hidden drive shares for workstations or servers.

- From the Windows NT Remote Access section, you can set the maximum number of unsuccessful authentication attempts and for the system to automatically disconnect.

- From the Windows NT System\Logon section, you can specify a specific logon banner or make sure the name of the last user who logged on is not displayed.

System Policy vs. Registry Mode

How does System Policy mode differ from Registry mode? System Policy mode is like Registry mode, but with an *attitude*. If there is a setting in the registry and a system policy conflicts with the registry, the system policy takes precedence.

You can find the system policy file. For NT systems, the file is named NTCONFIG.POL. Suppose you want to impose a set of restrictions on machines that the user cannot change. How is that accomplished?

Use the System Policy Editor to make the changes you want replicated across the network. Save the file as NTCONFIG.POL in the \WINNT\System32\Repl\Import\Scripts folder on the boot partition of the domain controllers.

NOTE   If system policy information is being stored for Windows 95 machines, the filename should be CONFIG.POL instead of NTCONFIG.POL.

When a computer attempts to log onto the network, it will check for the system policy. When the computer finds the NTCONFIG.POL file that affects the user or the computer, it brings this information into the registry and configures the workstation accordingly.

NOTE   If the changes are made in System Policy mode rather than Registry mode, the changes will overwrite the local registry. What a great topic for an exam question!

Necessary Procedures

The previous section examined the different types of profiles, but did not address how to create or change the settings. For a local user profile, there is not much to do, because it is automatically created and administered by NT. The configuration and dissemination of the roaming user profile are more challenging.

Creating a Local User Profile and a Mandatory User Profile

Local user profiles are created when the user logs on and makes changes to the computer. When the user logs off, these changes are saved in the file \WINNT\Profiles\UserName\NTUSER.DAT. To change this profile to a mandatory profile, change the extension from .DAT to .MAN. This changes the file to read only. Remember that with a mandatory user profile, if the NT domain controllers fail, the user will not be able to log onto the domain.

Creating a Roaming User Profile

Roaming user profiles are created from User Manager for Domains, which is accessed as follows:

1. Choose Programs ➢ Administrative Tools ➢ User Manager for Domains.

2. Double-click Administrator.

3. Select Profile. (See Figure 3.2 earlier in the chapter.)

4. In the User Profile Path, enter a universal naming convention (UNC) path to the \WINNT\Profiles directory. The syntax for a UNC path is *Servername**Foldername**Subfoldername*\Winnt\Profiles.

5. Close the User Environment Profile box by clicking OK.

6. Close the User window by clicking OK.

7. Close User Manager for Domains.

You may think nothing has changed. However, go to a different machine and log on as administrator. Your new profile will follow you.

Copying a User Profile to Make It a Remote User Profile

Create a central repository for user profiles on a server attached to the network, such as *Servername**Profile**Username*, and share the directory. Then, do as follows:

1. Start Control Panel.

2. Double-click System.

3. Choose the User Profiles tab.

4. Select the profile for the user you want to copy and click Copy To. You will be prompted to enter a path to the location of the share: *Servername**Profile**Username*.

5. Under Permitted to Use, make sure the appropriate user name is selected.

Creating and Implementing a System Policy

There are many ways and reasons to set system policies. In this example, a system policy will be created to ensure that the name of the last user to log onto a system is not displayed. This policy will be replicated throughout the network to all NT systems.

Log on as administrator and do as follows:

1. Choose Programs ➤ Administrative Tools ➤ System Policy Editor.

2. Choose File ➤ New Policy.

3. Click Default Computer.

4. Click Windows NT System.

5. Click Logon.

6. Check the box next to Do Not Display Last Logged On User Name.

7. Select OK.

8. Choose Save As and save the file as NTCONFIG.POL on the domain controller in the \WINNT\System32\REPL\Import\Scripts folder.

Exam Essentials

There was lots of useful information in this section. The exam writers love to concentrate on questions of filenames and locations, so as you read this section, pay close attentionto those topics.

Know where user profiles are stored.   User profiles are stored in the \WINNT\Profiles*Username* folder of any Windows NT computer.

Know the name of the user profile file.   The user profile file is called NTUSER.DAT.

Know how to make a local user profile a mandatory profile. Change the name of NTUSER.DAT to NTUSER.MAN.

Know what happens when the domain controller that contains the mandatory user profile is down and the user logs onto the network.   The user's locally cached profile will be used. If a mandatory profile is set, the user will not be able to log on.

Know where shortcuts are stored on a local machine.   Shortcuts are stored as part of the local user profile. The information will be stored in the \WINNT\Profiles*Username*\Desktop directory.

Know how profiles are accessed.   During logon, NT looks for a local user profile. If it does not find a local user profile, it will look for a roaming user profile. If it cannot find a roaming user profile, it will create a local user profile using the default user settings.

Know how to create a roaming user profile.   Copy the user's workstation local profile to a shared network path. Enter the UNC network path in the User Environment Profile dialog box.

Know what happens when a local user profile and a roaming user profile both exist. If a local user profile is older than a roaming user profile, the roaming user profile is used. If the local user profile is newer than the roaming user profile, NT will ask which profile the user wants to use.

Know the two modes available in the System Policy Editor. The two modes are Registry mode and System Policy mode.

Know the difference between Registry mode and System Policy mode. Registry mode changes the registry. System Policy mode allows you to control system policies for all NT computers in the domain. If a system policy exists that conflicts with the registry entry, the system policy entry will be used.

Know the name of the system policy file for NT and where it is stored for replication. The system policy file is called NTCONFIG.POL. It is saved to the \WINNT\System32\Repl\ Import\Scripts directory on the primary domain controller.

Know the name of the system policy file for Windows 95. The name of the policy file for Windows 95 workstations is CONFIG.POL.

Key Terms and Concepts

CONFIG.POL: The name of the file that stores system policies for Windows 95 client workstations.

Local profile: Information stored on a local computer that reflects how the end user has configured the system.

Mandatory profile: A local profile that the end user cannot change.

NTCONFIG.POL: The name of the file that stores system policies for Windows NT workstations and servers.

NTUSER.DAT: The name of the file stored in the \WINNT\ Profile*Username* directory that contains all the settings in the local profile.

NTUSER.MAN: The name of the file stored in the \WINNT\ Profile*Username* directory that contains all the settings in the mandatory user profile. When you change the extension of .DAT to .MAN, it turns the profile file into a read-only file.

Registry mode: A way the System Policy Editor can be used to edit the registry of either local computers or other computers in the domain.

Roaming profile: Profile created for a user who accesses more than one computer. The user's look and feel will remain the same, no matter what computer is being accessed.

System Policy Editor: The utility used to create system policies. Available through Programs ➤ Administrative Tools ➤ System Policy Editor.

System Policy mode: A way the System Policy Editor can be used to mandate registry settings throughout the domain. Settings changed in the system policy files will override local registry settings.

Sample Questions

1. Suppose that your boss is a control freak. They want to make sure that each NT workstation has exactly the same system policies. Each workstation is attached to the network, and the users must always log onto the domain before starting work. How can you keep your boss happy?

   A. Create a system policy file and export it to each workstation the first time it logs on.

   B. Create a system policy file for each end user and copy it to the user profiles directory on the domain controller.

   C. Create a system policy file and copy it to each workstation's WINNT folder.

   D. Create a system policy file that will affect all end users and copy it to the NETLOGON folder of the PDC.

Answer: D—Create a system policy file that will affect all end users and copy it to the NETLOGON folder of the primary domain controller.

2. After you created a system policy and stored it in the NETLOGON directory so that people can access it, you find that the policy is virtually ignored by several systems on your network. What is a possible cause?

   A. The computers may have a local policy that conflicts with the system policy.

   B. The user on the computer is logging onto the domain as administrator, nullifying any policy changes.

   C. The user on the computer is logging onto the domain as guest, nullifying any policy changes.

   D. You screwed up.

   Answer: A—If there is a conflict between a local policy and the system policy, the local policy takes precedence. Answer D is never an option, is it?

3. How do you change a user profile to a mandatory user profile?

   A. Change the extension in the NTUSER.MAN file to NTUSER.DAT.

   B. Change the extension in the NTUSER.DAT file to NTUSER.MAN.

   C. That is covered in the rights and permissions section of this book, and you haven't gotten that far yet.

   D. Store the profile in the \NETLOGON directory of the PDC with the filename NETUSER.DAT.

   Answer: B—If you change the extension in the NETUSER.DAT file to .MAN, it makes the user profile a mandatory user profile.

Administer remote servers from various types of client computers. Client computer types include:

- Windows 95
- Window NT Workstation

It is not always possible to go directly to the server to perform administration tasks. After all, servers are usually stored in locked rooms on the other side of the building. It is much more convenient to be able to perform routine tasks, such as checking the event log or starting User Manager for Domains, directly from your desktop workstation.

If your desktop workstation is running Windows 95 or Windows NT Workstation, you are in luck. Within five minutes, your system can access the tools necessary to administer a network remotely.

Critical Information

When Microsoft designed the remote administration tools, it considered the usual administration mind-set. Let's face it, you want the fastest, biggest, baddest computer your company can afford for your workstation. If you can run Windows NT Workstation, you will have more flexibility than if you have "just" a Windows 95 computer. Actually, the tools are somewhat different for each operating system, but, hey, any excuse to get a new computer.

Windows 95

If your workstation is running Windows 95, has an extra 3MB of disk space, and runs the Client for Microsoft networks, you can configure the system to access the following items:

- Event Viewer—viewer used to view the system log.

- Server Manager—powerful utility that allows you to monitor and manage all aspects of your network, including active users, shares, replications, alerts, and services.

- User Manager for Domains—utility that allows you to create and manage users and groups. This utility allows the administrator to set account policies, user rights, and audit accounts as well as manage trust relationships with other domains.

- File Security—the ability to set rights and permissions for files.

- Print Security—the ability to set rights and permissions for various print objects.

- Some utilities to help you manage NetWare services.

NOTE   The system must be at least a 486DX/33.

Windows NT Workstation

If, on the other hand, your workstation is running Windows NT Workstation and is a 486DX/33 with at least 2.5MB of disk space, you can access the following items:

- DHCP Manager—gives you the ability to configure a dynamic host control protocol (DHCP) manager on a network segment. A DHCP host will pass out IP addresses to workstations on the network segment.

- Remote Access Administrator—utility that allows you to administer RAS connections to the system.

- Remote Boot Manager—utility for the administration of images for diskless workstations.

- Services for Macintosh—administration tools for the Macintosh environment.

- Server Manager—powerful utility that allows you to manage all aspects of your network, including users, shares, replications, alerts, and services.

- System Policy Editor—utility that allows you to edit system policies. In Registry mode, you can edit any computer on the network.

- User Manager for Domains—utility that allows you to create and manage user and group accounts.

- WINS Manager—utility that allows you to manage Windows Internet name service (WINS). WINS is the Microsoft method of resolving Internet protocol (IP) addresses to Microsoft networking names.

As you can see, the list is different for each OS, but definitely skewed toward the NT Workstation side.

Necessary Procedures

Before you can configure your workstation to be able to remotely administer an NT server, you have to teach NT Server to work and play well with others. The NT Server installation does not prepare the system to pass out administrative tools to every Tom, Dick, and Windows 95 machine. Once the preliminary work of preparing the server is done, it is easy to install the workstation configuration tools.

Copying Client-Based Administration Tools

Installing client-based administration tools is a two-step process. First, you prepare the server. Second, you install the tools on the workstation.

1. Start Network Client Administrator by selecting Start ➤ Programs ➤ Administrative Tools ➤ Network Client Administration.

2. Select the Copy Client-Based Network Administration Tools radio button and click OK.

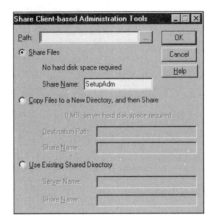

3. You can share files by providing a path name to the files, you can copy files to a new directory and then share, or you can use an existing shared directory. At the top of the dialog box, enter the path to the NT installation CD. Then, select the second option. You are given a destination path of C:\Clients\Srvtools by default and a share name of SetupAdm. At this point, the files will be copied and the share will be created automatically.

Now that the share has been created, you can go back to your workstation and use NT Explorer to attach to the share you have just created. Once you have attached to the share, go into the \WINNT folder and execute SETUP.BAT by highlighting the filename and double-clicking it. When the installation is finished, the remote tools will be available.

Exam Essentials

The exam writers did not spend much time covering the objectives in this section. However, there may be a few questions, revolving around operating systems and setup procedures.

Know the two operating systems that can be used to administer a Windows NT server remotely. The two desktop operating systems that can be used to remotely administer a Windows NT server are Windows NT Workstation and Windows 95.

Key Terms and Concepts

Remote administration: Administering an NT network from a Windows 95 workstation or Windows NT Workstation, rather than directly from the server.

Sample Questions

1. Remote administration is accomplished by:

   A. Dialing in and using a RAS connection

   B. Using RCONSOLE and an SPX connection

   C. Using a workstation running Windows for Workgroups

   D. Using a workstation running Windows NT Workstation

   Answer: D—Remote administration can be accomplished from either a properly configured workstation running Windows 95 or a Windows NT workstation.

2. Which operating system provides the best remote management ability?

   A. DOS

   B. Windows 3.1

   C. Windows 95

   D. Windows NT Workstation

   Answer: D—Windows NT provides the greatest flexibility.

Manage disk resources. Tasks include:

- Creating and sharing resources
- Implementing permissions and security
- Establishing file auditing

It's about time! We work in the Information Technology business, and so far, all we have talked about is technology. We finally get to start talking about what to do with information. Information needs to be managed and protected, which is what this objective is all about.

Let's explore how NTFS and FAT work together. What happens to the attributes given to a file stored on an NTFS system when it is moved to a FAT system? When NTFS was mentioned earlier, there were references to permissions and file rights. What are those things and how are they implemented?

Users access files through network share points. How are these share points created and what characteristics do they have? When should a share point be created? Can you hide a share point? How do you control access to information on the share point? Can you make sure that unauthorized users do not get into the payroll section? Worse yet, how will you know if someone does get into a private area and accesses a file they are not supposed to access?

Even though a lot of information is presented, don't panic. This is more real-world material than exam material. The exam writers seem to have skipped much of it. Go figure.

Critical Information

Before beginning this objective, let's take a look at the logistics behind the layout. The objective starts out with a discussion of the effects on a file when that file is moved or copied from one file system to another. You know from the discussion of file systems in Chapter 1 that the NT file system (NTFS) has some capabilities that plain, old FAT doesn't have, such as local directory- and file-level security and compression. The first part of this objective traces what happens to the compression attribute when the file is moved from a compressed area to an uncompressed area and what happens if the file is copied.

Once the user has access to an area using a share point, some restrictions may need to be placed on what a user can do in a particular share. For example, if you have created a share to reference a Human Resources policy manual, you may not want everyone to be able to rewrite the vacation policy to suit their own needs. This is where folder- and file-level security come into play. NT has several levels of share access security. In addition, if the share is located on an NTFS partition, additional local security can be applied to the folder or file. Each of these levels of security is applied in a specific order with predictable results.

To summarize, the file exists on a disk. That disk may be compressed. If the file is moved or copied, you know what happens to it. The file is accessed through a share point. The procedure for creating share points will be covered. The file is protected by share-point security and (if the file is on an NTFS partition) NTFS security. Is there a way to monitor and ensure that the file is accessed only by those users who are supposed to be allowed to access it? Yes, it's called auditing. The last section of this objective examines how you can audit a file to make sure only the right people are gaining access to it.

NOTE For a complete discussion of the differences between NTFS and FAT, see the section in Chapter 1 on file systems. The current section will assume that you understand the differences between the two file systems.

Creating and Sharing Resources

In this case, sharing resources means sharing folders. Folders are shared so that other people on the network can use the information or applications in the folder. You create a share so users can put their stuff on your network, in the *Servername*\Users*Username* subfolder. You also put shares on the network so users can access the network version of Excel, from *Servername*\Apps\Excel. Another share might point to the *Servername*\Shared\Data\Budgets area.

Just because you have created a folder called Data with a subfolder called Budgets, it does not mean that anyone else can see the folders. On the contrary, nothing is visible by default. For users to see a directory, the administrator must make the concerted effort to share the directory. Do your users want to remember all those UNC paths? These are the same people who have a difficult time remembering their password—you don't want them to have to remember *Servername*\Shared\Data\Budgets. To make sure users can remember where things are, administrators create shares and make them available under a readable share name.

The administrator can share any directory on the network if the administrator has been given the LIST permission. If a user on a remote computer has blocked the administrator from having the LIST permission, chances are the user does not want the information spread across the network, so the administrator cannot create a share.

NOTE If you are not sure what the LIST permission is or what it is good for, don't worry. A discussion of all permissions comes up next.

So, how are shares created? For a deeper look at creating and implementing sharing, skip ahead to the "Necessary Procedures" section. The current section will offer just a broad overview. Shares can be created using NT Explorer, My Computer, the command prompt, or Server Manager.

Look closely at Figure 3.7. To access this dialog box, open My Computer, browse to the folder and highlight it, right-click, and choose Sharing. Once the Sharing tab is displayed, choose Shared As and enter the share name—in this case, Applications. You can also add a comment so users will know what the share is for. You will notice that you can set a limit of users who can hack away on this share. You can allow the Maximum Allowed for the server or set a number of users with which you feel comfortable.

FIGURE 3.7: Sharing a drive using My Computer

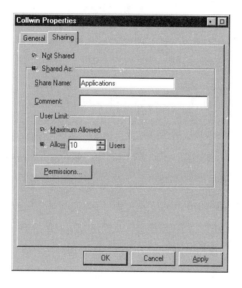

Using NT Explorer or My Computer to create a share is not the only way of doing it—it is just one of the most convenient. You can also create a share using File Manager (if you still use File Manager). If you happen to work in Server Manager, you can also create a share while doing normal management tasks. For the GUI-challenged or those of us who still feel most comfortable at a command prompt, you can use the Net Share utility. Each of these methods will be discussed in the "Necessary Procedures" section.

In addition to the shares that the administrator creates, if you are using an NT-based system that has a hard-coded access control list (ACL), you will find that there are at least two hidden shares. These hidden shares are the C$ share, which shares the root computer's C: drive, and the ADMIN$ share, which shares the root of the NT installation. These shares give administrators a path to the \WINNT directory or the operating system directory. Remember that a share name ending in $ results in a hidden or nonvisible share.

Implementing Permissions and Security

Shares have been created. It is time to start thinking about what kinds of permissions you want to grant users or groups of users for each one of the shares. The best way to start this process is to ask yourself some simple questions. Using the answers to the questions, you can make some decisions on share permissions.

To start, realize that by default all shares are granted Full Control to the Everyone group. Look at each share and ask, Who needs to do what to this share? If the share you are looking at is a data directory, your users will need to be able to see the filenames, open the files, write to the files, and even delete the files. If the directory you are looking at is a folder that houses an application, your users may just need to read the filenames and execute the files. Why do the permissions for the folders differ? You don't want your users to be able to go in and delete an executable file on which the rest of the network depends.

TIP For exact information on permissions to run a specific application, be sure to read the documentation that came with the application.

Permissions are applied at various levels by various processes. For example, there is a share-level permission. If the share points to a folder on an NTFS partition, local computer permissions can point to the folder or directory.

Share-Level Permissions

Taking this one step at a time, let's start with share-level permissions. When you create a share using NT Explorer, you open NT Explorer, track to the folder you want to share, highlight the folder, and right-click. Click Share to open the Properties page for the folder.

NOTE For more information on creating shares using NT Explorer, please review the "Necessary Procedures" section of this objective.

Looking closely at the Share tab of the Properties page, you will notice a button marked Permissions. Click the Permissions button to bring up the Access Through Share Permissions (or ATS permissions) screen (see Figure 3.8).

F I G U R E 3.8: Access Through Share Permissions

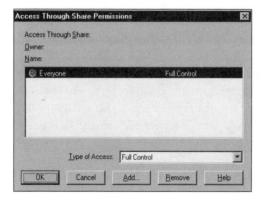

By default, the ATS share allows the group Everyone to have Full Control access to the share. If you use the Type of Access drop-down menu, you will see four types of share permissions you can control: Full Control, Change, Read, and No Access. See Table 3.1 for more information on these ATS share-level permissions.

T A B L E 3.1: Share-Level Permissions

Access Through Share Permission	Permissions Granted
Full Control	The user can read or see a folder, subfolder, or file; execute an application; write to a closed file; and delete a folder or file. If the share resides on an NTFS partition, the user can also take ownership of the resource and change permissions.
Change	The user can read or see a folder, subfolder or file; execute an application; write to a closed file; and delete a folder or file.
Read	The user can read and execute permissions to the share, folders, subfolders, and files.
No Access	The user can connect to the share, but will not be able to access any resources.

Share permissions deal with shares, and shares can point to folders regardless of the file system on which the folder resides. So, you can have a share that points to a folder on a FAT file system partition. If the share is on a FAT partition, once you assign the ATS permissions to the share, you are done. If there is a subfolder or file that needs more or less restrictive access, you are out of luck. Folder level is as deep as security gets on a FAT partition. If deeper security is necessary, the folder or file should reside on a drive that is based in NTFS.

If the share resides on an NTFS partition, another set of permissions can be granted to the local file or folder. This can get a little tricky. For example, suppose you are going to the bank to get some documents out of your safe-deposit box. When you arrive at the bank, you have to sign in to get the permission to go down to the vault; this is your logon security. Once you are down in the vault, you have to show identification to prove that you are whom you say you are. This second level of security could be considered share security. Once you prove whom you really are, you give your key to the person in charge of the vault so that they can open your box and give you access. When the teller finally takes the key to determine your access, that is NTFS security.

When determining what a user can really do, you must consider the share permissions granted to the share and the NTFS permissions granted to the folder or file. This is called the user's effective permissions to a folder. A user may get conflicting permissions from a variety of sources. One group may grant Full Access, another group may grant Limited Access, and the end user may have been given No Access as an individual permission. Is it possible to sort it all out? Yes, if share and NTFS permissions are applied, the most restrictive permissions take precedence. This is especially true of the No Access permission. If you have been given the No Access permission, either as an individual user or as a member of a group, you have no access, regardless of any other permissions you may have been assigned by other group memberships. You can attach to the share, but you cannot see anything.

WARNING It is common for a question about permissions to have the sample user be a member of a group that is granted No Access. The question will usually be long and involved, and then asks what the user can actually do. If the words No Access show up in relation to a user, the answer is *nothing*.

Do all these share permissions appear to be Greek to you? Let's examine permissions and what all those funky letters mean.

To do anything, each permission is made up of one or more actions. There are six basic actions, four of which apply to both share and NTFS permissions (see Table 3.2).

T A B L E 3.2: System Actions

Permission	Actions
Read (R)	Users can read or see a file. Usually used in conjunction with Execute.
Write (W)	Users can add data to a file.

T A B L E 3.2: System Actions *(cont.)*

Permission	Actions
Execute (X)	Users can execute a file. Usually used in conjunction with Read.
Delete (D)	Users can delete a file.
Change Permissions (P)	NTFS permission—users can change the access level of other users on this file or folder. Granted as part of Full Control if the share is on an NTFS partition.
Take Ownership (O)	NTFS partition—users can claim ownership of a file. Granted as part of Full Control if the share is on an NTFS partition.

NOTE   These actions also play a role in the auditing of files.

Given this information, let's reexamine the ATS share permissions. Full Control is self-explanatory. By default, when you create a share, the group Everyone has Full Control over the share and its folders, subfolders, and files. The newest user on your network can delete anything on the share. If security is an issue on your network, this could pose a problem.

Change gives the user or group the ability to perform the following actions: Read (R), Execute (X), Write (W), and Delete (D). So, the user or member of the group can read, execute, write, and delete information in the share.

The share Read permission grants the user or group the ability to read and execute files on the share. It is usually granted to application executable files—files with the extension .EXE or .COM.

No Access lets the user or member of the group attach to the share, but they cannot access any information from the share.

Directory-Level Permissions

What about the NTFS permissions? NTFS permissions are permissions granted to *local* files and directories on a host computer. These permissions can be granted by the owner of the directory. Separate permissions can be granted at the directory and file levels. The directory-level permissions are listed in Table 3.3.

T A B L E 3.3: NTFS Directory-Level Permissions

Directory-Level Permission	Permissions Granted
No Access	Users cannot access the directory at all.
List	Users cannot access the directory, but can see the contents of the directory.
Read	Users can read data files and execute application files.
Add	Users cannot read any information from the directory or even see the files that are stored in the directory, but can add data to the directory.
Add and Read	Users can see information in the directory and add information (new files) to the directory. Users cannot modify existing files in the directory.
Change	Users can see files in the directory, add files to the directory, modify files in the directory, and delete files from the directory (or even delete the whole directory). Users can also change the attributes of the directory.
Full Control	Users can do everything they can do with Change, but can also make changes to resources they do not own.

Permissions given to a directory flow down into the directory. If you have given the group EXCEL_Users the Read permission to the folder D:\Applications\Excel, a member of that group can execute the file EXCEL.EXE.

File-Level Permissions

There are times when security needs to be taken one step further, down to the individual file level. Suppose you have a folder that contains files with the payroll information for the next fiscal year. During the budget process, the payroll file is open so certain users can make changes. When the payroll process for the year has been finalized, you want users to be able to read the file, but not make changes to it. Meanwhile, in the same folder, there are files that the management team needs to change. In this case, you would simply change the permissions on the payroll file to allow people to only read the file. When you make the change to just one file, all the other files are not affected. See Table 3.4 for an explanation of file-level permissions.

TABLE 3.4: NTFS File-Level Permissions

File-Level Permission	Permissions Granted
No Access	Users cannot access the file at all.
Read	Users can read a data file or execute it if it is an application file.
Change	Users can read, execute, modify, or delete the file.
Full Control	Users can read, execute, write to, or delete the file, and change permissions or take ownership away from the owner of the file.

To set NTFS permissions for a folder or file, highlight the folder or file, right-click, and select Properties. From the Properties page, select the Security tab and then choose Permissions.

NOTE Step-by-step directions for setting ATS and NTFS permissions are found in the "Necessary Procedures" section, following the discussion of auditing.

Establishing File Auditing

How security-conscious is your place of business? Some businesses consist of only family members and security is nonexistent. Everyone has full access to everything. Other businesses are *very* security-conscious and make every effort to ensure against the inappropriate use of corporate information.

One way to check the security of those ultra-sensitive documents or folders is to enable auditing. Auditing will not allow you to choose which folders, subfolders, and files you want to audit, but it will provide you with a way of determining who is accessing the files.

You can audit the success or failure of the following actions by any user or group of users:

- Read

- Write

- Execute

- Delete

- Change Permissions

- Take Ownership

After you enable auditing, the results of the audit are written to the event log.

NOTE For more information on enabling auditing, see the "Necessary Procedures" section.

Necessary Procedures

For some system administrators who have been around for a while, the FAT file system may offer some solace, because it is understood. If, however, you want features such as security or data compression, NTFS is a must. There is a one-way conversion method.

Creating a Share

There are several ways to create a share—by using NT Explorer, My Computer, Server Manager, or the Net Share utility.

To create a share using NT Explorer:

1. Open NT Explorer.

2. Open directories until you locate the folder that you want to share.

3. Highlight the directory name and right-click.

4. Select Sharing from the drop-down menu. This will open the Sharing tab of the Properties dialog box.

NOTE You can also reach the Properties dialog box by highlighting the directory name, right-clicking, and choosing Properties. From the Properties menu, select Sharing.

---

5. When you reach the Sharing tab, you will notice that the default share name is the name of the directory. Some users are not excited about having a share name such as APPS_EXCEL. So, you can enter a new name for the share—one that is more user friendly. When you change the name of the share, it does not change the name of the directory—it just presents users with a name that makes sense to real people rather than computer people.

There is an opportunity to change the path, but if you have to do that, why did you choose this folder in the first place?

You will notice there is also a spot for comments. Comments are optional, and be careful, because what you enter will show up next to the share in NT Explorer.

To create a share using My Computer:

1. Open My Computer.

2. Click the drive letter on which the target folder resides.

3. Open directories until you locate the folder that you want to share.

4. Highlight the directory name and right-click.

5. Select Sharing from the drop-down menu. This will open the Sharing tab of the Properties dialog box.

6. When you reach the Sharing tab, you will notice that the default for the directory is Not Shared. Click the Shared As radio button. The usual share name is the name of the directory. Some users are not excited about having a share name such as APPS_EXCEL. So, you can enter a new name for the share—one that is more user friendly. When you change the name of the share, it does not change the name of the directory—it just presents users with a more user-friendly name.

To create a share using Server Manager:

1. Log onto the computer as administrator.

2. Start Server Manager by choosing Start ≻ Programs ≻ Administration Tools ≻ Server Manager.

3. Highlight the server name.

4. Choose Computer from the top menu, then select Shared Directories.

5. In the Shared Directory menu, click New Share.

6. Fill in the information on the New Share page, including Share Name, Path, and a comment.

7. Finally, you can add the maximum number of users allowed or choose to allow a specific number of users.

Net Share is a command-line utility. As such, you start the process by opening a command prompt. To create a share using Net Share, choose Start ≻ Programs ≻ Command Prompt. The syntax for the Net Share utility is shown below.

```
MS-DOS Prompt                                          _ □ ×
Microsoft(R) Windows NT(TM)
(C) Copyright 1985-1996 Microsoft Corp.

C:\>net share /?
The syntax of this command is:

NET SHARE sharename
          sharename=drive:path [/USERS:number | /UNLIMITED]
                              [/REMARK:"text"]
          sharename [/USERS:number | /UNLIMITED]
                   [/REMARK:"text"]
          {sharename | devicename | drive:path} /DELETE

C:\>
```

As an example, suppose you need a temporary share to point to D:\Applications\Excel. You want to call the share Excel and allow 10 users to access the share.

From the command prompt, the syntax would be as follows:

```
Net Share Excel=d:\applications\excel /users:10
```

To delete the share, the syntax would be as follows:

```
Net Share Excel /delete
```

Setting Share Permissions

You can set share permissions only on network shares. ATS permissions are usually assigned to a group, rather than an individual.

NOTE   As you have already seen from the discussion of creating shares, there are several ways of accessing the Properties page for a share, folder, or file. In the examples that follow, NT Explorer is the utility of choice.

To set ATS permissions:

1. Log onto the network as administrator or a user with Full Control over the share.

2. Start NT Explorer by selecting Start ➤ Programs ➤ Windows NT Explorer.

3. Browse to the share where the permissions will be applied. Highlight the share and right-click.

4. Click Sharing.

5. Click Permissions.

6. With the Access Through Share Permissions screen showing, click Add, which brings up the Add Users and Groups window.

7. Select the group that will receive the permissions, highlight the group, and click Add.

8. In the lower half of the Add Users and Groups window, use the Type of Access drop-down menu to choose No Access, Read, Change, or Full Access.

9. Click the appropriate choice. This will bring you back to the Add Users and Groups window.

10. Click OK to return to the ATS Permissions screen.

11. Click OK to return to the share's Properties window.

12. Click OK to return to NT Explorer.

Setting NTFS Folder- and File-Level Permissions

To set lower-level (folder or file) permissions, you must use NTFS permissions. NTFS permissions are not available for FAT partitions.

NOTE NTFS permissions are usually assigned to a group, rather than an individual.

To set NTFS permissions:

1. Log onto the network as someone who has ownership over the folder or file.

2. Start NT Explorer by selecting Start ➤ Programs ➤ Windows NT Explorer.

3. Browse to the folder or file where the permissions will be applied. Highlight the folder or file and right-click.

4. Click Sharing.

5. Click Security.

6. Click Permissions. This brings up the Directory Permissions window.

7. With the Directory Permissions window showing, click Add, which brings up the Add Users and Groups window.

8. Select the group or user that will receive the permissions, highlight the group or user, and click Add.

9. In the lower half of the Add Users and Groups window, use the Type of Access drop-down menu to choose No Access, List, Read, Add, Add and Read, Change, or Full Access.

10. Click the appropriate choice. This will bring you back to the Add Users and Groups window.

11. Click OK to return to the Directory Permissions window.

12. At the top of the Directory Permissions window, there are two radio buttons.

  • If you select Replace Permissions on Subdirectories, it will push the changes down to any subdirectories.

  • If you select Replace Permissions on Existing Files, it will push the changes down to any files.

13. Click OK to return to the folder's Security tab.

14. Click OK to return to NT Explorer.

Establishing File Auditing

Before you can configure auditing, you must turn it on. Auditing is turned off by default. To enable auditing:

1. Start User Manager for Domains by selecting Start ➤ Programs ➤ Administrative Tools ➤ User Manager for Domains.

2. Click Policies.

3. Click Audit.

4. Select the Audit These Events button.

5. Enable the checkboxes for the events you want to audit. Your choices involve the success or failure of the following items:

  • Logon and logoff

  • File and object access

  • Use of user rights

- User and group management
- Security policy changes
- Restart, shutdown, and system
- Process tracking

6. Click OK. Auditing is now enabled for the domain.

To start auditing activities of a specific folder or file, access the Auditing tab by choosing Properties ➢ Security ➢ Auditing. To select auditing:

1. Log on as an administrator or equivalent user.

2. Start NT Explorer by selecting Start ➢ Programs ➢ Windows NT Explorer.

3. Browse to the folder or file you want to audit. Highlight the folder or file and right-click.

4. Select Properties.

5. Click the Security tab.

6. Click Auditing.

7. At the top of the Directory Auditing window, you can select Replace Auditing on Subdirectories or Replace Auditing on Existing Files.

- Replace Auditing on Subdirectories will start the audit process for all current and new subfolders.
- Replace Auditing on Existing Files will start the audit process for all current and new files.

8. Click Add.

9. Select the users or groups you want to audit. Click Add after each selection.

10. When the selection of users and groups is complete, click OK.

11. Enable the appropriate checkboxes for the actions you want to audit.

12. After you have selected the actions to audit, click OK to begin auditing.

Auditing writes the information to the event log. This is a processor-intensive task and should be undertaken with great care.

Exam Essentials

Exam questions for the objectives in this section will show up on exam after exam. Know the different file systems and understand what each can do.

Know the various methods of creating a share.   You can create a share by using NT Explorer, My Computer, Server Manager, or the Net Share command-line utility.

Know how to create a hidden share.   You can create a hidden share by adding $ to the end of the share name—for example, C$ or ADMIN$.

Know how to set ATS permissions.   You can assign ATS permissions through the Properties page of the share. From the Properties page, select Permissions.

Know how to set NTFS folder- and file-level permissions.   You can assign NTFS permissions through the Properties page of the share. Select the Security tab to begin the process.

Know the effect when a user or group has the No Access permission to a share.   If a user has been given the No Access permission to a share or folder, either by an individual assignment or through a group assignment, the user will not be able to access that share. Assignments granted through other means cannot override the No Access assignment.

Know the effects of file auditing.   When you enable file auditing, it lets the administrator see what has been done with a file. The audited information is displayed in the event log.

Key Terms and Concepts

Access control list (ACL): Hard-coded list of users and groups with permissions to various hidden shares. Also, a list of users and groups that have been provided permissions or rights to a resource.

Access Through Shares permissions (ATS permissions): Permissions granted at the share point, at the folder level.

Add: Directory-level permission that allows the user to add information to the directory. With just the Add permission, the user cannot read any information from the directory or even see other files stored in the directory.

Add and Read: Directory-level permission that allows the user to add information to a directory and see information already stored in the directory.

Change: Permission that allows the user to read, execute, write, and delete folders, subfolders, and files at the share level and below.

Change permissions: An action that allows the user to change permissions to the file for others.

Delete: An action of deleting a file.

Execute: An action of running or executing a file.

File auditing: Configuring the server to keep track of various actions or events that occur to a given resource.

Full Control: Permission that gives the user full rights to the share, including the permission to determine ownership.

List permission: Directory-level permission that allows the user to see the contents of the directory, even if the user cannot gain access to the directory.

Macintosh-accessible volume: Server-based share that is available to users of Apple's Macintosh.

No Access: Users can connect to a share, but will not be able to access any resources.

Permission: Windows NT settings you set on a shared resource that determine which users can use the resource and how they can use it.

Read: Assigns Read and Execute permissions to the share, folders, subfolders, and files. Also an action of reading a file.

Share: To make resources, such as directories and printers, available to others.

Share name: A name that refers to a shared resource on a server. Each shared directory on a server has a share name, used by PC users to refer to the directory. Users of Macintoshes use the name of the Macintosh-accessible volume that corresponds to a directory, which may be the same as the share name. *See also* Macintosh-accessible volume.

Share permissions: Used to restrict the availability over the network of a shared resource to only certain users.

Shared directory: A directory to which network users can connect.

Shared network directory: *See* shared directory.

Shared resource: Any device, data, or program that is used by more than one other device or program. For Windows NT, shared resources refer to any resource that is made available to network users, such as directories, files, printers, and named pipes. Also refers to a resource on a server that is available to network users.

Take Ownership: An action that allows the user to take ownership of a file.

User rights: Define a user's access to a computer or domain and the actions that a user can perform on the computer or domain. User rights permit actions such as logging onto a computer or network, adding or deleting users in a workstation or domain, and so forth.

Write: An action of writing information to a file.

Sample Questions

1. Given the default permissions assigned to groups, which groups would you need to belong in to create a share?

    A. Administrators

    B. Backup users

    C. Guests

    D. Users

    Answer: A—Administrators can create shares.

2. Suppose that a user is a member of three groups—Administrators, MIS, and Apps_Acctg. There is a share created called Accounting. The Administrators group has Full Control permissions to the Accounting share. The MIS group has been assigned No Access permissions, and the Apps_Acctg group has been given the Change permission. What can the user do with the share?

    A. The user has full rights to the share, granted to them through their membership in the Administrators group.

    B. The user can read or see a folder, subfolder, or file; execute an application; write to a closed file; and delete a folder or file. These are inherent in the Change permission the user received through their membership in Apps_Acctg.

    C. The user can attach to the share, but cannot see or do anything. This is a result of the No Access permission given to the MIS group.

    Answer: C—In the Microsoft security model, all bets are off when the No Access permission is granted. If you are given No Access permission because of your membership in any group or by an explicit assignment to your user account, you have no access to the share.

3. A user has been given Change permission to the H_R share. The share points to a folder that resides on a FAT partition. The Human Resources Director comes to you and asks that the user retains Change permissions to the share, but the Director would like more restrictive permissions placed on the Salary_99 file. Can you help the Human Resources Director?

   A. Yes—NT will allow you to add file-level permissions to the Salary_99 file. Because the file is on a FAT partition, file-level security is allowed.

   B. No—NT will not allow you to add file-level permissions to the Salary_99 file. Because the file is on a FAT partition, file-level security is not allowed.

   C. Yes—The user is accessing the file through a share, which implies that they are a remote user. Because the user is a remote user, the format of the drive the share resides on has no impact.

   Answer: B—Because the share points to a folder on a FAT partition, only share-level permissions will apply.

CHAPTER

4

Connectivity

Microsoft Exam Objectives Covered in This Chapter:

▶ **Configure Windows NT Server for interoperability with NetWare servers by using various tools. Tools include:** *(pages 193 – 203)*
- Gateway Service for NetWare
- Migration Tool for NetWare

▶ **Install and configure multiprotocol routing to serve various functions. Functions include:** *(pages 203 – 215)*
- Internet router
- BOOTP/DHCP Relay Agent
- IPX router

▶ **Install and configure Internet Information Server.** *(pages 215 – 218)*

▶ **Install and configure Internet services. Services include:** *(pages 218 – 227)*
- World Wide Web
- DNS
- Intranet

▶ **Install and configure remote access service (RAS). Configuration options include:** *(pages 227 – 247)*
- Configuring RAS communications
- Configuring RAS protocols
- Configuring RAS security

There are very few "pure" networks in the world. Most networks are a combination of a legacy system purchased over the years, a couple of servers with operating systems mandated by some piece of software, a few odds and ends purchased by the "last guy," and a few new pieces of technology (mostly new toys bought for image not function).

Into this mess, you wish to bring a little order and stability—good luck! Given the state of many networks, one of the most important criteria for new systems is interoperability. When you add to this the ability to grow with technology, you have only a handful of potential operating systems worthy of consideration.

Microsoft Windows NT has a few design features that make it the perfect choice for today's networks. One of these features is NT's modular design. Every function that an NT server can perform is designed as a separate subsystem of the operating system. This modular design means that NT can be updated to meet the needs of future technologies. It also means that third-party developers can add functionality to the base operating system. These are important features in a business world that can't decide what the power tie of the week should be, let alone standardize a set of services for the network.

By the end of this chapter, you should be comfortable discussing the various tools available to connect an NT network to the world.

Configure Windows NT Server for interoperability with NetWare servers by using various tools. Tools include:

- Gateway Service for NetWare
- Migration Tool for NetWare

No discussion of networking is complete without discussing Novell's NetWare. In the not-too-distant past, Novell owned over 90 percent of the worldwide networking market. Even today, that percentage is probably still over 50. Given this, you will probably have to connect to a NetWare server at some point in your career.

Even if you believe the experts who claim that NetWare is a *legacy* operating system and that Novell is on a downward spiral to oblivion, common sense tells you that NetWare servers will be around for a long time. With Novell's current market share, it will take years for NT to replace the NetWare servers currently installed.

One of the features of Windows NT is its ability to coexist with a Net-Ware environment. This means companies can ease into an NT network, while maintaining the NetWare services that they currently use.

Critical Information

Because of the number of Novell networks in existence, Microsoft tests heavily on the skills necessary to add an NT server to a Novell NetWare environment. You will find NetWare-related questions on many of the MCSE examinations. Make sure that you are comfortable with the topics covered for this objective before you take the MCSE exam.

Gateway Service for NetWare

There are two ways to configure your network so that your clients can access NetWare servers:

- Install Client Service for NetWare (CSNW) on each NT workstation that might need to access a NetWare server

- Install Gateway Service for NetWare (GSNW) on an NT server and use it as a gateway to the NetWare environment.

CSNW is not listed in the exam objectives, but you should know what it is and when to use it. CNSW is software loaded on the *client* computers. This software allows them to directly connect to and communicate with NetWare servers. (The clients will also have to have the NWLink IPX/SPX-compatible network protocol installed and configured as one of their protocols.) CSNW should be used if your clients extensively use the NetWare servers or if you have a lot of users who will use the NetWare servers simultaneously.

It might not be convenient or necessary to configure CSNW on your clients. Another option is to install GSNW on an NT server. GSNW acts as a gateway to the NetWare environment. When clients need to access services on a NetWare server, they send the request to the

GSNW service on the NT server. It, in turn, passes the request to the NetWare server.

GSNW offers two benefits to the network administrator. First, only one computer (the NT server) has to have special software installed (GSNW). Second, the gateway server is the only computer that has to have NWLink installed and configured. Anytime you can bring management of a service to your server, rather than your workstations, you save time and effort. In addition, the GSNW connection uses only one NetWare connection regardless of the number of clients connected through it, while each CSNW connection uses an individual, which can be limited by the number of access licenses held.

The downside to this configuration is that all of your clients that need to access NetWare services must share this one connection. If you have a large number of users or your users access the NetWare server continuously, you will get better performance by using CSNW on your clients.

When configuring GSNW, you need to configure the NT side and the NetWare side. On the NetWare side, you must:

1. Create a user account with the same name and password configuration as on the gateway account on the NT server.

2. Assign to the NetWare user account created in step 1 all necessary trustee rights to NetWare network resources.

3. Create a group account named NTGATEWAY.

4. Make the user (from step 1) a member of this group.

WARNING   Since all users share this one account to access the NetWare server, the account must include all permissions that any GSNW user might need. In other words, you cannot set up different permissions for each NT client that might access the NetWare server. This might be a security issue in your environment.

Once the NetWare accounts are created, you configure the GSNW on the NT server. This process will be explained in the "Necessary Procedures" section. Once you have configured, you create shares on your NT server that point to a resource on the NetWare server. From the user's perspective, these shares look like any other share points on the NT server.

Remember that GSNW is designed for an environment in which Net-Ware access is light and intermittent. If your clients need continuous access to the Novell servers or you expect a high level of traffic, you should configure CSNW on your clients.

Migration Tool for NetWare

There are many reasons to migrate from a NetWare to an NT environment—you might purchase software that requires NT (an issue that is becoming more and more common), you might want to limit your network to a single operating system for ease of administration, or you might just be pushed into it by upper management. Whatever the reason, Microsoft has provided a tool to make the migration process smooth and painless.

The Migration Tool for NetWare (MTFN) can be found on your NT server in the *Windows root*\System32 directory. The executable file is named NWCONV.EXE. MTFN allows you to easily transfer information from a NetWare server to an NT server. MTFN performs the following tasks:

- Preserves user account information, including logon and station restrictions.

- Preserves user login scripts. Microsoft Windows NT supports network login script commands.

- Offers control over how user and group names are transferred.

- Offers control over passwords on the transferred accounts. NT cannot read network passwords, so all passwords must change.

- Offers control over how account restrictions are transferred.

- Offers control over how administrative privileges are transferred.

- Creates a volume for network users.

- Selects which files and directories to transfer.

- Selects the directories to which transferred files will be copied.

- Preserves effective rights on files and directories (only if copied to an NTFS volume).

This tool transfers user information and data from one server (NetWare) to another (NT), but it does not upgrade an existing NetWare server to Windows NT. This is actually the best form of migration. If, at any time, you are not happy with the results, you can reformat the new NT server to get back to where you started.

TIP   If you are migrating multiple NetWare servers, you do not have to replace each computer. Migrate each one in turn, testing the results before moving on. After you have confirmed that the migration was successful, you can take down the NetWare server. At this point, if the hardware supports NT, you have the computer for your next NT server.

Necessary Procedures

Microsoft has spent a lot of marketing dollars trying to convince users of Novell's NetWare to move to Windows NT Server. One of the biggest selling points is that the network does not have to be moved completely to NT—the two operating systems can coexist on the same network. You will see questions about this topic on many of the MCSE exams, and most of those questions will be of a "how to" nature. So, spend some time getting familiar with the procedures involved in connecting to a NetWare environment.

Configuring Gateway Service for NetWare

GSNW is installed like any other NT service. In the Services tab of NT Server's Network applet, click Add. There are no configuration options during the installation, but as in all network service changes, you will be asked to restart your server. After this restart, you will be presented with a window that asks for your preferred NetWare server or Tree and Context. The former is used in bindery-based

NetWare 3.*x* environments, the latter in NetWare 4.*x* NDS (Novell directory service) environments.

1. In Control Panel, you will find a new applet, GSNW, which is used to manage your NetWare gateway. The opening screen of GSNW allows you to change the default server, set some default print parameters, and determine whether clients should run a login script when they connect to the NetWare server.

2. Click the Gateway button. Enable the gateway and enter the NetWare gateway account and password defined earlier.

3. You are ready to allow your clients access to resources on the NetWare server. Create shares that point to those resources. In the Configure Gateway dialog box, click Add to get the New Share dialog box.

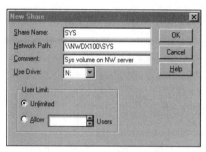

4. Give the share a name and define the UNC path to the resource. Define the mapped drive letter if desired. You can also limit the number of users that can simultaneously access the resource, although the default is Unlimited.

5. Once the share is configured, you can set permissions like on any NT share. Click the Permissions button in the Configure Gateway dialog box.

Remember that the Novell permissions set on the gateway account, which are more restrictive in nature, will overrule any permissions you set here.

From the client, the new share appears as if it is located on the NT server, which is acting as the Novell gateway.

Using Migration Tool for NetWare

Migration Tool for NetWare is found in the *Windows root* System32 directory. The executable is NWCONV.EXE. When you run it, it will ask you for the source and destination servers.

You can then configure the migration itself. Click the User Options button in the next dialog box and configure the migration parameters for user and group accounts. You can configure:

- How passwords should be handled. Remember that NT cannot read the NetWare password. You have three options: Users will have no password, password will be the same as the user name, or users will have a default password. You can also force users to change their new password the first time they log onto the NT domain.

- How Migration Tool should deal with duplicate user names. You have four options: Log an error but do nothing, ignore the problem and skip the user, overwrite the existing NT account, or define a prefix to be added to the user name.

- How to deal with duplicate group accounts. You have three options: Log an error and skip the group, ignore the duplicate group completely, or define a prefix to be added to the group name.

- How to handle accounts with supervisor privileges on the NetWare server. You can add those accounts to the domain admins group. (By default, they do not inherit any administrative privileges in the NT domain.)

The next step is to configure the file transfer between the two servers. On the MTFN main screen, click the File Options button. Here, you can decide which files and directories should be transferred and where they should be copied. By default, everything is copied to the NT server—remember to change the default settings so that the Novell management directories are not copied (you won't need NetWare management tools on an NT server).

This utility has a great function that can save you hours of time and prevent a catastrophic failure—the ability to run a trial migration. The trial migration attempts the migration without actually transferring any information. This allows you to determine any problems you will run into and correct them before they occur. The trial migration creates a series of three log files:

- LOGFILE.LOG—Describes the setting you configured for the migration.

- SUMMARY.LOG—Summarizes the activity, reporting which servers were involved, how much disk space was required, how many user accounts were migrated, and how many files and directories were migrated.

- ERROR.LOG—This is probably the most useful log file during a trial migration. It lists areas where the utility encountered a problem. It lists duplicate user names, duplicate group names, etc. This provides you with a list of problems that you can correct before performing the actual migration.

Once you're ready to go, click the Migrate button. Remember that this process will take quite a bit longer than the trial migration and places a huge system load on the servers. Schedule this to be done during low usage times. This time, the files actually have to be copied from server to server.

Exam Essentials

Interoperability with NetWare is very important to the success of Windows NT Server. Be sure you're comfortable with the following topics.

Understand Gateway Service for NetWare (GSNW). GSNW is a service that creates a connection between an NT server and a NetWare server. This connection can then be used as a point of access to NetWare resources. The point is to allow the clients of your NT domain access to NetWare resources without having to configure any special software on each client.

Understand the network setup for GSNW. On the NetWare server, you must create a user account that the GSNW service can use to log onto the network. You must also create a group named NTGATEWAY and make the user account a member. Assign any necessary trustee rights to this network group account.

Know when it is appropriate to use GSNW and when it is not.
GSNW is best when your users need occasional access to NetWare
resources. Remember that all users share one channel to the NetWare
server. If too many users access it, performance will decrease. On the
plus side, however, only one licensed connection will be established to
the NetWare server, which reduces the number of client licenses you
will have to purchase for your NetWare environment.

Understand the migration process from NetWare to NT.   Use
Migration Tool for NetWare to migrate users, groups, files, and
directories from a NetWare server to an NT server. This tool allows
you to configure which users and groups will be migrated and what
should happen in the event of duplicate names. It provides a method
for controlling NT passwords for migrated NetWare user accounts
since the passwords cannot be transferred. It also allows you to control the data that are migrated, both the content and the destination.

Key Terms and Concepts

Client Service for NetWare (CSNW):   Software loaded at the
client that allows a direct connection to a NetWare server.

Gateway Service for NetWare (GSNW):   An NT server service
that provides a point of access to NetWare servers.

Migration Tool for NetWare (MTFN):   A utility that migrates users,
groups, files, and directories from a NetWare server to an NT server.

Sample Questions

1. Which of the following items is loaded on client computers to
allow direct access to Novell NetWare servers?

A. CSNW (Client Service for NetWare)

B. GSNW (Gateway Service for NetWare)

C. NCS (Novell connection software)

D. Novell TCP/IP services

E. NWLink IPX/SPX Compatible Transport

Answer: A, E—To allow a client to access a NetWare server directly, you must load both the appropriate protocol (NWLink) and a NetWare redirector (CSNW).

2. Which of the following features are benefits of GSNW?

A. Only the server needs to load NWLink.

B. NetWare resources look like NT shares to your clients.

C. Each user can have their own set of permissions on the NetWare server.

D. Since only one session is created to the NetWare server, performance is enhanced.

Answer: A, B—The server providing the GSNW service is the only NT computer that must communicate directly with the Novell environment. Thus, it is the only computer that must load NWLink. Since all NetWare resources look like a shared resource on that NT server, no retraining is necessary for your users.

Install and configure multiprotocol routing to serve various functions. Functions include:

- Internet router
- BOOTP/DHCP Relay Agent
- IPX router

This section discusses routing—how to set up your server as a router in both an IP and an IPX network. A few more details about the DHCP Relay Agent will be provided—the process of acquiring a TCP/IP address from a DHCP server and how this process is affected by a routed network.

Routers are critical pieces of today's networks. Routers are the traffic cops of your network. They control the flow of traffic, decide the route that traffic will take, and can influence the pace of traffic. If you think of your network as a little town with the wiring as the roads, routers are little information booths. They can provide directions to any place on the network or at least point you in the right direction. Without routers, you would have to connect all your devices to a single network segment. This would be like having only one road through town—rush hour would be a real mess, and you would have way too much traffic through your residential areas.

Microsoft expects that you not only know how to implement routing, but that you understand it. That's not necessarily a bad thing—to understand routing, you have to understand network traffic. If you understand network traffic, you will have a much easier time troubleshooting network-related problems in the troubleshooting section of the exam.

Critical Information

Without the ability to route the TCP/IP protocol, an operating system is unable to connect to the Internet or any other networks outside of its own subnet. Of all the protocols available to NT, TPC/IP is the protocol chosen by default during the installation process. Know it inside and out!

Internet Router

The phrase *Internet router* is really a marketing invention. An Internet router is just a router that can route the TCP/IP protocol suite. Understanding the process of routing TPC/IP traffic has become very important as more and more businesses connect to the Internet.

Routing

Routing is the process of finding a path between networks. Routers are devices that perform the routing function. The process of how a router decides the best path to a given network segment differs with the protocol in use—each protocol has its own procedure for building a list of networks, called a routing table. The router uses its routing table to determine the path that a packet should take to reach its destination.

NT servers can be configured to act as routers. Physically this entails putting more than one NIC (network interface card) in a server and configuring it appropriately for each protocol that it will route. Microsoft calls a computer with more than one NIC a multi-homed computer. After you have determined the proper physical settings for the additional card(s) and installed them in the server, you add the driver in the Network applet, within the Adapters tab.

The routing table on an IP router contains information on where a packet should be sent to reach a given network segment. In Figure 4.1, there are three networks. Each router knows about the segments that it is physically attached to, but not any other segments.

The IP addressing has been simplified by giving each interface a two-digit identifier—IP addressing is a complex subject that is beyond the scope of this exam. The description of the processes used to route traffic has also been simplified. For the Enterprise exam, you just need to understand the theory—you do not have to completely understand the processes involved.

FIGURE 4.1: Three networks with two routers

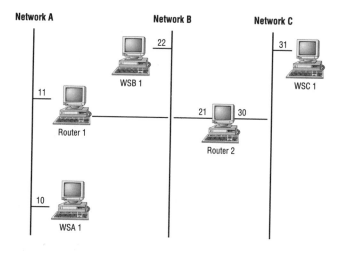

When a device needs to communicate with another device, it must first resolve the host name into an IP address. This can be done in a number of ways, but the Microsoft solution is to have a WINS server perform this function. Once the device has the IP address, it performs a calculation on the address to determine whether the destination is local or remote (on its network or another network). If the host is remote, the device will send the communication to its default gateway or router. The router is responsible for picking the next hop in the path to the destination.

In Figure 4.1, if WSA 1 needs to communicate with WSB 1, it would first determine whether WSB 1 is a local or remote host. Since WSB 1 is on another network segment, it would be a remote host. WSA 1 would then check its default gateway address and pass the packets of information to that address—WSA 1 *should* be configured with Router 1 as its default gateway.

Router 1 would then perform the same calculation to determine whether the destination is on a local network (one to which it is physically attached). If local, it would then pass the packets to the appropriate network segment.

Easy, right? Now, let's look at WSA 1 attempting to communicate with WSC 1. Everything would be the same, until the router determines that the destination is not on a network to which it is attached. At this point, the router would have to have a reference to look up the path to the destination network. This reference is the routing table.

The routing table contains a list of all known networks. This list contains information about which of the router's NIC cards should be used to send packets to a particular network and the address of the next router in the path.

The routing tables for each router in the example are shown in Tables 4.1 and 4.2.

T A B L E 4.1: Routing Table for Router 1

Destination Network	Local NIC Card	IP Address of Next Router
Network A	11	Local
Network B	20	Local
Network C	20	21

T A B L E 4.2: Routing Table for Router 2

Destination Network	Local NIC Card	IP Address of Next Router
Network A	21	20
Network B	21	Local
Network C	30	Local

When WSA 1 tries to communicate with WSC 1, it determines that the destination is remote. It then sends the packets to its default gateway—Router 1. Router 1 determines that the destination network is not local, so it checks its routing table. It discovers that to reach Network C, it must send the packets to the next router—out its own interface 20, addressed to IP address 21. Router 2 will then make the same calculations and discover that it is physically attached to the destination network.

There are two types of routing tables: static and dynamic.

Static routing   As an administrator, you can manually build the routing tables at your routers. This would involve typing in the appropriate information at each router in your network. This method is not favored by many administrators—it's a lot of work and can lead to mistakes. If you build static routing tables, you must update the tables every time you change your network.

Dynamic routing The TCP/IP protocol suite has a protocol specifically designed to pass this routing information between routers. Each router can then incorporate this information into its routing table. The protocol used to pass this information is RIP (routing information protocol). You must install RIP on you NT server as a separate service. Once RIP is installed, your NT server-based routers will begin exchanging route information.

RIP is a broadcast-based protocol. Every 30 seconds, RIP-enabled routers broadcast the contents of their routing table on each network to which they are attached. Since it is a broadcast, all routers on those segments will analyze the content of the broadcast and add any information to their own routing table. In Figure 4.1, if RIP is enabled on our routers, every 30 seconds both Router 1 and Router 2 will broadcast their routing tables on all of the networks to which they are attached. Each router's table begins with information about the networks to which they are attached. In this way, Router 1 will inform Router 2 about Network A and Router 2 will inform Router 1 about Network C. Note that both routers then know about the entire network, and the administrator does not have to configure the routing tables manually. RIP also has a mechanism built in to remove routes that have become unavailable, so the routing table will be a current representation of the network.

NOTE RIP was first made available on NT server in version 4. For older servers, you have to create static routes.

BOOTP/DHCP Relay Agent

DHCP is a great administrative tool—it saves time and effort, and reduces mistakes. It does, however, have one small drawback—the way communication occurs. All DHCP communication is accomplished with broadcast traffic using the BOOTP protocol, which is a protocol specifically designed to configure network clients.

When a client accesses a DHCP server, all traffic is maintained as broadcast-based traffic. Four packets are generated every time a client attempts to acquire an IP address:

- Request—In this packet, the client asks for an IP address. It has to be a broadcast because, at this point, the client has no IP configuration—in other words, it has no IP address and cannot communicate using IP in any other way. The request packet is sent to all DHCP servers on the network.

- Offer—All DHCP servers that receive the request will respond with an offer. This is also done as a broadcast packet. It has to be a broadcast because the recipient has no IP address. All DHCP servers that send an offer mark the address as "offered" in their scope.

- Selection—The client receives the offers from the DHCP servers. Whichever offer is received first will be chosen. This packet is sent out as a broadcast for two reasons. First, the client still does not officially have an IP address. Second, it lets all other DHCP servers know that it has made a choice (they can now unmark the address they offered so that they can offer it to another client).

- Acknowledgment—The DHCP server sends another broadcast acknowledging the selection by the client. The server then marks the IP address as "in use" and begins the lease time. The client now has an IP address and default mask (and often, information such as the default gateway) to use.

In most environments, a client is given an IP address for a specific amount of time, known as the lease period. The client will reestablish the lease on the IP address when the time has expired. The protocol used for these broadcasts is BOOTP. In the TCP/IP protocol suite, BOOTP is defined as both a service and a protocol used to deliver this service. It was designed for use by diskless workstations when booting from files stored on a server. Windows NT DHCP services take advantage of the fact that BOOTP is a fast and efficient protocol designed to pass configuration information to clients. NT does not, however, implement the BOOTP service to facilitate booting diskless workstations from a central server.

Because BOOTP was designed with a very specific purpose, most routers are not configured to pass BOOTP packets. (Actually, by default, most routers do not pass broadcast packets at all.) This leads to a problem in a DHCP environment—users can contact the DHCP server only if it is located on the same network. In other words, the DHCP server cannot, by default, service any clients located on the other side of a router. You can overcome this problem by configuring your router to pass BOOTP packets, but most system engineers would agree that this is not a good idea. You don't want to flood your network with broadcast packets every time a client boots. A better solution is to implement a DHCP Relay Agent on each network.

A DHCP Relay Agent is an NT server configured to pick up the clients' DHCP packets and forward them to the DHCP server. The Relay Agent must have a manually configured IP address and be configured with the IP address of the DHCP server. Since it has an address, it can use directed packets to reach the server. The bottom line is that the Relay Agent makes it possible for clients to receive their IP addresses from a DHCP server located on the other side of a router.

IPX Router

IPX has its own mechanism for building a routing table. It works much like IP in that it uses a protocol named RIP (routing information protocol) to pass information about the network from router to router.

To implement IPX routing on an NT server, you must first install RIP for NWLink IPX/SPX Compatible Transport. This service is installed from the Services tab of the Network applet. After the installation, you must restart your NT server.

As in IP, IPX routers use RIP to pass network information. An IPX routing table holds the network addresses of known networks and the number of networks that have to be crossed to reach each destination. Each network that has to be crossed is known as a *hop*. The RIP packets in Figure 4.2 would contain the information listed in Table 4.3.

FIGURE 4.2: IPX network

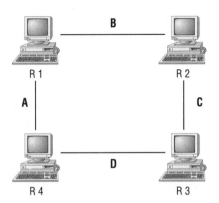

TABLE 4.3: RIP Packets from Router 1 (R 1)

Destination Network	Number of Hops	Send To Router ID
Network A	0	Local
Network A	3	Router 2 (R 2)
Network B	0	Local
Network B	3	Router 4 (R 4)
Network C	1	Router 2
Network C	2	Router 4
Network D	1	Router 4
Network D	2	Router 2

Each router will have a similar routing table. Note that in this example, the router keeps track of all possible routes to each destination. If communication fails on a given route, the router will automatically switch to another route to the destination.

RIP for IPX is a broadcast-based protocol. As such, since every router announces every route it knows, the amount of traffic can be prohibitive. Many companies refuse to allow IPX routing information across slow (and costly) WAN links. Full implementations of the IPX/SPX protocol suite allow filtering of this traffic. They usually have other tools to decrease the amount and frequency of traffic. NWLink and Microsoft's implementation of RIP for IPX do not include these tools. When you need to be able to control IPX traffic, it is better to purchase a dedicated router with these tools.

Necessary Procedures

Installing and configuring the Internet routing components is simply a matter of knowing where to look and then reading the screen. Remember that the Internet routing pieces are managed through the Network applet found in Control Panel.

Installing RIP for Internet

Select Control Panel ➤ Network ➤ Services ➤ Add ➤ Rip for Internet. There are no configurable options.

Enabling IP Routing

Select Control Panel ➤ Network ➤ Protocols ➤ TCP/IP Properties ➤ Routing. Check Enable IP Forwarding.

Configuring a DHCP Relay Agent.

Select Control Panel ➤ Network ➤ Protocols ➤ TCP/IP Properties ➤ DHCP Relay. Add the IP address(es) of your DHCP server(s).

Installing RIP for IPX

Select Control Panel ➤ Network ➤ Services ➤ Add ➤ RIP for IPX. There are no configurable options.

Enabling IPX Forwarding

Select Control Panel ➤ Network ➤ Protocols ➤ NWLink Properties ➤ Routing. Check Enable RIP Routing.

WARNING   RIP for IPX must be installed before IPX forwarding becomes available. This option is checked by default when you install RIP for IPX.

Exam Essentials

For this exam, you must understand the functions behind the routing of Internet protocols. Be sure to understand the following items before taking the exam.

Know what an IP routing table is used for.   An IP routing table is used to store directions to specific networks in your enterprise. Without a routing table, clients will be able to communicate only with hosts on their own network or hosts on networks directly attached to their default gateway.

Know the function of RIP for IP.   RIP for IP is the protocol used by routers to exchange information about the enterprise. Every 30 seconds, each router broadcasts its routing table on each network to which it is attached. Other routers pick up this information and add it to their routing tables. This dynamically propagates network information to each router on the network.

Know the four packets used in the DHCP client initialization. The packets (and steps) of the DHCP process are Request, Offer, Selection, Acknowledgment.

Know why a DHCP Relay Agent is used.   DHCP traffic utilizes the BOOTP protocol for communication. BOOTP is a broadcast-based protocol that most routers do not route. This means that if a client is on the other side of a router from the DHCP server, they cannot communicate and will not be able to acquire an IP address.

The DHCP Relay Agent picks up these broadcasts and relays them across the router, using directed traffic, to the DHCP server on behalf of the clients. If a network segment does not have a DHCP server, it should have a Relay Agent.

Know when to install RIP for IPX and enable IPX forwarding. Install RIP for IPX and enable IPX forwarding when clients that use IPX/SPX need access to resources on the other side of your router. Without this service installed, the server will not route packets from one network to another.

Key Terms and Concepts

BOOTP: A protocol designed to carry client configuration information. It was first developed to be used in the boot process of diskless workstations. It is also used for all DHCP traffic.

DHCP Relay Agent: A device that passes DHCP traffic across a router on behalf of clients.

Hop: A term used to specify the number of networks a packet will have to cross to reach a destination.

Multi-homed: A computer with more than one network interface card installed.

RIP for IPX: A protocol used by IPX routers to pass network information.

Routing: The process of finding a path between networks.

Routing table: A list of network segments available on your network and the routes to get to them.

Sample Questions

1. When creating an NT Server-based TCP/IP router, in what order are the following actions taken?

   A. Select Enable IP Forwarding.

   B. Configure the NIC cards.

C. Install TCP/IP.

D. Install the NIC driver.

E. Assign each NIC an IP address.

Answer: B, D, C, E, A

2. Which of the following services allows for a dynamic exchange of routing information between routers?

A. DHCP

B. WINS

C. RIP

Answer: C—RIP (routing information protocol) is used by routers to exchange information about the layout of the network.

Install and configure Internet Information Server.

Internet Information Server (IIS) is not even mentioned in the Enterprise course, but it is listed in the objectives—this should tell you something about its importance in Microsoft's view of the world. However, you will find IIS questions in many of the MCSE examinations, and this exam is no exception.

Over the past few years, Microsoft has tried to change its focus from the desktop to the network. An important part of that change is the inclusion of tools for connecting a Microsoft network to the world at large—mainly through the Internet. IIS is one of the main pieces of this philosophy.

Critical Information

By default, IIS 2 is installed when you install NT server. If you don't want to install it, you must clear the checkbox on the appropriate page. If you didn't install IIS 2 and want to install it at a later time, you can start the process in one of three ways:

- If IIS 2 is not installed, the NT installation program will put an icon on your desktop. This icon will start the installation of IIS.

- If you removed the icon from your desktop, you will also find it in Control Panel.

- If all else fails, you can access the installation program on your NT Server CD-ROM. It is in the \I386\Inetsrv directory. The executable is named INETSTP.EXE.

TIP   The NT Server CD-ROM includes IIS version 2. You should apply the latest NT service pack to upgrade IIS to the latest version. At the time of this writing, the latest version is 4. You can find the NT service packs at www.microsoft.com.

This objective concerns the installation process of IIS 2. Most of the critical information will be found in the "Necessary Procedures" section.

Necessary Procedures

There is very little involved in installing IIS on your NT server. For the exam, you will want to be aware of the choices you will be asked to make and the services that are added to your server.

Installing IIS 2

Here are the steps for installing IIS 2:

1. Start the installation program and work through the opening screen that warns you to close all programs before continuing. The first dialog box allows you to configure the options you will install on your server. (The various options that are relevant to the exam will be described in the next section.)

2. After making your choices, click OK. The next window allows you to configure where the various services will store their published material. These default directories for WWW, FTP, and Gopher services should be used and placed on a partition formatted with NTFS so that you can use NT security to protect these data. Based on the decisions you made in these windows, the installation program will then copy files to various locations. For this exam, you will not need to know what is copied or where these files are placed.

3. Your next decision is which OBDC drivers, if any, you wish to install on your server. These drivers allow IIS to access data stored in files created by various database programs. Highlight the appropriate drivers and click OK. The drivers will be copied to your system.

This ends the installation and configuration process for IIS 2.

Exam Essentials

This is a short but important objective for the exam. You should install IIS a few times before taking this exam.

Understand the options that are available when installing IIS 2. You should expect questions about which components to install and which directories to use to publish material for those services.

Key Terms and Concepts

OBDC driver: A set of DLLs that allows a service to access a data source created using another program.

Publishing directories: The directories used to hold information that the selected service (WWW, FTP, or Gopher) makes available to connected users.

Sample Questions

1. What is the function of an OBDC driver?

A. To allow access to OpenBase data-store software

B. To act as an interface between IIS and a database

C. To act as an interface between IIS and Exchange Server

Answer: B—OBDC drivers act as interpreters between IIS and a particular type of database (depending upon which driver you install).

Install and configure Internet services. Services include:

- World Wide Web
- DNS
- Intranet

O nce a company decides to move forward with Internet technologies, quite a few more services can (or must) be added to the network. Configuring these services is critical to an efficient and secure network. In this section, tips and techniques for configuring three of the most common services will be examined.

Critical Information

Microsoft has placed a lot of emphasis on the various Internet technologies available within an NT environment. The MCSE examination reflects this emphasis. While you are not expected to be an expert in any of the following technologies, you are expected to understand what they are, how they are used, and how to configure them.

World Wide Web

Many companies are finding a need to build a presence on the Internet. Most companies will do this by installing and designing a Web site. A Web server is nothing more than a server that provides file-retrieval privileges using a specific set of protocols, namely HTTP.

Configuring a Web server concerns more than just creating content. In many ways, content is secondary to the major concern—security. If you read any trade magazine, you'll find an article about the dangers of connecting to the Internet—hackers deleting data, viruses spreading like wildfire, and insecure transmissions being intercepted on the wire. All of these dangers are very real, but with proper configuration, you can avoid the majority of problems.

One of the best features of IIS is that it integrates very well with NT. When using IIS as your Web server, you can protect files using the same tools and techniques that you use in NT, such as the SAM database and the NT security model. When you install IIS, it creates a user account that is used to define the security assigned to anonymous users. That user account, named IUSER_*SERVER NAME*, can be granted limited permissions—just like any other NT account.

WARNING   The Internet anonymous-access account is a normal user account in all respects. Any resource that the group Everyone has permissions to is accessible to this account. Some administrators remove the group Everyone from the access control list (ACL) of *all* shares when they create anonymous-access accounts, thereby avoiding any potential problems.

The IIS environment is managed using the Microsoft Internet Service Manager, which is accessible by choosing Start ➤ Programs ➤ Microsoft Internet Server. In addition, the Web-based version of this utility is also available. This utility allows you to accomplish the following tasks:

- Connect to IIS servers and view their properties

- Start, stop, and pause a service
- Configure services

The three services provided by IIS are as follows:

- WWW service—This service allows users to connect to and view your Web site. You can configure a default page so that users do not have to specify a particular file when they connect.

- Gopher service—This service was primarily designed to allow administrators to index files and directories.

- FTP service—This service allows users to use FTP (file transfer protocol) to view, upload, and download files on a server FTP site.

You do not have to know any of these services intimately for the examination. However, you will need to be aware of the available options. The configuration of these three services will be examined more closely in the "Necessary Procedures" section.

DNS

DNS (domain name service) is the service used on the Internet to resolve user-friendly fully qualified domain names (more commonly called domain names) into IP addresses. When you send your browser to www.royal-tech.com, DNS finds the IP address of that Web server and returns it to your client so that communication can occur.

Basically, DNS is just a giant database. Its basic function is to hold records that have a host name and the IP address of that host. The DNS database is divided into domains (also known as zones). The piece of the DNS database that a DNS server holds—a domain—contains records that define the host name and IP address of resources.

NOTE   Other types of records are defined in the DNS specification. DNS can store everything from simple host/IP address records to records that define how e-mail should be handled.

When a user wants to find a resource, www.royal-tech.com for instance, they send a request to their DNS server. The DNS server performs a search for the associated record. It will first compare the request against its domain—in this case, the domain is royal-tech.com. If the domain holds that piece of the DNS database, it will return the IP address of the WWW server to the client. On the Internet, each DNS server is configured with a list of root servers. These root servers contain the IP addresses of all registered domain names.

If the local DNS server cannot resolve the domain name, it will query a root server for the IP address of the DNS server that holds royal-tech.com. Your DNS server will then query that DNS server for the IP address of a server named WWW.

NOTE DNS includes the ability to use aliases for hosts. Most companies do not name their Web server WWW. They create a record that acts as a pointer to the actual host-name record.

SEE ALSO A full discussion of DNS is outside the scope of this examination. For more information, check out *Mastering TCP/IP for NT Server* by Mark Minasi and Todd Lammle (Sybex, 1997).

DNS is installed as a service on your NT server. Once DNS is installed, you manage the DNS service using the DNS Manager utility found in your Administrative Tools group.

Intranet

The term *intranet* refers to an internal network that utilizes the tools and techniques of the Internet to provide services limited to local network users. For example, you can use the Web server to host an intranet Web site that contains internal policy memos that wouldn't be appropriate on a public Web site. Many companies are starting to realize the benefits of a total network solution, rather than having a network comprised of a series of servers, each installed, maintained, and managed as a separate entity.

For the examination, this objective revolves around a series of tips for securing an intranet or connection to the Internet.

- Remember that if you are going to allow anonymous access, the anonymous user (IUSR_ *SERVER NAME*) is made a member of the domain guests group. Be aware of this fact when assigning permissions to this group.

- You can configure both the WWW and the FTP services to require a valid user name and password for access. Two types of authentication are available:

    Basic—Transmissions are not encrypted, so the user name and password are sent as clear text. FTP supports only Basic authentication.

    Windows NT Challenge/Response—Supported by Microsoft Internet Explorer 2 and above, and provides a secure login over the network.

- Require passwords on all user accounts; require a minimum length of six or more characters and frequent changes.

- Lock out accounts after multiple failed logon attempts and require an administrator to unlock locked-out accounts.

- Use time restrictions and automatically disconnect users whose time has expired.

The bottom line for configuring an intranet is using all of the tools available in Windows NT to provide security.

Necessary Procedures

You are not expected to be an expert in the following subjects for this examination. However, you are expected to be able to install and configure them for basic services.

Configuring the WWW Service

IIS and its services are configured using the Internet Service Manager utility (the normal or HTML version) found in the Microsoft Internet Server (Common) group. The opening screen displays the IIS services running on your NT server. You can connect to another NT server by choosing Properties ➤ Connect to Server. If you right-click on any service, it will bring up a menu with options that allow you to start, stop, or pause the service, or access its Properties page for more advanced configuration options.

Numerous configuration options are available for the WWW service:

1. On the Service tab, you can configure various TCP connection parameters, decide whether you will allow anonymous access, and if so, which account should be used, and configure which levels of password authentication your Web server will use. It is recommended that you leave the default settings unless the Web server is on an intranet where all users are using Internet Explorer 2 or a later version; in that case, the Allow Anonymous checkbox should be cleared.

2. On the Directories tab, you can configure which directories will be made available to the WWW service and which HTML page should be shown by default if the user does not request a particular document.

3. The Logging tab allows you to configure the logging of WWW activity to a log file. Several file types are available, including SQL formats. Note that you can make the system add the log files to a SQL database.

4. Finally, the Advanced tab allows you to control which computers can access the WWW service. You can allow access to only selected IP addresses or domain names, or you can exclude all computers except certain IPs or domains.

Each of the other services installed as part of IIS has similar options, but you will not be required to be familiar with them for this examination.

Installing the DNS Service

The DNS service is installed like any other service on an NT server:

1. Open the Network applet in Control Panel.

2. Choose the Service tab.

3. Click Add.

4. Choose DNS from the list.

Configuring DNS

A full discussion of configuring DNS is outside of the scope of this examination. You should, however, be familiar with the DNS Manager tool found in the Administrative Tools (Common) group.

1. Add your server's IP address as a member of DNS by choosing New Server from the DNS menu. You will be asked for the IP address of the new DNS server.

2. Create the domain information by choosing New Zone from the DNS menu. You will be asked whether this is to be a primary or secondary DNS server. A primary DNS server holds the master copy the domain database. A secondary DNS server holds a copy and helps the primary server resolve domain names. If you choose Primary, you will be asked for the domain name.

3. Once you have set up your zone, you are ready to start creating DNS records for the resources in your environment. Choose New Record from the DNS menu (the New Resource Record dialog box is shown below) and start building your DNS database.

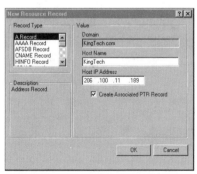

NOTE For this examination, you will not be required to know the details of configuring DNS—just the tools used.

Exam Essentials

Windows NT Server has taken a beating in the press when it comes to security. From Microsoft's perspective, it is imperative that MCSEs know how to provide a secure NT environment. Be very aware of the security issues discussed in this section.

Understand how IIS takes advantage of NT security. The IIS installation program creates an NT user named IUSER_*SERVER NAME*. This user is used to define the security context for anonymous access, which allows you to control what data are accessible to anonymous users by implementing NT security for the IUSR user and all other NT user accounts.

Know the three services installed by default as part of IIS. The three services installed by default are WWW, Gopher, and FTP.

Understand the function of DNS. DNS is a database used to resolve fully qualified domain names (FQDNs) into IP addresses. Each DNS server contains a piece of this database. When a client requests the IP address of a domain name resource, the DNS server will first determine whether it contains the requested information. If not, it will then query a root server for the address of the DNS server that does contain the appropriate domain information. It will then query that DNS server for the requested IP address.

Know Microsoft's rules for securing an intranet. Remember that if you are going to allow anonymous access, the anonymous user (IUSR_*SERVER NAME*) is made a member of the domain guests group. Be aware of this fact when assigning permissions to this group.

You can configure both the WWW and the FTP services to require a valid user name and password for access. Two types of authentication are available:

- Basic—Transmissions are not encrypted, so the user name and password are sent as clear text. FTP supports only Basic authentication.

- Windows NT Challenge/Response—Supported by Microsoft Internet Explorer 2 and above, and provides a secure login over the network.

Require passwords on all user accounts; require a minimum length and frequent changes. Lock out accounts after multiple failed logon attempts and require an administrator to unlock locked-out accounts. Use time restrictions and automatically disconnect users whose time has expired.

Key Terms and Concepts

Domain: A logical grouping of resources in the DNS database.

Domain name server (DNS): A database containing the IP addresses for hosts available on the network.

FTP service: A service that allows file transfers to and from a server.

Gopher service: A service primarily designed to index files and directories.

Intranet: An internal network that utilizes the tools and techniques of the Internet to provide services limited to local network users. Most commonly refers to an internal Web or FTP server.

IUSER_SERVER NAME: A user account created for IIS. Security assigned to this user defines the access allowed to anonymous connections to your Web server.

WWW service: The service that provides Web pages in HTML format to users connected to your Web server.

Sample Questions

1. Which of the following services provides the ability to index files and directories?

A. WWW

B. Gopher

C. FTP

Answer: B

Install and configure remote access service (RAS). Configuration options include:

- Configuring RAS communications
- Configuring RAS protocols
- Configuring RAS security

RAS allows a workstation computer running NT to connect to remote systems using just the POTS (plain old telephone system). When the client connects, the workstation is treated just like any other client. The user can access the network, check e-mail, get documents, and do just about anything they would do from their desk, except that now they are using a laptop.

NOTE There is a lot of testable material in this objective. Although the exam designers have not given it the attention of printing or disk configuration, there are some questions out there. Be aware and study hard!

Critical Information

The purpose of RAS is to allow for communications between a local host and hosts that operate from remote locations, utilizing just telephone lines. RAS can, however, be configured to work with ISDN and X.25 connections, as well as some WAN implementations such as asynchronous transfer mode (ATM). The purpose of this book is not to describe the multiple ways that RAS can interface with the telephone company. This book is designed to give you a broad overview of the product and get you through the exam, so it will stick to client-to-network communication using a dial-up connection.

For RAS to work, you need to create a mini-network. A network is nothing more than two systems with some information to share, a physical communication medium to share the information over, and rules to govern the transmittal of information. The first part of the objective involves the server piece of RAS—how to configure the server so it can "answer" the call when it comes. When the server answers the call, it must "talk" with the client using a specific set of rules. So, the available protocols and how to configure them to work with a dial-up client will be discussed. Finally, there have to be some rules for this discussion. The server needs to prove that the workstation is who it says it is, so RAS security will also be covered.

Configuring RAS Communications

The best place to start is always the beginning. If you are going to configure a system to which your workstations can call in and get information, something should be there to answer the phone. In this case, it will be your NT server. In an earlier chapter, communication products that allow you up to 256 dial-up connections from a single multiport expansion modem card were mentioned. RAS will take advantage of systems like that, as well as just a plain old modem hooked up to a COM port.

The first question to ask yourself is, What is the main goal of this communication channel? In some cases, your main goal may be to provide dial-up service to all those sales people and executives out there traveling around the country. If your company is small, you may not have a lot of sales people or high-powered executives traveling all over the country selling your company's wares. You may, however, have a remote site that needs to communicate with the home office and doesn't need all the power of a T-1 line. In that case, an ISDN line may be just the ticket. ISDN stands for integrated services digital network. ISDN is a faster, better version of what you normally think of as a modem connection. However, an ISDN does not use a modem. In fact, it is a purely digital data path from start to finish. It does require an adapter, which most people casually call a modem, but no modulation or demodulation actually occurs. A modem, on the other hand, requires an analog connection provided by the public switched telephone network (PSTN), generally referred to as the phone company.

NOTE   Anytime you want faster and better, that usually translates into *more expensive.* Costs vary on ISDN service around the world, but it is safe to say that it is more expensive than a standard dial-up line.

Modems modulate and demodulate the signals between two computers, sending the signal over the phone line. Your computer speaks digital. The phone company speaks analog. A modem turns a digital signal into an analog signal on the sending end, and turns the same signal from analog to digital at the receiving end.

The key word in the definition of ISDN is digital. With ISDN, you are now using a phone line that speaks digital, so there is no translation necessary. The ISDN modem or router just sends digital signals over a line that understands how to deal with ones and zeros. You have a cleaner, faster communication link. If you are planning on connecting two sites, you may look at installing ISDN service. However, in some places, it may not even be available. In others, the cost may be prohibitive. In some areas, it may be just the solution for which you are looking. When judging cost, keep in mind that ISDN service is like having two phone lines. Therefore, you would expect it to cost twice as much as a single phone line. Because there are two channels, you get twice the speed. Because it is digital, and analog modems rarely give you their rated speed, it is usually more than twice as fast.

You are now over the first hump—should you use ISDN or a regular phone line? If you are going to use the dial-up capabilities of the phone company, the phone line has to be dedicated to RAS communications. RAS is *very* selfish—it doesn't want to share. So, if your system is configured to dial out and notify you when the power goes out, or if you are running a fax-server solution using a modem and phone line, you need to add more hardware. RAS requires its own line with its own modem.

If you are installing an ISDN device, follow the manufacturer's directions. The ISDN device is slightly more challenging to install than a modem. Make sure you have somewhere to connect to (another ISDN connection) and make sure you have all the paperwork the phone company left for you when they installed the ISDN line. There are some interesting parameters that you will need to configure, such as SPIDs (service profile IDs). SPIDs identify which services the ISDN line is providing. The SPID looks like a normal 10-digit phone number, except that there are two of them.

NOTE   Installing modems was covered in Chapter 2. This section will assume that the modem is installed and dedicated to RAS communications.

After all these decisions have been made and all the hardware has been installed, the installation of RAS is really anticlimactic. Since RAS is a networking service, it is installed through the Network applet in Control Panel. It is just a matter of NT copying some files off the installation CD and linking the RAS with the modem or communication device you already have configured. Part way through the installation process, the system will begin asking you questions about protocols, which is a great segue into the next section of this objective.

TIP   For a step-by-step discussion of the installation of RAS, see the "Necessary Procedures" section of this objective.

Configuring RAS Protocols

RAS supports the big three protocols—TCP/IP, NWLink, and Net-BEUI. How it supports all those protocols does require some explanation. The explanation even requires some explanation, because you are about to be buried in a flow of acronyms.

TDI

The first acronym is TDI (transport driver interface). The TDI is an interface specification to which all Windows NT transport protocols must be written so that they can be used by higher-level services such as RAS. In other words, you will read that all of the dial-up protocols must be TDI-compliant.

PPP and SLIP

The next two acronyms deal with communication-framing protocols—the set of rules that allows communication devices to negotiate how information will be framed or blocked as it is sent over the network. The two framing protocols that RAS can use are point-to-point protocol (PPP) and serial line Internet protocol (SLIP).

Since SLIP is the granddaddy of framing protocols, it is just an implementation of Internet protocol (IP) over a serial line. Developed for use by UNIX computers, SLIP has been improved on and replaced, by and large, by PPP.

PPP is a data-link-layer transport that performs over point-to-point network connections such as serial or modem lines. PPP can negotiate with any TDI-compliant protocol used by both systems involved in the link and can automatically assign IP, domain name service (DNS), and gateway addresses when used with transmission control protocol/Internet protocol (TCP/IP).

Now that the terms are defined, an overview of protocols can be provided. When a dial-up client accesses a RAS server, it will use PPP as its network-layer protocol. Think of PPP as the Ethernet or token ring of the dial-up world.

NOTE SLIP is an older version of PPP. Although you *can* configure an NT RAS server to dial out using SLIP, in most environments, SLIP has gone the way of CP/M.

Once a modem is connected to a RAS server, it can support TCP/IP, NWLink, and/or NetBEUI. Each protocol can be bound to a modem, and a modem may have more than one protocol bound to it. Each of the three protocols have advantages and disadvantages, depending on the job you are configuring the system to do.

TCP/IP

TCP/IP is the standard protocol suite of the Internet. TCP/IP is a mature, stable, robust protocol suite that brings a lot to the table, including routing capabilities and the ability to handle less-than-perfect phone connections. However, while it is robust, it is not necessarily the fastest protocol out of the gate.

RAS using TCP/IP will allow the administrator to configure whether the client computer can access just the RAS server or the entire NT network. In addition, the RAS server controls how the client receives its TCP/IP address.

NWLink

NWLink is an Internet packet exchange/sequenced packet exchange (IPX/SPX) wanna-be. It is fast and efficient, and works well with interconnecting NetWare clients and servers. If you have a mixed environment with NetWare servers and NT servers, you are probably already aware of the advantages of NWLink. If you configure your RAS to use the NWLink protocol, you will not have to add a second protocol to those dial-up clients.

Like TCP/IP, NWLink can be configured to allow a RAS connection access only to the server or the entire network. You can also specify network-addressing and node-addressing selections through RAS protocol configurations.

NetBEUI

Of all the transport protocols, NetBEUI is the lightweight. NetBEUI is an efficient, simple protocol that protects against overuse of the network bandwidth. If you don't need to use TCP/IP or NWLink, NetBEUI is the protocol of choice.

NetBEUI configuration allows the administrator to determine only whether a user can access just the server or the entire network from the RAS connection.

NOTE   See the "Necessary Procedures" section for a step-by-step discussion of the configuration of each of the protocols.

Configuring RAS Security

Once the client computer has called the RAS server and has connected, how do you protect your network against intruders? RAS has some built-in security features. You can configure the RAS connection security using permissions, encrypted passwords, point-to-point tunneling protocol (PPTP), and call back. If you look at the Administrative Tools menu, you will see a new utility listed, Remote Access Admin.

Permissions

When a user dials in and authenticates to a RAS, permissions are the first line of defense for the network. If a user has been granted Remote Access Permission, the user can log onto the RAS server. Using the Remote Access Admin utility, RAS permissions can be granted to all users of the server, revoked for all users of the server, or granted to individual users. Notice that permissions cannot be granted to global groups or local groups. Basic RAS permissions can also be granted through the User Manager utility. The Remote Access Permissions screen is shown in Figure 4.3.

FIGURE 4.3: Remote Access Permissions

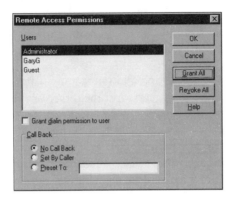

Call Back

One of the ways RAS enforces security is to call back the initiating client system to reestablish communication. This way, RAS is sure that the system calling is really what it says it is and can record the number it called to validate the user and minimize long-distance charges borne by the client. Call-back features can be set for each user with dial-up access. Notice in Figure 4.3 that you can configure three choices per user:

- No Call Back—Disables the call-back feature.

- Set by Caller—Prompts the caller for a number.

- Preset to—Calls back a user at a predefined phone number. The server will call back this number only for the user.

You cannot set call-back authentication for groups of users or a particular modem.

Passwords and Data Encryption

By now, just about everyone in the free world has heard the trials and travails of passing passwords and other information over phone lines and (gasp) the Internet. There are several ways of protecting information sent over phone lines—the most common is encryption.

When the client and the server begin to communicate, they use point-to-point protocol (PPP). To authenticate over PPP, RAS supports three authentication protocols:

- Password authentication protocol (PAP)
- Challenge handshake authentication protocol (CHAP)
- Microsoft extensions of CHAP (MS-CHAP)

You might anticipate that protocol selection is done through the Remote Access Admin tool, but your anticipation would be misguided. The protocol selection is done from the Network Configuration window of Remote Access Setup (see Figure 4.4).

FIGURE 4.4: Network Configuration of RAS

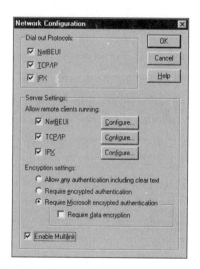

As you can see from Figure 4.4, the three settings show up under the heading Encryption Settings. The default selection is MS-CHAP, although that does not appear to be an option. It is just camouflaged by calling it Require Microsoft Encrypted Authentication. When you configure a client to call the RAS, it will encrypt its password via MS-CHAP. Using MS-CHAP ensures that the system on the other end of the phone is at least using Windows 95 or above for an operating system.

If the Require Data Encryption button is selected, not only is MS-CHAP used, but the data that are sent over the phone lines are also encrypted.

Suppose that you have a diverse environment that is not Microsoft-centric. That is the politically correct way of saying that you have some bit-head who wants to dial in from a UNIX box. Since that system cannot use MS-CHAP, something else needs to be provided. You can require encrypted authentication. This option sets up the system to run CHAP as well as MS-CHAP.

The final selection you can make involves those systems that do not support encrypted password authentication. In that case, you can check Allow Any Authentication Including Clear Text. This is the free-for-all method of system access.

Another security feature mentioned above is point-to-point tunneling protocol (PPTP). PPTP is a new NT 4 feature. It is Internet centered and uses a two-step approach to connecting the client to the server:

1. Connect the client to the Internet.

2. Use the Internet to create an encrypted link to the RAS server. In some areas, this is called creating a virtual private network (VPN).

NOTE   If you use this approach, the RAS server must be attached to the Internet.

Multilink
By filling the Enable Multilink checkbox in Figure 4.4, you are allowing RAS to combine multiple serial signals into one. This is especially helpful when dealing with the two channels of ISDN, because now you can take full advantage of both channels. Multilink will also allow you to link regular modems together.

There is a catch—to use multilink, both computers have to be running NT and both must have multilink enabled. Furthermore, it is important to remember that multilinking is not possible with the call-back option enabled.

Necessary Procedures

There is a lot to do in this section. This objective is all about configuring. While the first section of the objective gave an overview of the decisions to be made and the items to be ordered, this section is where the meat of the process lies—actually doing the work.

The exam developers approached this section in a logical fashion. The first three areas examine how to install RAS on the server, how to configure the protocols that the systems will use, and how to lock down security.

Configuring RAS Communications

RAS is a network service and is installed like most of the other network services—from the Network applet in Control Panel. Before beginning to install RAS or any network service, be sure to have the NT installation CD handy, or at least have access to the files it contains. To install and configure RAS:

1. Log onto the computer as administrator.

2. Choose Start ➤ Settings ➤ Control Panel.

3. Double-click the Network icon.

4. Open the Services tab by clicking it. Since RAS is not installed, click Add. This will open the Select Network Service window, which is a selection of all the services available but not currently installed on your server.

5. Scroll down to Remote Access Service, highlight it with a single click, and then click OK. This will open the Windows NT setup screen. This window asks for the location of the NT setup files. Provide the appropriate location and click the Continue button. At this point, the Installation Wizard copies the files it needs to the places it needs to put them.

6. The next window you are presented lists all the RAS-capable devices attached to the server. If you have more than one modem attached to the server, the drop-down menu will allow you to

select the device for RAS communications. If you haven't installed a modem, you can choose Install Modem or Install X.25 from this screen. Once you have chosen your RAS-capable device, click OK.

NOTE RAS is selfish. The communication channel must be dedicated to RAS. If you want to use the channel for something else, you will have to stop RAS and restart it when you are finished.

---

7. At this juncture, you should see the Remote Access Setup screen. Instead of continuing at this time, click Configure.

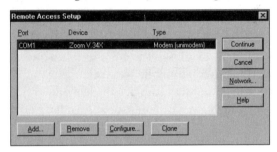

8. When you click Configure, it opens the Configure Port Usage screen, which allows you to specify how you want the port used. Make your selection from the choices below and click OK to return to the Remote Access Setup screen.

   - Dial Out Only—If you are configuring this server to dial into another RAS connection and you want this machine only to dial out, this is the appropriate selection.

   - Receive Calls Only—If your RAS connection will not be going out looking for work and dialing into other servers, this is the appropriate selection. It is also the default selection.

   - Dial Out and Receive Calls—This selection provides two-way communication.

9. You should now be back at the Remote Access Setup screen. Click Continue to open the RAS Server NetBEUI Configuration window.

Configuring RAS Protocols

The first protocol that is configured is the simplest, most basic network protocol—NetBEUI. You will also be prompted to provide information about TCP/IP and NWLink.

1. The RAS Server NetBEUI Configuration window allows you to choose how far your NetBEUI clients can go. Do you want them to access the entire network or just this particular computer? Make your choice by selecting the appropriate radio button and then click OK.

2. The next screen is the RAS Server TCP/IP Configuration screen. This screen is a little more complicated than the NetBEUI screen. There are several decisions to make before continuing.

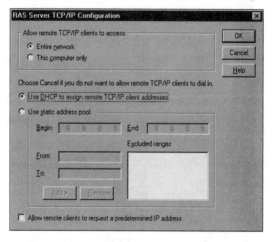

- The first set of radio buttons will allow you to decide how far the TCP/IP client will be allowed to go. Again, as with NetBEUI, the choices are Entire Network or This Computer Only.

- Now, things begin to get interesting. You will have to make some decisions about TCP/IP addressing.

- The first radio button is a "cop out" button. By selecting Use DHCP to Assign Remote TCP/IP Client Addresses, the server will pass the buck to a DHCP server to provide the IP address.

- If you choose Use Static Address Pool, it will let this service decide which of the IP addresses to assign to each connecting device.

- You can also check the box at the bottom of the screen that allows the remote client to request a predetermined IP address from either the DHCP server or the static pool. After making the appropriate selections, click OK.

NOTE Notice that there are Begin and End selections as well as Excluded Ranges under Use Static Address Pool. For a more complete discussion of TCP/IP addressing, read Sybex's *MCSE: TCP/IP Study Guide*.

---

3. When you click OK, it brings up the next (and last) protocol to configure—IPX. There are several decisions to make here also.

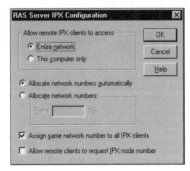

- The top selection of radio buttons allows you to choose whether the IPX client uses the entire network or just this computer.

- The next selection of radio buttons allows you to choose whether network numbers are allocated automatically or within the range you provide.

- In the bottom of the screen, there are two checkboxes. If you check the first, it will give the same network segment number to all IPX clients. If you check the second, it allows the client computer to select its own node address.

4. Click OK and close the RAS installation wizard.

5. Agree to allow NetBIOS broadcasts for IPX clients.

6. Click OK to close the Network Configuration window

7. Finally, select Yes to restart the computer.

Configuring RAS Security

RAS security is configured using both the Remote Access Admin utility and the Network Configuration window from the Remote Access Setup screen. The security settings involved with the Admin tool revolve around granting dial-up access rights to the server and call-back selections.

Encryption information and selections are made through the Network Configuration tool.

To provide dial-up access:

1. Start the Remote Access Admin utility by selecting Start ➤ Programs ➤ Administrative Tools (Common) ➤ Remote Access Admin.

2. From the Remote Access Admin screen, click Users to show users with access to this server. To provide access to users from another domain or another server, even if it is across a slow link, choose Server ➤ Select Domain or Server, and then choose the domain you would like to administer. To actually select the domain, double-click the domain name in the Select Domain window. Once this has been accomplished, the users in the other domain will show up in the Remote Access Admin screen.

3. Click Permissions to show the Remote Access Permissions screen.

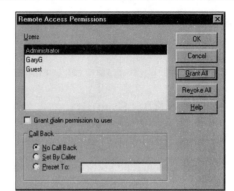

4. The Remote Access Permissions screen will show you the users associated with this system. By using the selection buttons to the right, you can Grant All access to dial-up networking or Revoke All access from dial-up networking. To grant individual users the right to dial up, highlight the user account and select the Grant Dialin Permission to User checkbox at the bottom of the screen. (Remember that RAS permission can also be granted in the User Manager utility.)

5. You can also use this screen to provide three levels of Call Back support:

- No Call Back—Disables the call-back feature.

- Set by Caller—Prompts the caller for a number.

- Preset to—Calls back a user at a predefined phone number. The server will call back this number only for the user.

To change the default encryption scheme for passwords and data:

1. From the NT Server desktop, highlight Network Neighborhood and right-click.

2. Click Properties.

3. Click the Services tab and highlight Remote Access Services.

4. Click the Properties button to bring up the Remote Access Setup screen.

5. Click the Network button. This brings up the Network Configuration window.

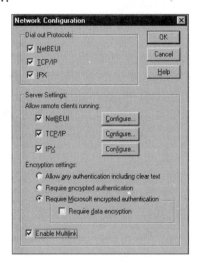

NOTE   The selection and configuration of protocols has already been discussed, so the items in the top half of the Network Configuration window will be skipped in the current discussion.

---

6. The default encryption setting is Require Microsoft Encrypted Authentication. This provides for MS-CHAP. If you fill the Require Data Encryption checkbox, it will encrypt not only the password, but any data flowing between the RAS server and the client.

- Select Require Encrypted Authentication if you are providing access to non-Microsoft-based operating systems, such as UNIX. This provides for CHAP-based encryption in addition to MS-CHAP.

- Select Allow Any Authentication Including Clear Text, which allows all three methods, including no encryption.

Exam Essentials

The exam writers really like the objectives in this section, so study carefully.

Know the three call-back modes and when they should be used. The three call-back modes are No Call Back, Set by User, and Preset. No Call Back bypasses call-back security. Set by User prompts the user for a number where they can be reached. Preset makes the system always call a specific number.

Use No Call Back if security is not an issue. Use Set by User if your users are travelling or at a client site. Use Preset when dealing with remote sites that will not move around.

Call-back options cannot be set if multilink is enabled.

Know the differences between SLIP, PPP, and PTPP. SLIP (serial line Internet protocol) is IP over a modem. This is an outdated protocol. PPP (point-to-point protocol) is used with serial or modem communications to provide IP communications, and it can provide additional features such as data compression and DNS and gateway addressing. PPP has largely replaced SLIP. Windows NT servers can establish SLIP connections only when dialing out or originating a SLIP session. PPTP (point-to-point tunneling protocol) is PPP with security and is used with the Internet to create an encrypted link to the RAS server. In some areas, this is called creating a virtual private network (VPN).

Key Terms and Concepts

ATM (asynchronous transfer mode): WAN communication implementation.

Call back: A part of RAS security. You can configure the RAS server to return the call of the system needing access.

CHAP (challenge handshake authentication protocol): Password security protocol used by RAS systems to communicate with non-Windows systems.

IPX: Internet packet exchange protocol.

ISDN (integrated services digital network):   Provides communications over special phone lines using digital communications.

Modem: From modulate/demodulate. Computer hardware that will turn a computer's digital signal into an analog signal that can be sent over a phone line. The modem at the receiving end will then turn the analog signal into a digital signal that the computer can understand.

MS-CHAP: Microsoft's implementation of CHAP. Default RAS selection. Used to provide secure password authentication between a RAS server and Microsoft Windows 95 or Windows NT clients.

Multilink: RAS can combine several serial signals into one, using either ISDN or modems.

NetBEUI: Microsoft networking protocol. Efficient, simple protocol that will not provide routing, but can be used in RAS sessions.

NWLink: Microsoft's implementation of the IPX/SPX protocol. Installed to be compatible with Novell networks. Can be used by RAS servers as a networking protocol.

PAP: Password authentication protocol.

POTS: Plain old telephone system.

PPP (point-to-point protocol):   A data-link-layer transport that performs over point-to-point network connections such as serial or modem lines. PPP can negotiate with any transport protocol used by both systems involved in the link and can realize data-transfer efficiencies, such as software compression, and automatically assign IP, domain name service (DNS), and gateway addresses when used with transmission control protocol/Internet protocol (TCP/IP).

PSTN (public switched telephone network):   The phone company.

RAS: Remote access service.

RAS permissions: Front-line security to determine whether the user has the right to log onto the RAS server.

SLIP (serial line Internet protocol): An implementation of Internet protocol (IP) over a serial line. SLIP has been replaced, by and large, by PPP.

SPID (service profile ID): ISDN-required configuration information. The ISDN phone number.

SPX: Sequenced packet exchange protocol.

TCP/IP (transmission control protocol/Internet protocol): The standard protocol suite of the Internet.

TDI (transport driver interface): A specification to which all Windows NT transport protocols must be written to be used by higher-level services such as RAS.

Sample Questions

1. What are the three RAS call-back options?

 A. No Call Back

 B. Preset

 C. Set by User

 D. Only if asked

 Answer: A, B, C—The call-back options for RAS are No Call Back, Preset, and Set by User.

2. Which dialup line protocols does RAS support?

 A. PPP

 B. TCP

 C. SLIP

 D. IPX/SPX

 E. UDP

 Answer: A, C—PPP and SLIP are the only two dialup line protocols listed.

3. What is multilink?

    A. The ability to have two or more modems handling different calls at the same time

    B. The ability to have two or more modems call out at the same time

    C. The ability to use more than one communication channel for the same connection

    D. The ability to have two network interface cards in the same system at the same time

Answer: C

CHAPTER

5

Monitoring and Optimization

Microsoft Exam Objectives Covered in This Chapter:

▶ **Establish a baseline for measuring system performance. Tasks include creating a database of measurement data.**
  (pages 251 – 257)

▶ **Monitor performance of various functions by using Performance Monitor. Functions include:** *(pages 258 – 270)*
  - Processor
  - Memory
  - Disk
  - Network

▶ **Monitor network traffic by using Network Monitor. Tasks include:** *(pages 271 – 276)*
  - Collecting data
  - Presenting data
  - Filtering data

▶ **Identify performance bottlenecks.** *(pages 276 – 281)*

▶ **Optimize performance for various results. Results include:** *(pages 281 – 308)*
  - Controlling network traffic
  - Controlling server load

While studying for the various MCSE exams, you have probably learned about numerous tools, services, and applications that can be added to an NT server. Each change you make to a server will influence its ability to perform other functions. In this chapter, a few tools that measure the effects of change on both your servers and the network will be discussed. The objectives for this portion of the exam cover your ability to use tools to gather information about your network and analyze the data gathered.

Managing your server is much like managing your family budget. Your family budget has a limited amount of resources. Those resources have to be used to accomplish certain things—you must pay for housing, transportation, and food. These things are mandatory and must be budgeted before anything else. At the same time, you'd like to be able to provide a few luxuries for yourself and your family—a vacation, a second car, or maybe a pool for those hot summer days. Managing a family budget is often more about juggling expenses than managing money.

Your server is the same type of environment. You have a limited amount of resources—just so much memory, hard disk, and CPU with which to play. With those resources, you have to provide certain services to your users—e-mail, shared data, print services, and backups. Once again, the act of managing the environment involves balancing needs against resources.

To truly manage your network, rather than react to it, you need a set of tools that allow you to measure the impact of each service on both an individual server and the network as a whole. Once you have that information, you can manage your resources to optimize performance and efficiency.

By the end of this chapter, you will be able to gather information, analyze it, and make changes to optimize your network.

Establish a baseline for measuring system performance. Tasks include creating a database of measurement data.

Before you can effectively optimize your servers or network, you must gather data about how they are currently being used and how they are responding to the current workloads. Without these data, you cannot make informed decisions—your optimization technique becomes a "trying experience," as in, let's try this and see what happens. With the proper information, however, your optimization technique becomes a "vacation exercise," as in, let's do this and then go home.

This section covers the basic task of gathering enough data to make informed optimization or troubleshooting decisions.

Critical Information

A *baseline* is a set of statistics that can be used for comparison. You should gather a standard set of statistics from your network and servers on a regular basis. This information should be saved so that it can be used to provide trend analyses and plan for future growth over time.

In any given environment, there are four major subsystems—processor, memory, disk, and network. When creating a baseline, you should always start with these subsystems. Then, analyze the other resources that are critical on your server and add them to the list.

Performance Monitor

Performance Monitor is the tool provided by NT to gather statistics at the server. Performance Monitor uses objects and counters to describe the statistics that can be gathered. An object is a subsystem, while a counter is a specific statistic of an object.

Performance Monitor has a list of 12 objects that can be monitored. Some software creates its own counters when you install it. Specific objects and counters will be examined later in this chapter. Each of the four main subsystems has an associated object with counters that you should track.

When creating your baseline, you will often want to gather statistics while a specific process happens. Backups, for instance, often strain both the servers involved and the network. Unfortunately, most companies do their backups during nonpeak hours or, in other words, during your personal time. You can use the AT command to start Performance Monitor automatically. The AT command allows you to schedule a start time for any process or application. Using the AT command, you can make Performance Monitor load and begin collecting data automatically. This can come in handy when you want to gather information on a regular basis or you are not available to start the process manually.

Once you've collected your data, you'll want to analyze it. Performance Monitor can save data in a format that many commercial applications can read. When you dump the statistics into a database or spreadsheet, it is called *creating a measurement database*. If you use a database or spreadsheet, it allows you to track information over time. Performance Monitor does not have this innate ability—it shows either current information or statistics since the server was booted. You can easily export Performance Monitor data in a format that a program such as Microsoft Excel can import. This allows you to take advantage of the various tools that the application might have—such as Excel's excellent graphing abilities. When you present your data to management, it is much more effective to use a graph than columns of numbers.

When gathering information, you will often track a lot of counters and check those counters frequently. How often Performance Monitor checks the values of counters you are tracking is called the *interval*. If your interval is set low, NT will gather the values often, which can result in huge data files. Microsoft suggests that after you have analyzed the data, you relog the information with a larger interval. This will reduce the size of the log file, but still leave you information for trend analysis and comparison.

Performance Monitor offers many ways to view the statistics that it gathers. You will need to be familiar with each of them for the exam.

Chart View

Chart view provides a real-time chart showing the values of the counters you have chosen. The first step is to add the counters to your view, as shown in Figure 5.1. Highlight the appropriate object and then pick a counter from the list.

FIGURE 5.1: Add to Chart

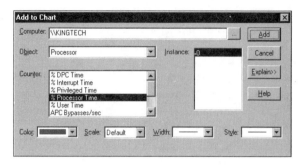

When you have added all of the counters you want to chart, click Cancel. The chart will show the value of those counters in real time, as shown in Figure 5.2.

FIGURE 5.2: A real-time Performance Monitor chart

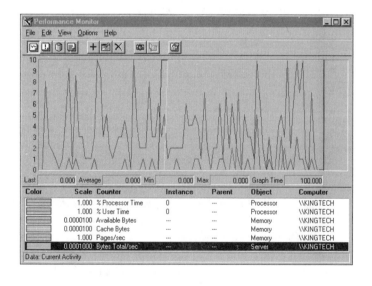

Report View

Report view shows the same information as Chart view. However, with Report view, the values are shown in the form of a text-based report. As in Chart view, the report data are updated in real time.

Log View

Log view allows you to save the data to a file. In Log view, you do not pick counters—all counters for the objects you chose will be tracked. Rather than the data being shown as they are collected, the data are saved to a file for later analysis.

Alert View

Alert view is different from the other three views. With Alert view, you set a threshold for a counter. When this threshold is reached, you can make Performance Monitor run an application that pages you, for instance.

Necessary Procedures

This objective primarily concerns your ability to use Performance Monitor. You must understand the available options before taking the exam.

Creating a Baseline Using Performance Monitor

To build a baseline, you use the Log view in Performance Monitor. First, pick the objects that you want to track. Remember to start with the four main subsystems. At a minimum, you will want to track processor, memory, disk, and whatever objects are available for protocols in use on your network. Save this log to a file. You will use this file—the baseline—as a basis for comparison. Performance Monitor can use this file later as the input material for graphs or reports.

Relogging Your Data at a Longer Interval

Use the Log view in Performance Monitor.

1. Choose Options ➤ Data from.

2. Choose Log File and browse to your baseline log file.

3. Build the log again, using the same steps as before—only this time, change the interval.

4. When you start the log, it will save information at the new interval, reducing the size of the log file.

WARNING Although this method is great for archiving trends, the resulting log file contains less-accurate data. Since you have reduced the sampling rate, the resulting information will be less detailed in terms of time.

Exporting Information to Another Program

Build a chart using your log file. Choose File ➤ Export Chart. Save the chart in a format your application can import.

Exam Essentials

This objective covers the tools needed to analyze a server. If you don't have the skills listed below, much of the rest of this chapter will make little sense.

Be able to explain what a baseline is. A baseline is a set of statistics gathered when the system is running normally. These statistics can be used for comparison at a later date.

Know the four main subsystems to track in a baseline. The four main subsystems are processor, memory, disk, and network.

Know the difference between an object and a counter in Performance Monitor. An object represents a subsystem; a counter represents a specific statistic of an object.

Key Terms and Concepts

Baseline: Stored statistics used for comparison.

Counter: A specific statistic that can be tracked.

Interval: In Performance Monitor, a setting that determines how often data are updated.

Object: An NT subsystem that can be monitored.

Sample Questions

1. Which of the Performance Monitor views displays a real-time graph?

   A. Chart

   B. Report

   C. Log

   D. Alert

   Answer: A

2. Which of the Performance Monitor views allows you to save data for later analysis?

   A. Chart

   B. Report

   C. Log

   D. Alert

   Answer: C

Monitor performance of various functions by using Performance Monitor. Functions include:

- Processor
- Memory
- Disk
- Network

When you troubleshoot any kind of complex system, one of the most important skills is knowing what to look for—the questions you ask and how you interpret the answers are critical to both problem solving and optimization on your network. In this section, the Performance Monitor counters to track on each of the major subsystems of an NT server will be discussed.

Critical Information

While any given environment might stress other particular components, there are four main physical components to any NT server: processor, memory, disk, and network. These four areas are good indicators of the health of your system. When monitoring any NT server, always start with these four components and then add any of the other additional NT objects that might be appropriate in your environment.

Processor

To determine whether the processor is the bottleneck, monitor the counters listed in Table 5.1.

T A B L E 5.1: Processor-Related Counters in Performance Monitor

Counter	Acceptable Value	Description
%Processor Time	Under 80 percent	If the processor is busy more than 80 percent of the time, it is likely that the processor is the bottleneck.
%Privileged Time	Under 80 percent	This is the amount of time that the processor is busy performing operating-system tasks.
%User Time	Under 80 percent	This is the amount of time that the processor is busy performing user tasks, such as running a program.
Interrupts/sec	Varies	This is the number of hardware interrupts generated each second. Each type of processor can handle a different number. On a 486/66, this number should be under 1,000; on a Pentium 90 system, this number could run as high as 3,500. If this number is consistently high, the system probably has an IRQ conflict or a piece of hardware that is going bad.
System: Processor Queue Length	Less than 2	This represents the number of threads that are ready to execute, but are waiting for the processor.
Server Work Queues: Queue Length	Less than 2	This represents the number of threads in the queue for a given processor.

If the bottleneck is your processor, you can:

- Add a faster processor
- Add another processor
- Move processing to another server

NOTE These are Microsoft's proposed solutions. In reality, you very seldom have the option of adding another or faster processor. Upgrading the processor in today's quagmire of choices (Pentium, Pentium Pro, Pentium II, etc.) is never as easy as it sounds. As for adding a processor, few administrators would buy a multiprocessor motherboard and leave a slot open.

Memory

Before the counters that determine whether memory is your system bottleneck are discussed, how NT uses memory needs to be reviewed.

Memory in an NT system can be divided into two classifications: paged and nonpaged. Paged memory is used by most applications. It can be made up of either physical RAM or virtual memory (hard disk space). Nonpaged memory is used by programs that cannot be "paged" to the hard disk. The operating system and its components use nonpaged memory.

NT uses a virtual memory model. In this model, applications that can use paged RAM are given a full set of memory addresses with which to work. The operating system keeps track of actual physical memory. When memory is full, the OS will move "pages" of memory to a file on the hard drive (PAGEFILE.SYS). If that code is needed later, it will be moved back to physical memory. By using a virtual memory model, your applications can use more memory than is physically available (up to the limits of your hard drive).

Whenever the data that a program needs are not in RAM, they must be acquired from the hard drive. This process is called a *hard page fault*. If you have a consistently high number of hard page faults (over five per second), it could indicate that performance is being significantly degraded since there is not enough memory available on the server. The goal on an NT server is to have enough memory in the server so that most data requested are found in memory. (Obviously, the first time the data are used, they will have to come from the disk. But after that, if you have enough memory for file caching, it can greatly increase performance.)

TIP To appreciate the importance of file caching, compare the access speeds of your memory and your hard disk. Hard-disk access times are measured in milliseconds or thousandths of a second. Memory is measured in nanoseconds or millionths of a second.

Monitor the counters listed in Table 5.2 to determine whether memory is your bottleneck.

T A B L E 5.2:   Memory-Related Counters in Performance Monitor

Counter	Acceptable Value	Description
Pages/sec	0–20	The number of pages that were either not in RAM when requested or needed to be moved to virtual memory to free up space in RAM. This is really a measurement of disk activity related to memory management.
Available Bytes	Minimum of 4MB	The amount of available physical RAM at any point in time. This number will usually be fairly low, because NT will utilize memory that is available and free it up as needed.
Committed Bytes	Should be less than the physical amount of RAM in the computer	This indicates the amount of memory in use. If the number is greater than the amount of physical RAM in the machine, you need more memory.
Pool Non-Paged Bytes	Should remain steady	This is the memory used by nonpaged processes (i.e., the operating system). If this number fluctuates, it could indicate that a process is not using memory correctly.

If memory is the bottleneck on your server, the fix is simple—add more RAM. With today's prices, you are shorting the true performance of your server by allowing a RAM bottleneck to occur.

Disk

The disk is usually the slowest component on your computer. NT compensates for this by using file caching and memory management to reduce the number of disk accesses. Often, what appears to be a disk problem is really just a lack of memory, so be sure to watch both subsystems—disk and memory.

Before you can track disk counters in Performance Monitor, you must turn on those counters. The disk counters are not activated by default, because tracking physical-disk access used to add measurable overhead to the workstations and servers that ran older Intel processors. Today's CPUs aren't affected to nearly the same degree, but the counters still must be turned on and off.

To activate the disk counters, type **diskperf –y** at a command prompt. If your disks are configured as a RAID set, type **diskperf –ye**.

NOTE The added overhead of tracking disk counters is constant once they are activated—not just when you are monitoring them. You should turn them off when you are not actively watching them. To turn them off, type **diskperf –n** at a command prompt.

Once you have activated them, you can monitor the counters listed in Table 5.3.

T A B L E 5.3: Disk-Related Counters in Performance Monitor

Counter	Acceptable Value	Description
%Disk Time	Under 90 percent	This is the amount of time that the disk drive is busy. If this number is consistently high, you should monitor specific processes to find out exactly what is using the disk. If you can, move some of the disk-intensive processes to another server.
Disk Queue Length	0–2	This value represents the number of waiting disk I/O requests. A high number indicates that I/O requests are waiting for access.
Avg. Disk Bytes/Transfer	Depends on use and type of subsystem	The larger this number is, the more efficiently your disk subsystem is working. This value depends on the type of access—are your users saving many small files or a few large ones? It also depends on the types of disks and controllers.
Disk Bytes/ sec	Depends on use and type of subsystem	The larger this number is, the more efficiently your disk subsystem is working. This value depends on the types of disks and controllers.

If you find that the disk subsystem is the bottleneck, you can do the following things:

- Add a faster controller and disk drive. (See Chapter 1 for a comparison of the various disk technologies.)

- If using RAID, add more disks to the set. This spreads the work across more physical devices.

- Move disk-intensive processes to another server to spread the workload.

WARNING None of these solutions is really a simple fix. If you add a faster controller, it will help only if your disks are compliant with the controller type. If they are not, you will have to replace the disks as well to gain any benefit. As for the RAID solution, to add a disk, you need to have a slot open and the funding for more hardware. As for moving the process to another server, you need to have a server that is not too busy to accept the extra workload. The proper solution to this problem is to have prevented the problem in the first place. Proper capacity planning (projecting throughput needs, comparing technologies, and implementing the best solution) is the best fix.

Network

Due to the complexity of today's networks, monitoring the network portion of your environment can be a difficult task. The network doesn't end at your NIC card—the network includes the entire infrastructure that makes up your enterprise. Everything attached to your network could be a potential problem. To monitor a network, you have to be familiar with all of the components on that network—the routers, the wiring, the protocols, the operating systems, etc.

Don't try to fix the entire network, try to find out which component is causing the problem and fix that.

Performance Monitor has a few counters, listed in Table 5.4, that can help you determine where the problem lies. A few of the counters analyze the overhead on the server itself, while others give an overview of what is happening on the wire.

T A B L E 5.4: Network-Related Counters in Performance Monitor

Counter	Acceptable Value	Description
Server: Bytes Total/sec	Varies	This counter shows the number of bytes sent and received through this server. It is a good indicator of how busy the server is.

T A B L E 5.4: Network-Related Counters in Performance Monitor *(cont.)*

Counter	Acceptable Value	Description
Server: Login/ sec	Varies	Use this value to determine the authentication overhead being placed on the server. If this number is high and other services are slow, it might indicate the need for another domain controller.
Server: Login Total	Varies	This is the number of login attempts this server has serviced since the last time the server was started. Can be used to justify another domain controller.
Network Interface: Bytes sent/sec	Varies	Used to determine whether a particular network interface card is being overused.
Network Interface: Bytes total/sec	Varies	This is the total number of bytes sent and received through a particular NIC.
Network Segment: %Network Utilization	Usually lower than 30 percent	This shows the percentage of network bandwidth in use. This number should be lower than 30 percent for most networks. Some network technologies can sustain a higher rate.

The Network Segment object is not available until you install the Network Monitor Agent as a service on the server. Once this service is installed, Performance Monitor will put the NICs in promiscuous mode when you are monitoring Network Segment counters. When in promiscuous mode, a NIC processes *all* network traffic, not just those packets destined for the server. This can add a tremendous amount of overhead to the server.

Each protocol that you add to your server also has its own counters. These counters allow you to determine the overhead being placed on your server by each protocol. Most of these counters have no acceptable range of values. The values will depend upon the hardware, topology, and other protocols used on your network.

NetBEUI and NWLink

These two protocols have similar counters, listed in Table 5.5.

TABLE 5.5: NetBEUI- and NWLink-Related Counters in Performance Monitor

Counter	Acceptable Value	Description
Bytes Total/sec	Varies	This is the total number of bytes sent and received using this protocol. This counter is an excellent way to compare network overhead created by various protocols.
Datagrams/sec	Varies	This is the total number of nonguaranteed datagrams (usually broadcasts) sent and received.
Frames sent/sec	Varies	This is the number of data packets sent and received.

TCP/IP

The counters listed in Table 5.6 will not be available unless both the TCP/IP protocol and the SNMP service are installed on the server.

TABLE 5.6: TCP/IP-Related Counters in Performance Monitor

Counter	Acceptable Value	Description
TCP Segments/sec	Varies	This is the total number of TCP frames sent and received.

T A B L E 5.6: TCP/IP-Related Counters in Performance Monitor *(cont.)*

Counter	Acceptable Value	Description
TCP Segments re-translated/ sec	Varies	This is the total number of segments retranslated on the network.
UDP data- grams/sec	Varies	This is the number of UDP-based datagrams (usually broadcasts) sent and received.
Network Interface: Output Queue Length	Less than 2	This is the number of packets waiting to be transmitted through a particular NIC. A high number can indicate a card that is too busy.

The following strategies are potential fixes if the network is your bottleneck:

- Upgrade the hardware at the server. Add a faster NIC, add RAM, or upgrade the processor.

- Upgrade the physical components of your network, such as routers and bridges. Shift to higher-speed network protocols such as 100BaseT Ethernet.

- Decrease the number of protocols used on your network.

- Segment your network to split the traffic between segments.

- Add servers to split the workload.

Exam Essentials

Trying to outsmart the exam writers at Microsoft is often an exercise in futility. There is one common thread throughout—they want to ensure that you have the skills necessary to provide your environment with an efficient NT network. The following items are critical to that goal.

Understand NT's virtual memory model. NT extends physical RAM by using disk space. When a program needs memory, NT will allocate physical RAM. IF there is not enough RAM available, NT will move a "page" of memory to the PAGEFILE.SYS file on the hard drive. To the application that originally placed that information in memory, it appears as if the data are still in RAM. When that application needs the data again, NT will page something else to disk and place it in physical RAM for use.

Know the difference between paged and nonpaged memory. Paged memory can be "paged" to the PAGEFILE.SYS file. Nonpaged memory contains data that cannot be moved to virtual memory (usually, this code will be part of the operating system).

Know how to activate the disk counters in Performance Monitor. From a command prompt, type diskperf –y. In a RAID implementation, type diskperf –ye.

Know the suggested fixes for bottlenecks in each of the four major subsystems. These fixes are as follows:

- Processor:
    - Add a faster processor.
    - Add another processor.
    - Move processing to another server.
- Memory:
    - Add RAM.
- Disk:
    - Add a faster controller and disk drive. (See Chapter 1 for a comparison of the various disk technologies.)

- If using RAID, add more disks to the set. This spreads the work across more physical devices.

- Move disk-intensive processes to another server to spread the workload.

- Network:

    - Upgrade the hardware at the server. Add a faster NIC, add RAM, or upgrade the processor.

    - Upgrade the physical components of your network, such as routers and bridges.

    - Decrease the number of protocols used on your network.

    - Segment your network to split the traffic between segments.

    - Add servers to split the workload.

Be familiar with the counters discussed in this section. Reread this section, paying close attention to the counters listed. They are the counters that are most likely to be mentioned on the exam.

Key Terms and Concepts

Datagram: A term usually used to describe a nondirected packet on the network (broadcasts, acknowledgments, etc.).

Frame: A term usually used to describe a directed packet of data.

Nonpaged memory: An area of memory that cannot use virtual RAM. Usually used by the operating system.

Paged memory: An area of memory that can be extended using virtual memory space.

Virtual memory model: A memory system that uses hard-drive space as if it were RAM.

Sample Questions

1. If the parameter %User Time is consistently over 80 percent, which of the following subsystems is most likely the bottleneck?

   A. Processor

   B. Memory

   C. Disk

   D. Network

   Answer: A—%User Time refers to the amount of processor time being used by user-mode processes.

2. The process of moving data from RAM to the paging file is known as what?

   A. Memory clearing

   B. Memory leaking

   C. Hard page fault

   Answer: C

3. Before tracking disk statistics, you must perform which of the following tasks?

   A. Use Disk Administrator to turn on the disk counters.

   B. Use Diskperf from a command prompt to turn on the disk counters.

   C. Install the disk statistics service in the Network control panel.

   Answer: B—Due to the overhead of tracking them, none of the disk counters are active until you turn them on.

Monitor network traffic by using Network Monitor. Tasks include:

- Collecting data
- Presenting data
- Filtering data

While Performance Monitor is a great tool for checking the health of a server, in a networked environment, you will occasionally want to look deeper into what's happening on the wire. For this, you will want to use a packet-analysis tool. Microsoft Windows NT ships with just such a tool—Network Monitor.

Critical Information

Network Monitor allows you to capture and analyze the packets flowing through your network. Unlike Performance Monitor, which shows you only the numbers of packets, Network Monitor allows you to page through the captured information to find specific types of communication and even look into the packets to see exactly what's happening on your network.

The goal of this objective is to ensure that you understand how to use Network Monitor to view and analyze traffic on an NT network. That traffic will be discussed later in this chapter. From a testing perspective, this objective is procedure-based. As such, the critical information will be found in the "Necessary Procedures" section. The opening screen of Network Monitor will be introduced, then specific tasks will be covered in the "Necessary Procedures" section.

Network Monitor

The opening screen of Network Monitor, shown in Figure 5.3, is divided into four panes. Each pane provides a specific type of information.

F I G U R E 5.3: Network Monitor

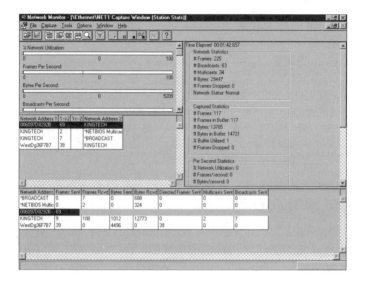

- Graph pane—Displays current activity.

- Session Statistics pane—Displays summary information about communication between two machines.

- Summary Statistics pane—Displays information about the data capture in progress.

- Station Statistics pane—Displays a summary of the traffic generated by each host.

Necessary Procedures

This is another section in which the objective concerns your ability to use a particular tool. Most of the critical information is actually here in the "Necessary Procedures" section.

Collecting Data

Network Monitor can capture the traffic on your network. To start this process, choose Capture ➤ Start. When the desired sampling interval has passed, choose Capture ➤ Stop.

Presenting Data

Once traffic has been captured, you can analyze its content. Choose Capture ➤ Display Captured Data. The data will be displayed in the order in which it was captured. When you double-click any packet, it will bring up three additional panes in the view.

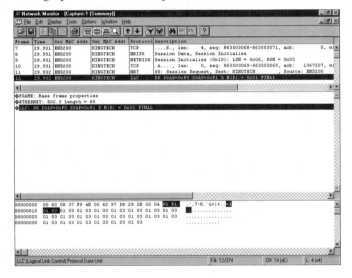

- The Summary (top) pane gives a summary of the traffic generated, including the protocol used, the sender and destination addresses, and a short description of the purpose.

- The Detail (middle) pane displays the contents of the highlighted packet in a text format. This is where you can analyze the contents of each packet.

- The Hex (bottom) pane shows the contents of the packet in hex and ASCII format.

Filtering Data

When you do a generic capture of the data on your network, it can create a large amount of data. Often, the amount of data presented can make it difficult to find whatever you are looking for. Network Monitor can filter the data as they are collected or as presented from the captured packets.

Filtering Data as They Are Collected

To specify the types of data to be included in your capture, choose Capture ➤ Filter. You will then be able to filter the packets collected by either address or protocol.

Filtering Data as Presented

View the captured data and choose Display ➤ Filter. You will be presented with the Display Filter dialog box, which will allow you to reduce the captured database using a number of options.

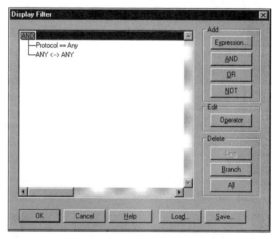

You can then choose to limit either the computers involved in the communication or the protocols that will be displayed. If you double-click the Protocol == Any line, you will be presented with the expression-builder windows shown below.

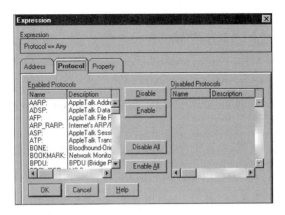

In these windows, you can enable or disable the presentation of any protocol.

Exam Essentials

This is a hands-on objective. Know the procedures discussed inside and out.

Understand the procedures described in the "Necessary Procedures" section of this chapter.   Review the "Necessary Procedures" section. If possible, practice using Network Monitor on a live network. Try finding the traffic described throughout this book.

Key Terms and Concepts

Capture: The act of collecting packets for analysis.

Network Monitor: An NT utility used to collect and view packets on the network.

Network Monitoring Agent (NMA):   An NT service that must be installed and running to support network object counters in Performance Monitor and Network Monitor. NMA also sets password controls on which users are allowed to access captured data and data files.

Sample Questions

1. Which of the following tactics would be used to reduce the amount of information presented in a Network Monitor capture?

A. Filtering the data collected by computers involved

B. Filtering the data collected by protocol

C. Filtering the data after the capture has occurred

D. Saving the data for later import into Performance Monitor

Answer: A, B, C—The amount of information on a network can be overwhelming. Network Monitor offers many ways to limit the amount of information presented so that you can concentrate on a specific area.

▶ Identify performance bottlenecks.

NT servers are used for a lot of different tasks. Microsoft defines three main server environments—File and Print, Application, and Domain. Each of these environments will stress different components of a server. In this section, each of these environments will be defined, and which components they will utilize most heavily and the specific objects and counters that you will track to analyze each environment will be discussed.

WARNING Microsoft has made a big assumption when discussing each type of server environment—the assumption is that the server is used to provide only one service. In most networks, servers perform multiple services. In a real-world network, you will have to analyze how each function affects all other functions that the server performs.

Critical Information

For each server environment, you will need to know its main function and the importance of each of the four main subsystems for each environment.

File and Print Server

A file and print server is used by users to acquire and save data, to load server-based software, and as a print server. A breakdown of this type of server is given in Table 5.7.

NOTE The values in the following tables represent relative importance. Some components may have equal values.

T A B L E 5.7: File and Print Server

Subsystem	Importance to Environment*	Critical Information
Memory	1	Servers use memory to cache the files that users request. Caching a frequently used file can increase process performance by over 100 percent.
Processor	2	Each network connection uses processor time at the server.
Disk	3	Since most connections are used to save or retrieve data, the disks can have an impact on performance. However, since servers use file caching, memory will have a bigger impact.
Network	3	Every transaction will add to the traffic on the network, but this is usually not the bottleneck on a file and print server.

*1= highest; 4=lowest

Application Server

An application server is a client/server environment. In a client/server environment, the actual processing happens at the server, not the client computer. A good example is a database server. The client runs a small piece of software called a front-end, which is used to formulate a query of the database. The server runs the actual database software. When the front-end sends a query, the server looks through the database and returns only the results. Notice that most of the processing happens at the server. The details of this environment are listed in Table 5.8.

T A B L E 5.8: Application Server

Subsystem	Importance to Environment*	Critical Information
Memory	2	Each application or service you add to a server will use memory. Most client/server-based applications use a lot of memory. Make sure the server has sufficient memory for both the operating system and the application.
Processor	1	As discussed above, most of the actual processing occurs at the server.
Disk	3	This is a tough one to categorize. If the application is disk intensive (a database, for instance), the disk could be a potential bottleneck. In most cases, though, its impact will be negligible compared to the processor and memory.
Network	4	Client/server-based applications put very little traffic on the network. Instead of transferring a large amount of data to be processed by the client, only the pertinent information is transferred.

*1= highest; 4=lowest

Domain Server

A domain server is a server that is involved in providing network management services. This server will be a domain controller, a DHCP server, a WINS server, etc. Most communication will be server to server, rather than client to server. The components of a domain server are listed in Table 5.9.

TABLE 5.9: Domain Server

Subsystem	Importance to Environment*	Critical Information
Memory	1	Each service the server provides will use memory.
Processor	2	Each network connection will use processing time. Domain controllers need to synchronize the SAM and act as login servers for users.
Disk	3	Domain servers are usually not disk intensive.
Network	1	All transactions will involve the network. Limited connection speed will slow down the overall operation of the workstations while waiting for server processes such as security authentication.

*1= highest; 4=lowest

Now that you know the different kinds of servers that might be found in your environment and which subsystem(s) is most important to each, you can use this information to choose what to include in your baseline. For each of the "big four" subsystems, you will need to know which counters to watch and what ranges of values are acceptable for each environment.

Exam Essentials

Most of the optimization techniques covered in the remaining chapter will assume that you understand the different types of environments in which an NT server might be used. Know these before continuing.

Know the three types of server environments and the importance of the four main subsystems for each. The three types of environments are File and Print, Application, and Domain. Review Tables 5.7, 5.8, and 5.9 to understand the relative importance of the four main subsystems to each environment.

Key Terms and Concepts

Application server: A server that acts as the back-end for a client/server-based application.

Client/server: An application process that is divided into two parts—the server code that does the actual request processing and client code that communicates requests to the server.

Domain server: A server that performs network management tasks.

File and print server: A server that provides data storage and print services to the network.

Sample Questions

1. On a file and print server, which of the four main components is most likely to be the bottleneck?

   A. Memory

   B. Processor

   C. Disk

   D. Network

Answer: A—Memory is used to cache users' data requests. If not enough memory is available, the system will spend too much time accessing its hard drives.

2. On an application server, which of the four main components is most likely to be the bottleneck?

   A. Memory

   B. Processor

   C. Disk

   D. Network

   Answer: B—Since most of the actual processing of data occurs at the server, the processor becomes a critical component.

3. On a domain server, which of the four main components is most likely to be the bottleneck?

   A. Memory

   B. Processor

   C. Disk

   D. Network

   Answer: A, D—The function of a domain server is to handle network management tasks. Also, keep in mind that every connection to a server uses memory.

Optimize performance for various results. Results include:

- Controlling network traffic
- Controlling server load

So far, the information in this chapter has been interesting, but not all that useful. Knowing what tools to use and what parameters to watch are of little use if you don't know how to interpret the data you collect. This section covers how to use the information provided by Performance Monitor and Network Monitor to optimize both your servers and the network that they use to communicate.

Critical Information

Most administrators would define *optimization* as the act of configuring a component for maximum performance. The problem is that this is not a complete definition of the term. You throw high-end components into your environment and spend hours tweaking configuration parameters. When you're done, you have the fastest network money can buy. Unfortunately, this network has as much in common with a normal business environment as an Indy 500 race car has with your family minivan.

Optimizing your network is a lot like purchasing an automobile. Before you spend any of your budget, you want to examine two things: function and need. The first step in optimization is to purchase hardware and software that are designed for the functions that they will perform in *your* network. The second step is to determine the minimum acceptable level of performance mandated by your environment. If your network will be used to do real-time reservations for a large airline company, you would need high bandwidth and redundancy. If your network will be used to do nightly updates of plant inventory, you could probably get by with less bandwidth and slower hardware.

When optimizing a network, you must consider the overall costs of ownership and compare those costs to business needs. Pure physical performance is usually insignificant compared to budget restraints and the need for reliability.

Controlling Network Traffic

Before you can control network traffic, you need to know what traffic will be generated on your network. In the Microsoft-instructor-led course 689, "Supporting Microsoft Windows NT 4.0—Enterprise Technologies," students spend two full days analyzing data captured by Network Monitor. While most of this information is not tested upon directly, it is assumed that the person being tested understands the implications of each type of traffic. Most of the questions for this objective will be scenario based. You will be given a description of an environment and will be expected to know how to optimize network traffic.

There are three main ways to optimize network traffic:

- Reduce the amount of traffic by removing an unnecessary service.

- Add services that reduce the amount of time it takes for users to accomplish a task. (Note that this might actually increase the amount of traffic generated.)

- Reduce or control the frequency of the traffic that is generated.

For each type of traffic, the methods that can be used to optimize your network will be discussed. For the examination, you will be required to understand the purpose of the traffic, the number of packets generated, and the frequency with which the traffic is generated. At the end of this section, you will find a table that summarizes this information.

Client-Initialization Traffic

The first type of traffic that will be discussed is the traffic that might be generated when a client attaches to the network or attempts to connect to another workstation or server computer. There are two things to remember about this type of traffic: it is usually not a significant percentage of your overall network load and it is necessary if your clients are going to use your network. Because of this, in the real world, most administrators do not spend a lot of time analyzing this type of burst, high-volume traffic that occurs infrequently for short periods of time—the reduction in traffic is usually not worth the amount of time that would be spent in optimization.

DHCP Traffic

Dynamic host configuration protocol (DHCP) is both a protocol and a service. It is an industry standard way to configure clients with TCP/IP configuration data such as IP addresses and subnet masks from a central server. There are two major types of traffic associated with DHCP: lease acquisition and lease renewal. Neither of these two types of traffic generates enough packets on the wire to be considered significant.

Each time a DHCP client initializes, it must contact the DHCP server to acquire its IP configuration. This process generates four packets on the network.

All DHCP acquisition traffic is accomplished through broadcast packets. There are two reasons for this. First, until the acknowledgment is received, the client does not have an IP address, so packets cannot be addressed directly to it. Second, all DHCP servers respond to the discovery packet if they receive it, which means that each DHCP server has earmarked an IP address for the client. When they receive the broadcast acknowledgment packet, they know that the client has accepted an address. If it is not theirs, the DHCP server can free up that address for another client.

If you use Network Monitor to view the contents of the DHCP packets, you will notice the following things:

- The Ethernet destination is set to FFFFFFFF. This denotes a broadcast packet.

- The IP source address is set to 0.0.0.0, and the IP destination address is set to 255.255.255.255. This combination alerts the DHCP server that it should process the packet.

- The UDP source and destination ports are listed as the BOOTP port.

Two frames will be generated to renew the lease. This will happen each time the client starts up or when half of the lease duration has been reached.

DHCP traffic has such a small impact on the network—four packets to acquire an address and then two packets to renew—that most administrators do not exert a lot of effort to optimize this service. There are, however, a couple of techniques to optimize this service of which you should be aware:

- Reduce the renewal traffic by increasing the lease duration.

- If your router is configured to pass BOOTP packets, you can usually configure the router with a retry count. This parameter configures the router to pass the packet only if the request has been outstanding for a specified period of time. This gives all local DHCP servers the chance to answer the client request, before that request is passed to another subnet.

WINS Client Traffic

Windows Internet network server (WINS) is a service loaded at an NT server. It provides two very important functions for your network: It acts as a registration agent for NetBIOS names, effectively preventing duplicate names on your network, and it builds a database of NetBIOS names and IP addresses that can be used to resolve a computer name into its IP address. By using a WINS server, you reduce the amount of broadcast traffic on your network and allow browsing across a routed network.

There are four types of WINS traffic generated: registration, renewal, resolution, and release.

Registration   During the initialization of a WINS client, it will contact the WINS server to register its NetBIOS name. The WINS server will search its database to confirm that the requested name is not already in use on the network. If the name is in use, the WINS server will return a negative response to the client.

The importance of this becomes apparent when you compare it to the process used in a non-WINS environment. Without a WINS server, the client will announce itself on the local subnet by broadcasting a packet. This packet announces the computer to the network. If another computer on the local subnet is using the name being announced, the local subnet will respond with a negative acknowledgment, telling the client that it cannot use the name with which it was configured. There are two major problems with this procedure. First, it adds broadcast traffic on the local subnet—traffic that all other computers must process. Second, since it is a broadcast packet, most routers will not pass it to other subnets. This results in an environment where duplicate names can exist on the network.

Renewal When a client registers its name with a WINS server, the server returns a lease duration. Like DHCP, this lease must be renewed on a regular basis to ensure that the WINS server's database of names is up to date. The client will begin the renewal process when half of the lease duration has passed. This is a two-packet process.

Resolution The WINS server also acts as a name-resolution database. When one NetBIOS computer needs to communicate with another, it sends a request to the WINS server. The server looks through its database to find the record for the requested computer. If it finds a record, it returns the IP address to the requesting computer. This process generates two packets on the network—a request and an answer.

Release The WINS database is supposed to contain records for computers that are online and available. Unlike DHCP, though, when a WINS client is properly shut down, one of the last things it does is send a packet to the WINS server releasing its lease on its registered NetBIOS names. This alerts the WINS server to remove those records from its database. This process consists of two packets for each name the computer has registered.

Since WINS generates such a small amount of traffic on the network, you probably won't spend a lot of time optimizing your clients. There are, however, a few steps you can take should the need arise:

- Remember that each client must register a unique name for each service that it provides. One way to reduce the amount of WINS traffic is to disable unnecessary services at your clients. This has the added benefit of reducing the size of the WINS database—which will help reduce the server-to-server traffic. That traffic will be discussed later in this section.

- You can also increase the NetBIOS name-cache parameter. Each time a name is resolved, the client will put it in its NetBIOS name cache. By default, this information is stored for 10 minutes. After 10 minutes have passed, the client will have to resolve the IP address again. Unfortunately, you must edit the registry to change this parameter. The registry setting is as follows:

```
HKEY_LOCAL_MACHINE\SYSTEM\CurrentControlSet\
Services\NetBT\Parameters\CacheTimeOut
```

- You can also configure a text file at each client, called the LMHOSTS file, that contains the NetBIOS name and IP addresses of computers the client is likely to communicate with. You can have these entries preload during initialization. Preloaded entries are placed in cache permanently, foregoing the need to use the WINS server to resolve the name.

- You can also increase the lease time for registered names. However, this choice doesn't make a lot of sense. By default, the lease duration is three days. This means that renewal traffic is two packets every one-and-a-half days. If you increase the duration, it will reduce the frequency of this action—but it will also take the WINS server longer to remove records from its database if a machine is not shut down correctly.

File-Session Traffic

Except when using broadcast-based services, computers must establish a "session" before communication can occur. The amount of traffic generated is not significant, but if you understand the process, it can help when you are analyzing other types of traffic. File-session traffic can be divided into the following six areas: address resolution, TCP session establishment, NetBIOS session establishment, SMB protocol negotiation, connection sequence, and session termination.

The six types of file-session traffic are used to manage the connection between two computers for data transfer. Because of this, the amount of network bandwidth utilized is usually negligible when compared to the overall transaction. The size of the actual files transferred will determine the amount of traffic generated for the process.

Address resolution   Once the host or NetBIOS name has been resolved to an IP address, using one of the methods discussed earlier, the IP address must be resolved to a hardware or MAC (media access control) address. This process is called address resolution, and it utilizes ARP (address resolution protocol) to accomplish the task. Basically, the computer sends a request to the destination computer asking for its hardware address. The destination computer replies with the requested information. Both computers then move this information into their respective ARP caches so that address resolution will not have to occur for every packet. This is a two-packet process, which occurs the first time the computers attempt to communicate.

TCP session establishment   Once the MAC address has been acquired, a TCP session must be established. This is known as the TCP *three-way handshake*. Three packets are involved—a request to communicate, an acknowledgment of the request, and an acknowledgment of the acknowledgment. This process occurs only once between the client and the server. Multiple file connections can be established over the same TCP session.

NetBIOS session establishment   Once the TCP session has been built, a NetBIOS session must be established. Basically, you are working your way up the OSI model, ensuring that communication can occur. As in the TCP session, this process occurs only once, because multiple file sessions can be established of the same NetBIOS session. This is a two-packet process.

SMB (server message block) protocol negotiation   The next step is for the two computers to agree upon an SMB version to use in communication. SMB is the language spoken internally by the operating system. Like any other piece of mature software, SMB has gone through numerous revisions and updates. The client sends a list of all SMB versions or dialects that it understands. The server looks through the list and returns a packet identifying the highest revision that both computers can utilize. This will be the SMB dialect that is used in communication between the two machines. This process occurs once, while the file session is being established. It generates two packets on the network.

Connection sequence   The last step in the file session establishment is for the client to connect to the shared resource on the server. This process will generate a varying amount of traffic depending upon the length of the names of share points and the SMB options that are used.

Session termination   When the data have been transferred, the client will disconnect from the server's resource. This generates two packets of traffic. When the client disconnects from the last resource on the server, the TCP session will be terminated. The termination involves another three-way handshake and generates three packets of network traffic.

Optimizing file-session traffic   There are two main methods of optimizing file-session traffic. First, remove all unnecessary protocols. Session requests are sent over all protocols simultaneously, so if you remove unused protocols, it can significantly reduce the amount of file-session traffic on the network. Second, ensure that the data users' access is located on a server near them (on the same TCP/IP subnet). While this does not reduce the amount of traffic generated, it does reduce the amount of traffic that must be routed across multiple network segments.

Logon-validation traffic

Before a user can take advantage of the resources on the network, they must log onto the network. This process is called logon-validation. The domain controllers in your NT domain handle this process. The relative impact of validation traffic on your network depends upon many variables. When designing your network, you will have to determine the number of domain controllers needed and the appropriate placement of those servers on your network. You will also have to think about when this traffic occurs—do all users log on at 8:00 A.M. every morning, or will logon traffic be randomly generated throughout the day?

Logon-validation traffic can be divided into four categories: finding a logon server, preparation, validation, and session termination.

Finding a logon server   Before the logon process can begin, the client must find a logon server (domain controller). There are two ways that this can be accomplished—through a broadcast request or through a query of a WINS server. The preferred method is, of course, using a Microsoft WINS server.

Preparation   The next step in the process is the establishment of a session between the client and the server. This is the same process used for establishing a file session.

Validation   Once the session is established, validation can proceed. On a Windows 95 client, this will entail approximately four packets. On a Windows NT client, more traffic will be generated because the server must return a list of trusted domains to the client.

Session termination   Upon completion of the logon process, the session must be terminated. This will generate approximately five frames of network traffic.

Numerous techniques can be used to optimize logon-validation traffic:

- Determine the number of domain controllers needed for your network. Microsoft estimates that one domain controller should be available for every 2,000 users. This should ensure that no domain controller is overwhelmed by the validation traffic. A couple of Performance Monitor counters can help determine the logon workload being placed on a server. *Server: logons/sec* monitors the number of logon attempts, both successful and unsuccessful, each second; *Server: logons total* monitors the total number of logon requests handled by a server since the last startup.

- By default, NT servers are configured to maximize throughput for file sharing. While this is appropriate for a file and print server, it is not necessarily the best configuration for a domain controller. In the Network applet in Control Panel, you can change this configuration to maximize throughput for network applications. This should increase the number of logon requests the server can handle from 6 to 7 per second to around 20.

- Place domain controllers so that they are near users. This reduces the amount of logon traffic that must be routed across multiple subnets or slow WAN links.

- Ensure that your server meets the hardware requirements for the task. Use your knowledge of Performance Monitor to ensure that no bottlenecks slow down the validation process.

Client-Server Traffic   Now that the client has initialized and logon validation has occurred, the other client-to-server traffic that will be generated on your network can be examined. Three types of traffic generate a predictable amount of traffic between the server and the client: browser, domain name system (DNS), and intranet.

Browser traffic   Browser traffic is generated by a server when announcing itself to the network and by clients when retrieving the browse list. The entire process will be examined later in this section.

There are various ways to optimize the browser traffic on your network:

- Disable unnecessary server service components. Remember that every computer that can act as a server must announce itself to the network every 12 minutes. These computers are also added to the browse list, increasing its size. Every server adds at least 27 bytes to the browse list.

- Control the number of potential browsers on your network. The number of backup browsers is determined automatically by the browser service on the master browser. When the master browser determines that an additional backup browser is needed, it will choose from the list of potential browsers. You can control which computers will be considered for this function, thus ensuring that only computers with the necessary bandwidth will be chosen. By default, all Microsoft computers on the network are potential browsers. You change this default setting in different ways depending upon the operating system in use. In NT you edit the registry, changing the value of HKEY_LOCAL_MACHINE\SYSTEM\ CurrentControlSet\Services\Browser\Parameters\Maintain-ServerList to No. On a Windows 95–based computer, use the Network applet in Control Panel to disable the master browser parameter. On a Microsoft Windows for Workgroups computer, edit the SYSTEM.INI file and add MaintainServerList = NO to the [network] section.

- Eliminate all unnecessary network protocols. All browser traffic is initiated on all protocols. Reducing the number of protocols in use can greatly reduce the amount of traffic generated.

DNS traffic DNS traffic is generated by using a domain name server to resolve host names. When users try to access a resource using TCP/IP commands, such as PING or a Web browser, the host name must be resolved to an IP address. This process, called host name resolution, can be accomplished using DNS.

DNS is a database that contains the host name and IP address of all hosts that can be resolved using the DNS process. Unlike WINS, the DNS database is static in nature—the administrator must manually create records in the DNS database for each host, and these records are available whether or not the host is online.

Three types of DNS traffic will affect your network:

Lookups—In the best of worlds, a DNS lookup consists of two packets: a request from the client and an answer from the DNS server. Since the client is configured with the IP address of the DNS server, all traffic is handled using directed, rather than broadcast, packets. After obtaining the IP address from the server, the client can then initiate communication with the destination host.

DNS recursion—If the DNS server does not contain the requested IP address, it must pass the request to another DNS server. This process is called a *recursive query*. The DNS server will act on behalf of the client, asking another DNS server for the requested information. If it receives an answer, it will return the IP address to the client.

Integration with WINS—Keeping the DNS database can be a hassle on a busy network. Every time you add a computer, move a computer, change an IP address, or make any other changes to your IP network, you must manually enter these changes into the DNS database. Another drawback to DNS is that the database does not indicate which computers are currently available on the network. A client could conceivably go through the process of host name resolution only to receive an error while trying to communicate with a machine that is not currently available. To avoid these drawbacks, Microsoft allows you to configure DNS to query the WINS database. Remember that the WINS database has a record for each computer currently available that includes the NetBIOS name and IP address of each machine. When the DNS server receives a request for a host that is not found in its database, it will convert the host name into a NetBIOS name and submit it to the WINS server. The WINS server will check its database for a corresponding IP address.

To optimize DNS traffic, you can do the following things:

- Do not configure your DNS servers for recursive lookups. While configuring your DNS servers for recursive lookups would reduce the amount of traffic, it severely curtails the effectiveness of DNS. If a DNS server does not contain the requested information, it will return an error to the client rather than attempting to find the information on another DNS server.

- Configure your clients so that the DNS server they use is most likely to have the information they need. Basically, this reduces the need for recursive lookups.

- Increase the TTL (time to live) setting on your DNS server. Each time a name is resolved, the DNS server moves the host name and IP address into cache. When a client makes a request, the first place DNS looks is in this cache. If the information is available, the DNS server will not need to look any further. If you increase the TTL from the default 60 minutes, it will reduce the number of recursive lookups.

Intranet browsing traffic   Intranet browsing traffic is generated by a Web browser when downloading information from a Web server. Browsing a Web server can generate a lot of traffic on your network. Unfortunately, there is no way to characterize the traffic generated while downloading each page. However, certain aspects of the traffic will be the same no matter what the content is of the Web pages accessed.

Connecting to a Web site—Before you can download the content of a Web page, you must establish a TCP session to the Web server. This session is established in the same way as any other TCP session—the three-way handshake.

Requesting a Web page—Once the TCP session has been established, the user can begin the process of requesting information, usually in the form of pages. Web pages are requested using the

HTTP protocol. Using HTTP, the browser must issue a "get" command for a page and another get command for each image or graphic that is part of that page. Each get command constitutes a separate packet of communication.

Browsing security—Most Web server software, including Microsoft's Internet Information Server (IIS), can be configured to use some sort of authentication process to control access to information. While this will add overhead to your network, both in network traffic and in processing, the type of information stored on the Web server might mandate it.

Web browsing, even on an intranet, can add a significant amount of traffic to your network. There are a few common-sense rules that you should follow to control the impact of this technology:

- Keep Web pages small. Good Web design takes advantage of linking in HTML documents. Users will download only the pages they request—a small opening page with well-defined links to other pages will reduce the amount of information that a user will have to download.

- Limit the number and size of images. While the graphical interface of Web technologies is what has made them so popular, images make up a large percentage of the download on many pages. Many sites mandate both a text- and a graphics-based page so that users can determine the type of information that they will see.

- Increase the size of the local cache at the client. Each time a client accesses a Web page, the browser looks in its cache to see if it already has the page available. The larger this cache is, the more likely it is that the user will receive a page from the local cache rather than having to access the Web server.

- Think about security. If your information is intended to be public, allow anonymous connections. If you have information that is not intended to be public, implement Web security, but be aware of the access costs.

Server-to-server traffic
Another type of traffic that will be generated on your network is traffic between servers as they carry out network maintenance tasks.

While these functions do not usually generate a significant amount of traffic, you should be aware of each type of traffic, its function on the network, and its frequency. Six types of server-to-server traffic will be discussed: account synchronization, trust relationships, server browsing, WINS replication, directory replication, and DNS server.

Account synchronization In a Microsoft Windows NT network, a domain controller—either the primary (PDC) or a backup (BDC)—authenticates user logon attempts. All changes to the accounts database must occur on the PDC. The PDC will, in turn, update the information stored on the BDCs. The process of updating the account database on a BDC is called account synchronization.

The traffic involved in account synchronization can be divided into five types:

Find PDC—Each time a BDC is started, it must find the name of the PDC for its network. This information is placed in cache, so this process occurs only once. Four packets are generated on the network.

Session establishment—Once the NetBIOS name and IP address of the PDC are found, the BDC will establish both TCP and NetBIOS sessions with the PDC. This process is the same as discussed earlier.

Secure-channel establishment—Next, the BDC must establish a secure channel to the PDC. This process generates approximately eight packets of network traffic and is done only once. This channel is held open until one machine or another goes offline.

Verify database—The BDC sends the version ID for each of the SAM databases to the PDC. The PDC compares this value with its own version of those files. If the BDC is out of date, the PDC will initiate the synchronization process.

Announcement of change—Every five minutes, the PDC looks for changes to any of the three databases that make up the SAM. When a change is noted, the PDC sends a message to each BDC notifying them that a change has occurred. Each BDC will then request the updated information from the NETLOGON service of the PDC.

Two types of updates can occur—partial and full. In a partial update, only the changed information is sent to the BDC. In a full update, the entire SAM database is send to the BDC. In most cases, it is preferable to do a partial update because this reduces the amount of traffic involved in the process.

The PDC keeps a log of all changes to the SAM. This log is of a fixed size (by default, it is 64KB) and will hold approximately 2,000 changes, depending on the size of the changes. Each change is given a version ID—think of this as a counter. The PDC keeps track of the highest version ID sent to each BDC. When it notes a change to the SAM, it compares the version ID of the change with the version ID of the last change sent to each BDC. If the version ID is higher than the last one sent, the PDC will notify the BDC of the change and a partial update will occur.

Occasionally, there will be more than 2,000 changes between updates. When this occurs, the change log will "wrap" or begin overwriting change information. When the PDC checks version IDs, it will notice that wrapping has occurred and institute a full update to the BDC.

You can change various registry parameters to optimize this traffic (see Table 5.10).

Each of these parameters will be found in the following area of the registry:

```
HKEY_LOCAL_MACHINE\CurrentControlSet\Services\Netlogon\
Parameters
```

T A B L E 5.10:   Synchronization Parameters in the Registry

Registry Parameter	Description
Pulse	Determines how often the PDC checks for changes in the SAM databases. The default value is 5 minutes. It can be set as high as 48 hours. Be very careful when increasing this value because a long interval could result in BDCs not being updated in a timely manner.

T A B L E 5.10: Synchronization Parameters in the Registry *(cont.)*

Registry Parameter	Description
Pulse-Maximum	Determines how often the PDC will send a message to each BDC even if no changes have occurred to the SAM database. The default is every 2 hours. This parameter can be set as high as every 48 hours.
ChangeLog-Size	Controls the number of changes to the SAM that can be stored. By default, this log has a maximum size of 64KB, or enough room to store approximately 2,000 changes. If you increase the size of the change log, it will reduce the number of full updates to the BDCs.
Pulse-Concurrency	By default, the PDC can send out change notifications to only 10 BDCs simultaneously. If you increase this number, the BDCs will be updated faster, but the process will use more network bandwidth. If you decrease this value, it spreads the synchronization process over a longer period of time.
Replication-Governor	Controls two aspects of the synchronization process—the amount of bandwidth that it can utilize and the amount of data that can be transferred. The default value is 100. This means that the synchronization process can use 100 percent of the available bandwidth and each transfer can be up to 128KB of data. If you set this number to 50, it would indicate that the NETLOGON service can use only 50 percent of the available bandwidth and can transfer only 64KB of data in a single synchronization process. If you set this value too low, it can result in the BDCs never fully synchronizing with the PDC.

Trust relationships There really isn't a lot of traffic generated to maintain an existing trust relationship. Most of the traffic will be generated when you access resources across the trust. Three types of traffic are specific to the trust relationship: establish trust, import accounts, and pass-through authentication.

Establish trust—There are three steps to establishing a trust relationship between two domains. First, the trusted domain must permit the trusting domain to trust it. This will generate synchronization traffic as the PDC lets the BDCs know that the trust has been permitted. The trust is added as a hidden user in the SAM database, and this record must be synchronized to all BDCs. Second, the trusting domain must add the first domain as a trusted domain. It must find the name and address of the trusted PDC, establish TCP and Net-BIOS sessions with that PDC, attempt to connect to the PDC (this first attempt will fail because the trust account is not yet valid, but it validates the creation of an account in the trusted domain), and then retrieve a list of all backup browsers and servers in the trusted domain. Finally, the trusting PDC will query WINS for a list of all domain controllers in the trusted domain. This traffic is generated only once during the establishment of the trust relationship. Once the relationship is established, very little traffic is generated to maintain the relationship. Basically, every time the trusting PDC is restarted, it must query WINS for a list of domain controllers in the trusted domain. Additionally, every seven days, the two domains change the password assigned to the trust relationship.

Import accounts—One of the main reasons to establish a trust relationship between two domains is to allow users from the trusted account access to resources in the trusting account. In User Manager for Domains, the administrator of the trusting domain can see a list of users and groups from the trusted domain. Every time this list is viewed, the list must be retrieved from a domain controller in the trusted domain. This can generate a lot of network traffic depending upon the number of user and group accounts defined in the trusted domain.

Pass-through authentication—The most frequent form of traffic generated across a trust relationship is pass-through authentication. If a user from the trusted domain sits down at an NT-based machine defined in the trusting domain and attempts to log in, the following things will occur:

1. The NETLOGON service will query a domain controller for a list of trusted domains.

2. The user picks their home domain from the drop-down list.

3. The NETLOGON service passes the logon request to a domain controller for its own domain.

4. That domain controller recognizes that the user's account exists in a trusted domain and passes the request to a domain controller in the trusted domain.

5. That domain controller authenticates the user and passes the security information for the user back to the domain controller in the trusting domain.

6. The domain controller in the trusting domain passes the security information to the NT computer from which the user is attempting to log on.

NOTE Notice that the domain controller from the trusting domain "trusts" the authentication information from the trusted domain. This is known as pass-through authentication.

Another type of pass-through authentication occurs when a user tries to access a resource in a trusting domain. Since the trusting domain does not contain the user's account information, the same process will take place.

There are two main ways to optimize the traffic generated by trust relationships—reduce the number of trusts and assign permissions to groups rather than individuals.

Server browsing For the MCSE examination, you will need to know what types of traffic are generated to maintain the browse list. Browser traffic can have a great impact on your network. Microsoft estimates that server browser traffic makes up approximately 51 percent of the "maintenance" traffic on your network. Because of this large percentage, it is imperative that you understand how the browser service operates.

Five types of browser traffic are generated in a Microsoft Windows NT network:

- Host announcements

- Local master announcements

- Workgroup announcements

- Elections

- Browse list exchanges

Before the individual types of traffic can be discussed, how the browser service works needs to be reviewed. First, a single domain environment will be discussed.

Each computer that has a server component configured will announce itself at boot and every 12 minutes thereafter. This announcement is made using a broadcast packet. The computer expects to receive a response from the segment's master browser. If no master browser responds, the computer will force the election of one.

There is a master browser on each network segment. The master browser collects and answers each computer announcement. It places the information contained in the announcement into a database. There are a few rules about which machines will become the master browser on a network segment. First, the PDC will always be the master browser for the segment to which it is attached. If there is no PDC on a segment, a list of election criteria will determine which machine will become the master browser. These criteria work their way down from NT Server to Windows for Workgroups—with the latest operating system having the highest criterion.

The master browser will then appoint a certain number of machines to act as backup browsers. These computers get a copy of the browse list from the master browser. This list is updated every 12 minutes.

The PDC is not only the master browser for its segment; it may also be the domain master browser—receiving the browse list of all master browsers in the network. It correlates this information into a domain browser list and then sends the domain list to all of the master browsers. The master browsers contact the domain master browser every 12 minutes to update their information.

Stop and analyze this arrangement. Basically, you have a computer on each network segment funneling information about the computers on its segment to a central location (the domain master browser). This machine, in turn, correlates the information from all over the network into a master list and sends it back to a computer on each segment. This is how the browse list is kept current. Now, think about the timing involved—these lists are exchanged every 12 minutes. This explains why a machine booted on a segment might not appear in the browse list for quite some time.

To make this even more complicated, there is a master browser on each segment for every domain that has machines on that segment. In other words, a particular network segment might have multiple master browsers—one for each domain represented by a computer. These master browsers announce their presence to each other with a broadcast packet every 12 minutes.

Now that you understand how the browse list is maintained, you need to understand how it is used by a client. When a user clicks Network Neighborhood, they see a list of all computers that have a server component configured. First, they must find out which computer is the master browser on their segment. They can either broadcast this request or query a WINS server. Once they have this information, they will ask the master browser for a list of backup browsers on their network segment. They will then ask a backup browser for the current list.

All in all, the traffic generated can have a pretty big impact on your network. You will probably look for ways to optimize this process. There are three methods of which you need to be aware:

- Reduce the number of protocols in use on your network. All browser traffic is generated on *all* protocols.

- Reduce the number of entries in the browse list. Disable the server service on computers that do not need to share resources.

- You can configure a couple of registry parameters. Both are found in the HKEY_LOCAL_MACHINE\SYSTEM\CurrentControlSet\ Services\Browser\Parameters subkey. The first parameter is the

MasterPeriodicity parameter. This parameter specifies how often a master browser contacts the domain master browser. The default is 720 seconds (12 minutes). The second parameter is the Backup-Periodicity parameter. This parameter specifies how often a backup browser contacts the master browser for a fresh copy of the browse list.

WINS replication   The WINS server serves two functions—name registration and name resolution. Computers use the WINS server to ensure that their NetBIOS names are unique on the network and to resolve their NetBIOS names into IP addresses. A single WINS server is sufficient in most LAN environments, but think about how this would work on a WAN. Every time a computer starts, it has to cross the WAN link to register its name. It also has to cross the WAN link to resolve the IP addresses of local hosts. This slows response times, and the ability to communicate with local hosts depends upon the WAN link being up and available. Having a single WINS server on a WAN is clearly not acceptable.

Most companies will configure a WINS server for each physical location. This keeps registration and resolution traffic off their expensive WAN links. However, clients will have no way to resolve the IP addresses of hosts in another physical location. This is where WINS replication comes into play. As an administrator, you can configure the WINS servers to replicate their local information to other WINS servers. In this way, each WINS server can have information about computers across your entire network. This replication process will generate traffic between the WINS servers.

There is no way to quantify the amount of traffic that will be generated by the WINS replication process. The amount depends upon the size of the network, the number of services each computer needs to register, and the number of changes to the WINS database. You will, however, want to optimize this service as much as possible.

The WINS partnership is configured as either a push or a pull relationship. Choosing the correct configuration is the best way to optimize this service.

In a push relationship, each WINS server will notify its partners when a certain number of changes have occurred to its database. Each partner will then request these changes when convenient. In this type of configuration, you have no control over when the replication of data will occur—when the threshold number of changes has been reached, the replication process will begin.

In a pull relationship, you configure each WINS server to request changes from its partner at a specific time interval. With this configuration, you can configure replication so that it occurs during off-peak hours on your network.

Microsoft suggests that you configure WINS servers as push partners within a physical site and pull partners across wide-area links.

Directory replication   The directory replication service allows you to store a master copy of data and automatically update copies of the data on other servers. This service was designed to allow the replication of logon scripts so that users will run the same logon script no matter which domain controller they have attached to for authentication. The amount of traffic generated by this process is fairly slight since logon scripts are usually small files that don't change very often. The process can also be used to replicate other types of data. In this case, the amount of network traffic generated depends upon the amount of data and the frequency with which it is changed.

The replication process is fairly straightforward. The computer that has the master copy is known as the export server. The computer that will receive a copy of the data is known as the import server. The export server checks its data for changes on an interval known as a pulse. By default, the pulse is five minutes. If there are no changes, the export server will send a packet out to the import servers letting them know that it is still up and running as an export server. If there are changes, it will notify the import computers of this fact.

The import computers will then request the changed information from the export server. Each import computer will establish a session with the export server. One of the first things the import computer will request is the NetRemoteTOD (the time of day) of the export server. The import server does this because replication cannot occur if the two servers' clocks are off by more than 10 minutes. The next step is to check various replication parameters and, if all conditions are met, request the changes.

In a normal environment, where replication is used only to replicate logon scripts, you should not need to spend a lot of time optimizing this service. If you are replicating a large amount of data, however, you can do a few things to make the process more efficient.

It is best to have a flat, shallow directory structure for the data being replicated. The replication process checks to see if any file in a directory or its subdirectories has changed. If *any* file has changed, the entire subdirectory will be replicated—not just the file that has changed.

You can change a couple of registry settings to control the frequency of communication between the export and import computers. These registry entries will be found in the HKEY_LOCAL_MACHINE\SYSTEM\ CurrentControlSet\Services\Replicator\Parameters subkey. The first registry setting is the Interval parameter. This parameter controls how often the export server checks for changes to its data. The second parameter is the pulse. This parameter controls how often the import computer contacts the export server if no communication has occurred. If an import computer has not heard from an export server in *Interval*Pulse* minutes, it will contact the export server and request changes.

DNS server   Large companies might have multiple DNS servers on their network. This can provide some fault tolerance to the DNS database and split the DNS workload between servers in a busy environment. With this configuration, one DNS server will be the primary one. It will contain the master copy of DNS. The other servers will be configured as secondary DNS servers. They will receive a copy of the DNS database from the primary server. The process of replicating the DNS database from the primary to a secondary is called a *zone transfer*.

The overall amount of traffic will vary depending upon the size of the DNS database, but a certain amount of traffic will be generated just managing the zone transfer process. First, the secondary server will query the primary server for changes, generating two packets on the network (query and response). If the response indicates that changes have occurred, the secondary server will then establish a TCP session with the primary DNS server. There is no process for determining which records have changed, so the entire DNS database will be sent to the secondary server.

Three parameters can be set in the DNS Manager tool to optimize the zone transfer process:

Refresh interval—The amount of time the secondary server will wait before querying the primary server to see if changes have occurred. The default is 60 minutes.

Retry interval—The amount of time the secondary server will wait to try the zone transfer in the event of failure. The default is 10 minutes.

Expire time—The amount of time the secondary server will continue to respond to name-resolution queries after it has lost contact with the primary server.

Controlling Server Load

Although Microsoft NT Server is optimized for an average workload, it does not mean that the generic configuration is best for all networks. Luckily, NT offers many ways to optimize its performance for varying network conditions.

Earlier in the chapter, various changes you can make to your server based upon information gathered using Performance Monitor were discussed. Although these suggestions were all valid, they are not the place to begin your optimization. NT can be optimized for various uses by accessing the properties of the server service. These properties can be found in the Services tab of the Network control panel.

Each of the optimization parameters is designed for a different type of server environment:

- Minimize Memory Used—Choose this option for servers that will support 10 connections or fewer.

- Balance—Optimizes the server for up to 64 simultaneous connections.

- Maximize Throughput for File Sharing—Allocates the maximum amount of memory for file-sharing applications. This option should be chosen for servers on a large network.

- Maximize Throughput for Network Applications—Optimizes server memory for client/server applications that manage their own memory, such as SQL Server or Exchange Server. This option should be used on servers that support large networks.

Exam Essentials

There is a lot of information in this objective. Most of it will not be tested on directly. Instead, you will see questions that assume you have the knowledge to choose the best solution for a given scenario.

Know the three ways to optimize network traffic. The three ways to optimize network traffic are as follows:

- Reduce the amount of traffic by removing a service.

- Add a service that will reduce the amount of time it takes to accomplish a task.

- Reduce the frequency with which a certain type of traffic is generated.

Understand how DHCP packets are addressed. The client-initialization traffic is broadcast based. Each packet has a destination hardware address of all *F*s, an IP source address of 0.0.0.0, and an IP destination address of 255.255.255.255.

Understand the browse service.   Each network segment has a master browser. This computer creates a list of all servers on the segment. The master browser for each segment sends its database to the domain master browser (the PDC), which maintains a domain-wide resource list. The domain master browser sends this list back to each master browser. When a client attempts to browse the network, it first gets the name and address of the master browser on its segment. Then, it requests a list of backup browsers from the master. Finally, it requests the browse list from one of the backup browsers.

Know the four optimization parameters and in what type of environment each should be used.   The four optimization parameters are Minimize Memory Used, Balance, Maximize Throughput for File Sharing, and Maximize Throughput for Network Applications.

Key Terms and Concepts

Account synchronization: The process of the PDC updating the copy of the SAM database on a BDC.

Address resolution: The act of resolving an IP address into the MAC (media access control) address for a node.

Backup browser: A computer, appointed by the master browser, that holds a copy of the browse list for access by users.

Domain master browser: The PDC of an NT network. It acts as the master browser for its network segment and as a go-between for all master browsers in the domain, building and distributing a domain-wide browse list.

Ethernet destination address: The MAC or physical address for which a packet is destined. A packet with the Ethernet destination address set to all Fs denotes a broadcast packet.

Master browser: Each network segment will elect a master browser to maintain a local browse list and communicate with the domain master browser to acquire the domain-wide browse list.

Pass-through authentication: The process used to authenticate an account from a trusted domain.

SMB (server message block) protocol: The language spoken internally by the NT operating system. There have been several revisions (dialects) of this protocol released. The client and server must agree upon the dialect to be used before communication can occur.

Sample Questions

1. Suppose that you are configuring an NT server for use by the graphics department of a small company. Six users will need to access this server. How should this server be optimized?

   A. Minimize Memory Used

   B. Balance

   C. Maximize Throughput for File Sharing

   D. Maximize Throughout for Network Applications.

Answer: A

CHAPTER

6

Troubleshooting

Microsoft Exam Objectives Covered in This Chapter:

▶ **Choose the appropriate course of action to take to resolve installation failures.** *(pages 311 – 314)*

▶ **Choose the appropriate course of action to take to resolve boot failures.** *(pages 315 – 326)*

▶ **Choose the appropriate course of action to take to resolve configuration errors. Tasks include:** *(pages 326 – 334)*
- Backing up and restoring the registry
- Editing the registry

▶ **Choose the appropriate course of action to take to resolve printer problems.** *(pages 334 – 342)*

▶ **Choose the appropriate course of action to take to resolve RAS problems.** *(pages 343 – 346)*

▶ **Choose the appropriate course of action to take to resolve connectivity problems.** *(pages 346 – 354)*

▶ **Choose the appropriate course of action to take to resolve resource access and permission problems.** *(pages 354 – 358)*

▶ **Choose the appropriate course of action to take to resolve fault-tolerance failures. Fault-tolerance methods include:** *(pages 358 – 366)*
- Tape backup
- Mirroring
- Stripe set with parity

▶ **Perform advanced problem resolution. Tasks include:** *(pages 366 – 375)*
- Diagnosing and interpreting a blue screen
- Configuring a memory dump
- Using the Event Log service

The objectives for this chapter cover the actions you should take to correct a specific set of problems. Some of these problems occur often in the workplace, while others occur rarely. Whether the problems are common or rare, knowing how to correct them is a very big part of being a network administrator.

Learning to troubleshoot technical problems is a lifelong process. You can pick up some useful tips by reading books or taking classes, but you can never know everything—experience plays a big role in developing troubleshooting skills. However, this book can act as a starting place to help you build a "troubleshooting database" in your head.

Each section features a specific set of steps to take when troubleshooting a particular problem. For the exam, it is important to know these steps.

Choose the appropriate course of action to take to resolve installation failures.

In the real world, installation failures can be fairly common. They are also the most fortunate type of problem, because they manifest before the server has been placed in production. While you are usually under a deadline during installation, there is usually less pressure to fix the problem immediately.

Critical Information

An NT installation might fail for many reasons. The easiest way to avoid installation problems is to purchase equipment that has been tested to be compatible with Microsoft Windows NT. Microsoft provides a tool—the NT hardware qualifier (NTHQ) utility—that will help you determine whether your equipment is on the tested list. This tool is found on your NT Server CD-ROM or can be downloaded from the Microsoft Web site. NTHQ tests your hardware to determine whether any components are not on the list.

WARNING Always download the latest version of NTHQ from the Microsoft Web site. The version found on your CD-ROM will not contain information about hardware that has been certified since the CD-ROM was created. Before you purchase equipment, you can access the compatibility list on the Web site. Make it a policy to specify *NT 4.0 certified* when you talk to vendors.

Some specific problems that you might encounter will now be examined.

Media Errors

If you get an error message that indicates that a particular file cannot be copied or is corrupt during an installation of NT, it could indicate a media error. Try using another CD-ROM if you have one. If not, try using another method of installation. For example, copy the I386 directory to the C: drive (assuming it is a FAT partition) and try the installation from there. Another option is to copy the I386 directory to another server, sharing the directory, and then install from that share point.

Nonsupported SCSI Adapter

If your CD-ROM is attached to a SCSI adapter that is not supported by NT, you can lose the ability to read from it halfway through the installation process, after the server has been restarted under NT. Unfortunately, even if the CD-ROM manufacturer provides an NT SCSI driver, you cannot use it until after NT is fully installed. If you run into this problem, you will have to use the techniques listed in the "Media Errors" section. Try installing from a share point on another server. Or, boot to DOS, copy the I386 directory to the C: drive, and install from there.

Insufficient Disk Space

Insufficient disk space is really just poor planning. Know the minimum requirements before you start the installation, and make sure your hardware meets or exceeds them. The only fix for insufficient disk space is to provide NT with enough disk space either by deleting an existing partition or by adding another drive.

Failure of Dependency Service to Start

When the dependency service fails to start, it is usually a configuration error. Most of these errors result from network interface card (NIC) problems, requiring you to go back to the network setup section of the installation and ensure that the protocols are configured correctly, that you have chosen a unique computer name, and that the NIC settings are correct.

Inability to Connect to the PDC

Ensure that you have entered the domain name correctly, that the NIC settings are correct, and that you have chosen the correct network protocols. This problem is quite common—it usually occurs when you try to install a BDC on a computer that has a nonsupported NIC. If NT doesn't provide a NIC driver, the card cannot initialize and you cannot communicate with the server.

Error in Assigning a Domain Name

When you install a PDC, ensure that the domain name is not already in use on your network. The domain name cannot be the same as any other domain or computer name.

Failure of NT to Install or Start

When NT fails to install or start, it usually indicates that a piece of hardware is not compatible with NT. Run NTHQ to determine which component is not on the hardware-compatibility list and replace the component.

Exam Essentials

If you know what problems you might encounter, it can help you avoid them.

Understand the various reasons that an NT installation might fail. The most common reasons for failure are either human error or incompatible hardware.

Key Terms and Concepts

HCL (hardware-compatibility list): A list of hardware that has been tested and approved for use with Microsoft Windows NT.

NTHQ (NT hardware qualifier): Software that checks your hardware to ensure that all components are on the hardware-compatibility list.

Sample Questions

1. Which of the following actions should you take if you encounter a media error when installing NT?

   A. Try another NT CD-ROM.

   B. Try another method of installation—across the network, copy the I386 to the local drive first, etc.

   C. Give up and try another operating system.

   Answer: A, B—Although answer C might seem like the easiest method in the short term, it is not a Microsoft-recommended solution.

Choose the appropriate course of action to take to resolve boot failures.

Nothing is worse than a server that won't finish the boot process. You are left staring at an obscure error message or, worse, at a blue screen filled with what appears to be hieroglyphics. In this section, the most common error messages, their causes, and the appropriate actions to take to correct the problems will be discussed. A discussion of blue screens will be found later in this chapter.

Critical Information

NT goes through four distinct phases during the boot process. For the MCSE examination, you will need to know what happens in each phase. After the stages have been examined, specific errors and possible solutions will be examined.

NT Boot Phases

The four boot phases are as follows:

- Initial
- Boot loader
- Kernel
- Logon

Initial Phase

During the initial phase, the computer performs a power on self test (POST), during which it determines how much memory is installed and whether the required hardware is available. During this process, the computer executes the BIOS and reads the information stored in CMOS to determine what storage devices are available, the date and time, and other parameters specific to the hardware.

In CMOS, the computer will read the type and configuration of possible boot devices. Based upon this information, it will determine which device it should examine to find operating system boot information. If your computer is configured to boot from the hard drive, your computer will read the first sector in an attempt to find the master boot record (MBR). The MBR contains critical information for the boot process—a list of partitions defined on the disk, their starting and ending sectors, and which partitions are active. (The active partition is the one that the computer will attempt to boot from.) If there is no MBR on the disk, the computer cannot boot to an operating system. This is why many computer viruses attack the MBR.

Once the computer has determined which partition it should look to for boot information, it will access that partition and read the partition boot sector (PBS). The PBS contains operating system-specific information. In the case of Windows NT, it directs the computer to load a file called NTLDR (NT loader), which is found in the partition root folder. If the PBS is missing or corrupted, you may see an error message that implies that no operating system was found, a nonsystem disk is being used, or a disk error has occurred. This is what happens when you restart your computer with a nonsystem floppy disk in the A: drive. There is no boot information on it, so the server doesn't know where to find the operating system.

Boot Loader Phase

Once NTLDR has been found and starts to load, the boot loader phase begins. During this phase, NT uses various programs to gather information about the hardware and drivers needed to boot. The following files will be utilized during this phase:

NTLDR—This is the operating system loader. It must be in the root directory of the active partition. NTLDR remains the overall conductor of the NT startup process.

BOOT.INI—This is an important text file that controls which operating system will be loaded. The user will see a menu offering various operating system choices. NTLDR expects to find this file in the root directory. The BOOT.INI file will be discussed in more detail later in this section.

BOOTSEC.DOS—If the computer is configured to dual boot between NT and another operating system, the NT installation program will gather all of the information needed to boot the other OS and place it in this file. When the user chooses to boot to another OS, NT will call this file.

NTBOOTDD.SYS—This is a device driver used to access a SCSI hard drive when the SCSI controller is not using its own BIOS.

NTDETECT.COM—This is a program that attempts to analyze the hardware on the computer; it passes this information to the operating system for inclusion in the registry later in the boot process. NTDETECT.COM can detect the following components: computer ID; bus/adapter type; video, keyboard, and communication ports; parallel ports; floppy disks; and mouse/pointing device. While NTDETECT.COM performs its function, it displays the following message on the screen:

```
NTDETECT V1.0 Checking Hardware…
```

NTLDR controls the initial startup of NT on the hardware. It also changes the processor from real-time to 32-bit flat memory mode, starts the appropriate miniature file system (NTLDR has code that enables it to read FAT and NTFS partitions), and reads the BOOT.INI file to display the menu of operating system choices.

Once NT has been selected and NTDETECT.COM has run its course, NTLDR will display the following message:

```
OS Loader V4.0
Press SPACEBAR now to invoke Hardware Profile/Last
Known Good menu.
```

If the spacebar is not pressed and there is only one hardware profile, NTLDR will load the default control set. If the spacebar is pressed, NTLDR will display a screen offering hardware profile choices and the option to use the last known good configuration. This is an important method to restore driver and configuration settings from the registry following changes that caused an operating system failure. The old settings are called from the registry's saved control sets and used in place of the erroneous settings.

Once the hardware configuration has been chosen, NTLDR will load the NT kernel—NTOSKRNL.EXE. NTLDR loads this kernel into memory, but does not initialize it at this point. Next, the boot loader loads the registry key—HKEY_LOCAL_MACHINE\ SYSTEM. NTLDR scans all of the subkeys in CurrentControlSet\ Services for device drivers with a start value of zero. These drivers are usually low-level hardware drivers, such as hard disk drivers, needed to continue the boot.

Kernel Phase

The boot loader phase ends when NTLDR passes control to NTOSKRNL.EXE. At this point, the kernel-initialization phase begins. The screen will turn blue, and you will see a message similar to the following one:

```
Microsoft  Windows NT™ Version 4.0 (Build 1381)
1 System Processor (16MB Memory)
```

The kernel then creates the HKEY_LOCAL_MACHINE\HARD-WARE registry key using information passed to it by the boot loader (gathered by NTDETECT.COM).

The next step is to load the device drivers. NTOSKRNL.EXE looks in the registry for drivers that need to be loaded, checks through their DependOnService and DependOnGroup values for dependencies, and determines the order in which drivers should be loaded. It then loads the services, reads and implements the specified parameters, and initializes the various services and drivers that are needed.

Logon Phase

An NT boot is not considered successful until a user successfully logs on. The Windows subsystem automatically starts WINLOGON.EXE. The Begin Logon box now appears on the screen. The user can press Ctrl+Alt+Delete to log on even though other services might still be initializing in the background.

The service controller performs one last sweep through the registry to locate any remaining services that need to be loaded. At this point, NT has just about finished the boot process.

When a user logs on, NT considers the boot to have been successful. Only then will it take the CurrentControlSet and copy it to create the last known good configuration (for use in the next boot of this computer).

Now that the boot process has been examined, some of the specifics required for the examination can be discussed.

BOOT.INI File

The BOOT.INI file is a text file located in the root of the boot partition. Here is an example of a BOOT.INI file for an NT server that is set up to dual boot with the Windows 95 operating system:

```
[boot loader]
timeout=30
default=multi(0)disk(0)rdisk(0)parition(1)\WINNT
[operating systems]
multi(0)disk(0)rdisk(0)parition(1)\WINNT="Windows NT
Server Version 4.0"
multi(0)disk(0)rdisk(0)parition(1)\WINNT="Windows NT
Server Version 4.0 [VGA mode]" /basevideo /sos
C:\="Windows 95"
```

A BOOT.INI file has two sections. In the [boot loader] section, you will find settings that control the defaults—how long the menu should be on the screen before a default is selected and which operating system should load if the user makes no selection. In the [operating systems] section, you will find the various choices that are presented to the user, and the path and switches for each of the operating system files. The ARC path conventions were discussed earlier. Now you see where that information is put to use. If there is no BOOT.INI file, the system will attempt to boot from the location where the NT installation program places boot files by default—the \WINNT directory on the active partition. If you have placed the operating system files in another location, the BOOT.INI file is critical to the boot process.

BOOT.INI Switches

You can use numerous switches within the BOOT.INI file to help control the way that NT boots. These switches are placed at the end of the line that describes the location of the operating system.

/basevideo—This switch forces NT to boot using a standard VGA driver, which allows an administrator to recover from installing an incorrect or corrupted video driver that disables video output. The NT installation program creates an operating system choice, annotated [VGA mode], in the BOOT.INI file that implements this switch. This allows you to fix a video driver problem by rebooting, choosing the VGA option, and replacing the bad driver.

/maxmem:n—This switch allows the administrator to specify how much physical memory NT can use. You can use this switch to troubleshoot various memory problems such as parity errors, bad SIMMs, etc.

/noserialmice=[COM x or COM x,y,z]—NT will occasionally detect a device on a communication port and assume that it is a mouse—even if it is another type of device. When this happens, that device will be unusable in Windows NT because a mouse driver will be loaded that uses that port. This switch disables detection on the communication port(s) specified. This can be used to prevent NT from issuing shutdown signals to a UPS during the boot process.

/sos—This switch will cause NT to display the names of drivers as they are loaded rather than the default progress dots.

/crashdebug—This switch enables the automatic recovery and restart capability in the event of a stop screen. This parameter can also be set in the System applet in Control Panel.

A number of switches relate to advanced troubleshooting techniques that will be covered later in this chapter. These switches configure NT to "dump" its memory contents into a file for analysis. You can configure where this memory dump file will be placed. Often, a problem will be so severe that the computer is inaccessible. With this type of error, you will want to configure the system to dump its memory to another computer's hard drive. The following switches control this transfer:

/baudrate=nnnn—This switch is used to configure the communication port if you are going to dump memory to another computer.

/debugport=comx—This switch sets the communication port to be used.

BOOT.INI Error Messages

Various error messages are commonly seen when there is a problem with the BOOT.INI file. If the BOOT.INI file is missing or the operating system line does not point to the NT operating system files, you will see the following message:

```
Windows NT could not start because the following file
is missing or corrupt:
   <winnt root>\system32\NTOSKRNL.EXE
Please reinstall a copy of the above file.
```

If the ARC path points to a nonexistent or inaccessible disk or partition, you will see the following error message:

```
OS Loader V4.0
Windows NT could not start because of a computer disk
hardware configuration problem. Could not read from the
selected boot disk. Check boot path and disk hardware.
Please check the Windows NT documentation about
hardware disk configuration and your hardware reference
manuals for additional information.
```

In either event, you can either edit the BOOT.INI file to correct the problem or restore the BOOT.INI file off of your emergency repair disk.

Last Known Good Configuration

If your Windows NT server refuses to boot after you have added new hardware or software, you can attempt to boot using the last known good configuration. The *last known good configuration* is the hardware configuration used during the last successful boot. Remember, though, that when you successfully log onto the computer, you will overwrite the last known good configuration with the current control set.

If one of the files used during the boot process has become corrupted, you can attempt to replace it with a good copy. You can accomplish this task in a couple of ways. If you boot to a FAT partition, you can boot to a DOS disk and copy the new file over the suspect file. The only file that is unique to the server's hardware is the BOOT.INI file. All of the other files are generic, so you can grab a copy from any other NT server. You can also expand a copy from the NT Server CD-ROM using the Expand –r utility.

Another way to replace suspect boot files is to use your emergency repair disk (ERD). You create the ERD by running the RDISK.EXE utility. This utility creates a disk with the following files on it:

SETUP.LOG—An information file that is used for verifying the system files

SYSTEM._—A copy of the system registry hive

SAM._—A copy of the security accounts manager database

SECURITY_—A copy of the security hive

SOFTWARE_—A copy of the software hive

DEFAULT_—A copy of the default hive

CONFIG.NT—The Windows NT version of the CONFIG.SYS file used to configure an NT virtual DOS machine

AUTOEXEC.NT—The Windows NT version of the AUTOEXEC.BAT file used to configure an NT virtual DOS machine

NTUSER.DA_—A copy of the *System Root*\Profiles\Default-User\Ntuser.DAT file

Files with an underscore (_) in their extensions are in compressed form and can be decompressed using the expand utility. By default, the repair disk utility will *not* back up the entire SAM or security files. Use the /s switch when running this tool to get a complete backup. If you do not use this switch, your repair disk will have a default user accounts database. If you have a problem with the registry and need to restore from the ERD, you will lose all of your user account information.

To restore from the ERD, you must boot from the setup disks provided with Windows NT Server (or create a set by using the CD-ROM). On the screen that asks whether you want to install NT or repair files, type **R** to select the repair option. After that, just follow the instructions.

The repair process can do the following things:

- Inspect the registry files—Replaces existing registry files with those on the ERD. Remember that you will lose any changes that have occurred since the last time you updated the ERD.

- Inspect startup environment—Attempts to repair a BOOT.INI file that does not list NT as an option in the user boot menu.

- Verify Windows NT system files—Verifies each file in the installation against the file that was installed originally (this is what the SETUP.LOG file is used for). If it finds a file that does not match the original, it will identify the file and ask whether it should be replaced.

- Inspect boot sector—Copies a new boot sector to the disk.

Exam Essentials

Understanding the boot process is critical to troubleshooting. For the exam, you should be comfortable with the information covered for this objective.

Know the four phases of the NT boot process and what happens in each phase. The *initial phase* is mostly hardware related. The computer does a POST, reads the CMOS, finds the boot device, and reads the master boot record.

In the *boot loader phase*, NTLDR gathers information about the hardware that is needed to boot. It reads the BOOT.INI file and displays the operating system menu, runs NTDETECT.COM to discover the computer's hardware, and loads NTOSKRNL.EXE.

The NT operating system initializes in the *kernel phase*. NTOSKRNL .EXE creates the hardware registry key using the information gathered during the boot loader phase, reads the registry to find out which device drivers need to be loaded, and loads services that are marked with a start value of zero in the registry.

The *logon phase* is the last phase. The WINLOGON service starts and displays the logon box. An NT boot is not considered successful until a user logs onto the machine.

Understand the function of the BOOT.INI file.   The BOOT.INI file has two sections—[boot loader] and [operating system]. The [boot loader] section contains information about defaults—how long the menu should stay on the screen before a default operating system should be chosen and where that default operating system is located. The [operating systems] section contains the choices that the user will be presented with and the location of the available operating system files.

Know the BOOT.INI command switches and what functions they perform.   These switches include /basevideo, /maxmem:n, /noserialmice, /sos, /crashdebug, /debugport, and /baudrate.

Understand the last known good configuration.   The last known good configuration is a saved copy of the CurrentControlSet in use the last time NT was successfully booted. It is overwritten when a user successfully logs on during the end of the WinLogon phase. Since the configuration information within it was sufficient to log on a user, you can always use it to bypass any major errors. You can then log on and correct the problem.

Understand the process involved in creating and using the emergency repair disk (ERD).   Use the RDISK.EXE utility to create an ERD. Remember to use the /s switch to ensure that your security and account information are backed up. You use the ERD by booting to the NT setup floppies and typing **R** for repair when asked whether you want to install NT or repair files.

Key Terms and Concepts

CMOS: Configuration information stored in a nonvolatile form that is used by the computer at boot. In the current discussion, this is how the computer knows which device to boot from.

Emergency repair disk (ERD): A floppy disk that contains replacement copies of critical system files. You can use this disk to recover from boot problems caused by the deletion or corruption of these files.

Master boot record (MBR): A section of the boot device that contains a list of the partitions on the disk and which partition is the active partition.

Partition boot sector (PBS): A sector of the disk that contains operating system-specific boot instructions.

Power on self test (POST): A process run by the computer to determine the amount of memory installed and confirm the existence of required hardware.

Sample Questions

1. What are the four phases of an NT boot (in the correct order)?

A. Initial, Boot loader, Kernel, Logon

B. Boot loader, Initial, Kernel, Logon

C. Boot loader, Kernel, Initial, Logon

D. Logon, Initial, Boot loader, Kernel

Answer: A

2. A user is given the chance to use the last known good configuration in which phase of the NT startup?

   A. Initial

   B. Boot loader

   C. Kernel

   D. Logon

   Answer: B

3. The current configuration becomes the last known good configuration at which point in the boot process?

   A. After all services have successfully loaded in the kernel phase

   B. After a user successfully logs on

   C. After the BOOT.INI file has executed

   Answer: B—An NT boot is considered successful when a user logs on at that computer. At that point, the current configuration is considered to be valid, so it is written to the last known good configuration.

Choose the appropriate course of action to take to resolve configuration errors. Tasks include:

- Backing up and restoring the registry
- Editing the registry

Almost everything you do on an NT-based computer will access the registry. The registry contains information about your hardware settings, the drivers needed to access that hardware, your user profiles, the software you have installed, etc. Each time you boot, the registry is read from and written to in order to determine what should happen. When you run a program such as Microsoft Word, the registry is read to determine where the program is located. When you log onto the system, the registry is read to build your security context. In other words, the registry is critical to the health of your server's operating system. Both Windows NT and Windows 95 have registry files, but the keys are not identical. This is one of the principal reasons that you cannot upgrade from Windows 95 to NT.

The objectives for this section involve the tools that you can use to back up the registry and edit its contents. Always remember to do these two things in *that* order—back up, then edit. Since the registry is so important, you want to always have a current backup before you make any changes to the registry.

Critical Information

Before the tasks listed in this exam objective can be discussed, what the registry is and how it is structured must be examined. The *registry* is a database that contains NT configuration information. This database is organized in a hierarchical structure that consists of subtrees and their keys, hives, and values.

NOTE Don't be intimidated by the term *hierarchical*. You are already familiar with a hierarchical structure—the DOS file system. If you understand the directory, subdirectory, and file structure of DOS, you can understand the structure of the registry. Hierarchical structures use a series of containers and subcontainers to organize the data that they hold.

The NT registry is made up of five subtrees, each of which holds specific types of configuration information. Each subtree holds keys that contain the computer or user databases. Each key can have specific parameters and additional subkeys. The term *hive* refers to a distinct subset of a key. You can back up a hive as a single file.

It is important that you know the five main subtrees and understand the type of information that is found in each one.

HKEY_LOCAL_MACHINE—Contains hardware and operating system configuration parameters for the local computer, such as bus type, processor, device drivers, and startup information. This is the subtree that is most commonly used in the troubleshooting process for operating system errors or crashes.

HKEY_CLASSES_ROOT—Defines file associations and configuration data for COM and DCOM objects.

HKEY_CURRENT_USER—Contains the user profile for the user that is currently logged in. You will find parameters for the user's desktop, network connections, printers, and application preferences.

HKEY_USERS—Contains all actively loaded user profiles, including a copy of HKEY_CURRENT_USER.

HKEY_CURRENT_CONFIG—Contains the current hardware configuration.

Backing up and Restoring the Registry

You can back up the registry in four ways:

- Choose Save Registry in the NT Backup utility found in the Administrative Tools (Common) group. This is the preferred method if you have a tape backup unit. This method can back up and restore the registry while Windows NT is running.

- Use the two command-line tools that can also back up and restore the registry while NT is running—REGBACK.EXE and REGREST.EXE. These tools are included in the Windows NT Resource Kit.

- On the Registry menu within the registry editor, click Save Key. This process saves a single key, and everything below it, to a file. Online restorations using this method are not guaranteed, so use the backup utility whenever possible.

- Create or update your emergency repair disk. Remember to use the /s switch to ensure a complete backup.

Editing the Registry

Most of the time, you will avoid editing the registry directly—you will use various tools to adjust the configuration of your environment, and these tools will write to the registry for you. There are, however, many optimization and troubleshooting techniques that will require you to use the registry editor. You use two modes when working with the registry—backup and read-only mode.

Backing up is a simple form of protection against a moment of clumsiness. Everyone makes mistakes; the trick is to be prepared for them. The best protection against yourself is a good backup.

An option in the registry editor allows you to use read-only mode. In this mode, you can look at parameters, do your research, and know that, at the very least, you didn't inadvertently make the problem worse. After careful consideration of your options, you can then go back into the editor and make changes to the registry (after making a good backup).

Many of the troubleshooting and performance optimization techniques that have been discussed required you to make changes to the registry. By default, only members of the administrator group can change the registry; normal users are limited to read-only access. NT ships with two tools designed for manual editing of the registry database—the Windows NT registry editor (REGEDT32.EXE) and the Windows 95 registry editor (REGEDIT.EXE). While both tools allow you to edit the registry, certain keys can only be edited using the NT version.

When you edit the registry, certain changes may take effect immediately, while others might require some action on your part. In general, when you edit values in the CurrentControlSet subtree, the computer must be restarted before changes will take effect. When editing values in HKEY_CURRENT_USER, the user will often be required to log off before changes take effect.

Necessary Procedures

Almost every course in the MCSE program includes at least one example of a change that you might have to make to the registry. If you understand the process, it will make your studying easier.

Using the Registry Editor to Back Up a Key

Both the NT and Windows 95 versions of the registry editor allow you to back up the registry. They accomplish this goal in different ways—the NT version, shown below, will save each subkey as a separate file, so you have to save each of the five main hives individually.

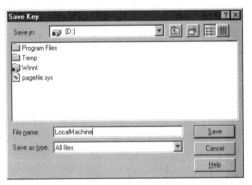

The Windows 95 version, shown below, will allow you to save the entire registry as a single file.

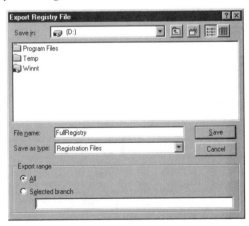

Creating or Updating an Emergency Repair Disk

The emergency repair disk creation utility, RDISK, allows you to create and update a repair disk as registry changes on your NT server. Run RDISK.EXE from a command prompt. The program will ask you for a floppy disk to copy the information to. Remember to use the /s switch when running RDISK.EXE so that you get a complete backup of the registry.

Using the Registry Editor to Search the Database

Both the NT and Windows 95 version of the registry editor allow you to search the database—there is, however, a difference in functionality.

REGEDT32.EXE allows you to search for any key by name; for instance, you could search for the CurrentControlSet key. The only problem with this is that you must know the correct name of the key.

REGEDIT.EXE gives you a few more choices as to what you can search for. You can search for the actual value or data within a key. This will come in handy if you are looking for information, but don't know which subkey it is in. For example, suppose that you have a problem with a device set to interrupt 5. In the NT version, you would have to know the name of the key in which this value was stored; in the Windows 95 version, you could search for the number 5.

Using the Registry Editor to Add or Edit the Value of a Key

To add or edit the value of a key:

1. Open REGEDT32.EXE.

2. Choose Edit ➢ Add Value.

3. You will have to determine what type of data will be entered. There are five types of data:

   - REG_BINARY—Represents data as a string of binary numbers

- REG_SZ—Represents data as a string

- REG_EXPAND_SZ—Represents data as an expandable string

- REG_DWORD—Represents data as a hexadecimal value with a maximum size of 4 bytes

- REG_MULTI_SZ—Represents data as multiple strings

Unless you are a software developer, you probably will not have to determine the type of data—just the value. You will choose the type based upon information found in a manual or reference material.

Using the Registry Editor to Troubleshoot a Remote Computer

You can use the registry editor to access the registry of a remote computer. You are allowed to access the HKEY_LOCAL_MACHINE and HKEY_USERS subkeys of the remote machine. Choose Registry ➤ Select Computer.

Exam Essentials

For this exam, you are not expected to understand every detail of the registry, but you are expected to know what it is used for, how it is organized, and the processes involved in backing it up and editing its content.

Know the five main keys and understand what type of data is contained in each. The five main keys are as follows:

- HKEY_LOCAL_MACHINE

- HKEY_CLASSES_ROOT

- HKEY_CURRENT_USER

- HKEY_USERS

- HKEY_CURRENT_CONFIG

Know the four methods of backing up the registry. To back up the registry, use the backup tool located in the Administrative Tools (Common) group, the two command-line utilities REGBACK.EXE and REGREST.EXE from the Windows NT Resource Kit, the registry editor, or the emergency repair disk.

Know the various functions of the registry editor utility. Reread the "Necessary Procedures" section above. Know what you can accomplish using the registry editor and how to perform those tasks.

Key Terms and Concepts

Hierarchy: A structure used to store information. The registry is a hierarchical database made up of keys and subkeys that hold values.

Hive: A subtree and its values, including any subtrees below it. Think of the hive as a branch of a tree.

Key: A subtree that contains per-computer or per-user configuration databases.

Registry: A database that contains the configuration parameters necessary for the NT operating system to function.

Value: Within the registry, a specific parameter's setting.

Sample Questions

1. Which of the five main registry subtrees holds system startup information?

   A. HKEY_LOCAL_MACHINE

   B. HKEY_CLASSES_ROOT

   C. HKEY_CURRENT_USER

   D. HKEY_USERS

   E. HKEY_CURRENT_CONFIG

   Answer: A

2. Which of the five main registry subtrees holds file association information?

   A. HKEY_LOCAL_MACHINE

   B. HKEY_CLASSES_ROOT

   C. HKEY_CURRENT_USER

   D. HKEY_USERS

   E. HKEY_CURRENT_CONFIG

   Answer: B

Choose the appropriate course of action to take to resolve printer problems.

How many times have you had to trek all the way across the building, up four flights of stairs, and through a crowded hallway, only to find a gaggle of people standing around a printer getting mad because the printer doesn't work? Once you have added paper to the printer, the users are happy, but now you are the one who is mad and frustrated.

Critical Information

Printing problems are easy to resolve if you understand the printing process. Experience has shown that printing problems fall into two basic categories—SEU (stupid end user) problems and system problems. The SEU problems are easy to solve:

- Plug in the printer.

- Turn the printer back on.

- Put paper in the printer.

- Clear the paper jam in the printer.

- Put the printer back online.

- Redirect the user to the proper printer.

Troubleshooting printing subsystem problems can be more difficult. One technique to use when troubleshooting printing problems is to generate a mental flowchart of where the print job goes. If you can figure out which step along the way is causing the problem, you can usually understand how to solve the problem.

Printing from the workstation starts when an application sends output to the software-based printer at the workstation.

NOTE   Remember from Chapter 2 that an HP LaserJet 5P is not a *printer*, it is a *print device*. The printer is the software that runs at the workstation to prepare the print job.

At this point, NT checks whether the workstation has the most up-to-date version of the printer driver. If it does, all is well. If it doesn't, NT downloads a copy of the print driver from the print server to the client.

The printer sends the job to the print spooler. The client (workstation) spooler writes the data to a file and sends a remote procedure call (RPC) to the server spooler. Then, the data are transferred from the workstation to the server spooler on the print server machine.

The print server machine sends the print job to the local print provider, which translates the information into something the printer can understand, and if necessary, adds a separator page to the print job. Separator pages are used, in some cases, to signal to the printer that a change in printer languages is coming—it needs to switch from Hewlett Packard's printer control language (HP PCL) to PostScript or back again.

When the local print provider is done with the job, it sends the job to the print monitor, which sends it to the appropriate printer port and printing device.

If you remember the process, you can check each step along the way. When you find out where the print job stops, you can reset the application that should handle the next step. If the job comes out garbled, make sure the printer driver is up to date or determine whether there is a SEU problem.

Necessary Procedures

Print troubleshooting can be divided into the following key areas:

- SEU (stupid end user) problems
- Applications (non-Windows)
- Print drivers
- Spooling
- Printing speed

Troubleshooting with SEU Tricks

When a group of end users has a printing problem, you usually find out about it when your pager goes off. Here is a list of SEU tricks:

1. Is the print device plugged in? The cleaning staff chooses the most creative places to plug in vacuum cleaners.

2. Is the printer cable attached at both ends?

3. Is the print device turned on? The end user may have told you that it is turned on, but is it really?

4. Does the print device have paper in it?

5. Does the print device need toner, ink, or a ribbon?

6. Is there a paper jam?

7. Is the paper the right size for the job the user wants to print?

8. Has someone replaced the letter-size input tray with the legal-size input tray?

9. Is the print device trying to tell you something? Check the control panel for messages or flashing lights. Read the manual and find out how to solve the problem.

10. Is there really something wrong with the print device, or is the SEU just confused? If the SEU is confused, straighten them out, politely.

11. Is the print device online? Did someone try to troubleshoot it themselves by taking the print device off-line and then forget to reset it?

Troubleshooting Non-Windows-Based Applications

Non-Windows-based applications can be tricky to troubleshoot, because they change the normal print routine. Here are some things to check:

1. Each non-Windows-based application needs to have its own set of print drivers. Does this application have the right drivers?

2. Each non-Windows-based application needs to be told where to go to print. Is this application network aware, do you have to use the NET USE LPT1: command or some other method of setting up the printer port? Read the manual.

Troubleshooting Print Drivers

Print driver problems manifest in strange ways—print jobs suddenly take on odd appearances. Here are the common print driver problems:

1. A print job is submitted for a small document. Instead of receiving their document, the user receives page after page of smiley faces or other strange characters. Make sure that the user has a PCL print driver selected in the application. This is a classic case of a print job using a PostScript driver to print to a PCL printer.

2. A print job is submitted for a document. You can trace the print job all the way to the printer, but nothing comes out. Other than with this job, the printer works fine. Check the print driver. The user may be sending a job formatted with a PCL driver to a PostScript printer. PostScript will not act on a job that is not formatted with the appropriate driver.

3. A print job comes out with garbage embedded in the document, especially in graphics. Check to make sure that tabs and form feeds are turned off for the job. This is primarily applicable to jobs going to PostScript printers and is a workstation setting.

4. When you find a print driver update, the update needs to be made only at the print server. Drivers need to be updated only at the print server—the print server will distribute the job to the clients.

Troubleshooting Spooling

Spooling is the act of copying a file from one spot to another. Spoolers must be running at both the print server and the workstation.

1. If print jobs get stuck in a print spooler, stop and restart the spooler. Choose Start ➤ Settings ➤ Control Panel ➤ Services ➤ Spooler.

2. You can also stop and start the spooler using the NET START SPOOLER and NET STOP SPOOLER commands from the command line.

3. By default, print spoolers are stored in the \WINNT\System32\ Spool\Printers folder. Be sure the disk that contains this folder has plenty of free disk space. Bad things happen when you try to print a 100MB file to a print spooler that resides on a drive with only 50MB free. Change the location of the print spooler from the Advanced tab of the Server Properties dialog box.

4. You can assign a separate spooler for each printer. Enter a path for the new spooler directory in the registry. The path will act as the data for the value SpoolDirectory . The printer name is also needed. The registry entry is HKEY_LOCAL_MACHINE\System\ CurrentControlSet\Control\Print\Printers*Printer*. Be sure to stop and start the spooler so that this will take effect.

5. If the computer that houses the print spooler suffers an unexpected shutdown, the jobs that are in the spooler should print when the print spooler is restarted.

NOTE Print jobs in the spooler are made up of two files, *.SPL and
*.SHD. The file with the .SPL extension is the actual spool file—the
.SHD file is a shadow file. Check the spooler directory occasionally to
clean out the old, corrupted files. You can tell which ones they are by
the date and time stamp.

Troubleshooting Printing Speed

A *very* common complaint of end users is the speed of the network.
Here are some things you can do to remedy this situation:

1. Print spooling is a background process. NT Workstation assigns it
   a process priority of seven. NT Server, on the other hand, gives it
   a higher priority of nine, which means that it is as important as a
   foreground application. If your NT workstation is just a print
   server, increase the priority. To change the priority, add a value
   called PriorityClass of type REG_DWORD to HKEY_LOCAL_
   MACHINE\System\CurrentControlSet\Control\Print and set it
   with the priority class you desire.

TIP Priority is a funny thing—what you give to one, you take away
from another.

2. Many times, third-party print servers are faster than NT-based
   print servers. Printers that have a built-in network card are usually
   the fastest providers.

NOTE One common printer manufacturer (Hewlett Packard)
requires that the dynamic link control (DLC) protocol is installed so
that a network interface can communicate with the rest of the
system.

Exam Essentials

Printing is a favorite topic of the exam writers. The questions they ask sometimes don't have obvious solutions, so make sure to understand the following material.

Know that HP (Hewlett Packard) is different.   Depending on which HP print device you use, it may require that the dynamic link control (DLC) protocol is loaded when you have a printer with an integrated network interface card. If, during installation, you do not see an option to install a port for the printer, DLC is not installed. Check the manual to see whether DLC must be loaded. On the exam, if the question mentions HP and not DLC, be suspicious.

Know that HP is different (part two).   Suppose that DLC is loaded at the workstation and at the printer, and you still cannot print. Using the HP utilities, check whether another computer is attached to the print device using continuous-connection mode. If that is the case, the other user is hogging all of your resources.

Know what happens when a printer jams.   If a job has been submitted and the printer jams, you can restart the document by going into the Printers folder and choosing Documents ➤ Restart.

Know what happens when a printer jams in a printer pool.   If one printer of a printer pool jams, the job that is printing at the time of the jam will be held at that printer until the jam has been cleared. Other jobs will be routed to different printers in the pool.

Key Terms and Concepts

DLC (dynamic link control):   A protocol that is necessary to manage HP printers that have onboard network interface cards.

Print device: The hardware that puts the ink on the paper.

Print driver: The software component that allows the print devices to interface with the operating system.

Print server: A computer to which printers are attached and that is connected to the network.

Print spooler: Temporary holding areas for print jobs. Print spooler files are stored in the \WINNT\System32\Spool\Printers folder.

Printer: A software applet that runs at the client workstation. The printer takes the print job from the applications, and prepares it to traverse the system and come out as ink on paper at the print device.

Printing pool: A number of print devices that are connected to the same printer. The printer directs the print job to an available print device in the pool.

Sample Questions

1. Suppose that a user is installing a new HP print device on the network. The print device has it own network interface card. When the user tries to configure the device, they find that there is no option to install a port for the printer. What is the most common cause of this situation?

    A. The printer is corrupted.

    B. The print spooler has some corrupted file in it.

    C. The print driver needs to replaced.

    D. This device uses both PCL and PostScript printing. Therefore, it doesn't need a printer port.

    E. The DLC protocol is not configured on the workstation the user is using for a print server.

    Answer: E—The most common cause of not being able to "talk" with an HP print device is the lack of a data link control (DLC) protocol configured at the print server. HP uses the DLC protocol to communicate with its print devices.

2. Suppose that a user has a big report due in the morning. They are trying to print that report to an HP printer that has an onboard network interface card using the DLC protocol. DLC is currently installed and working on their computer. Even after the user resets the printer, they still cannot print to it. What is the most likely cause of the problem?

   A. The user isn't sending their print job to the HP printer; they are using a printer on a different floor.

   B. The printer is out of paper.

   C. Somewhere on the network, there is another computer hooked to the printer using DLC in continuous-connection mode.

   D. The print device is currently servicing an Apple computer and will come back online when it is finished with the Apple print job.

   Answer: C—If DLC is being used by another computer on the network in continuous-connection mode, no other system can connect to the printer.

3. A print job appears to be stuck in the print spooler. What should you do?

   A. Sounds like lunch time!

   B. Stop and restart the print spooler.

   C. Go into the \WINNT\System32\Spool\Printers folder and delete all the files that are in the spooler, and then resend the job.

   D. Turn the printer off and back on to reboot it.

   Answer: B—If the print job becomes stuck, a quick fix is to stop and restart the print spooler. Investigate the size of the spooler file capacity and compare it to the total size of the print jobs being sent to it.

Choose the appropriate course of action to take to resolve RAS problems.

What is more frustrating than bringing a laptop home, getting set to do some work, dialing in, and not getting connected? You can take some actions to minimize this frustration.

Critical Information

When you troubleshoot remote access service problems, there is always two sides to the issue. You may know that your side is correct, but if the other side isn't configured exactly the same as your side, you are simply not going to talk. As a network administrator, the task is even more frustrating, because you are working with end users who are working with configurable software, cables, IRQs, internal or external modems, etc.—the list of things they can screw up is practically endless. Some common troubleshooting tools for RAS connections will be examined in the next section.

Necessary Procedures

Every administrator has their own troubleshooting style. One approach is to start from the wall and work back.

Troubleshooting Dialing Problems

Before you can establish modem communications, you have to be able to dial the phone. Here are some simple things to look for:

1. Does the phone line actually work? Is there an analog telephone you can plug into the line to make sure that there is a dial tone?

NOTE This sounds like common sense, but it is often the really simple things that haunt you. You can spend a long time reinstalling the modem, checking the connections, verifying the ports—only to find out that there was no carrier to begin with.

---

2. Now that you know there is a real phone line on the other side of the jack, are you sure the cable is good? Often, you use a different cable for your modem than you do for the phone. Replace the phone cable with your cable, if possible, and retest for a dial tone.

3. So, there is a real phone line running through your phone cable— plug the cable into your modem and try again.

4. If you still don't have a connection, start checking modem connections. If it is an internal modem, is it firmly in the slot? Did you screw it down? If so, unscrew it and reseat the card. Is it an external modem? Are the cables tight to the modem and the PC? Does the modem have power? Is the modem turned on? Is the modem working properly? Is it installed properly?

5. Is RAS installed properly? Have you selected Receive Calls Only? Have you selected Dial Out Only? Can you dial out with another simple terminal program such as HyperDialer?

Troubleshooting Connection Problems

Troubleshooting connection problems can be frustrating. Many different settings can get changed and mess up the works.

1. Are you dialing the right phone number?

2. Are both computers using the same type of authentication?

3. Are both sides of the conversation using the same protocols from within RAS?

4. Does the user account have dial-in privileges and is the call-back feature properly set?

5. Did you verify the user name, password, and domain name when dialing in?

6. If your user can dial in, appears to connect, and then gets disconnected after authentication, did you try to enable RAS logging? When in doubt, check the log file, DEVICE.LOG.

Exam Essentials

As you study this section, concentrate on where things are and how to get to them.

Know where the DEVICE.LOG file is kept.   DEVICE.LOG is kept in the \Winnt\System32\RAS directory.

Sample Questions

1. All else has failed—it is time to read the log. Where are entries made for RAS logging?

   A. WINNT\DEVICE.LOG

   B. WINNT\System32\RAS.LOG

   C. WINNT\System32\RAS\DEVICE.LOG

   D. WINNT\System32\RAS\Ras.LOG

   Answer: C—The RAS log is kept in the WINNT\System32\RAS\ DEVICE.LOG file.

2. How do you view the RAS log?

   A. Use Event Viewer

   B. Use a text editor

   C. Only through Word

   D. Only through WordPerfect

   Answer: A—The RAS log is viewed through the Event Viewer.

3. Your RAS connection is using call back with multilink over a regular phone line. How many numbers can you configure RAS to call back per call?

A. Unlimited

B. 1

C. 3

D. 5

E. 7

Answer: B—RAS can be configured to call back only one number using call back. Multilink is disabled when call back is set.

Choose the appropriate course of action to take to resolve connectivity problems.

Troubleshooting connectivity problems can be a complex process. At least two computers could be the cause of the trouble, not to mention the network components between them. In this section, assume that the problem is a configuration issue on an NT-based server.

In reality, before you start troubleshooting your NT configuration, you should ensure that the network is functioning properly. Luckily, this is usually an easy task. If two computers are having problems communicating, the first step is to see if *any* computers can communicate. Pick a computer on the same physical network and try to connect from there. If you can successfully attach, the problem is probably a configuration issue. If you cannot connect, you should begin by troubleshooting your network components, such as the wiring, routers, and other physical aspects of your network. Determine whether your outage is system wide or just located on a network segment.

Once you have determined that the problem is confined to a particular computer, you can begin the process of troubleshooting its configuration. To do this, you must understand the networking architecture of Microsoft Windows NT.

Critical Information

Both user-mode and kernel-mode network components are in the NT architecture. Like the rest of the operating system, the network components are modular—distinct components perform each network function. If you understand the architecture, it makes troubleshooting easier. Once you have analyzed the symptoms of the problem, you can usually determine which components are involved.

The discussion will begin with the components at the network interface card and work up to the user-mode components. The overall structure of the NT networking architecture is shown in Figure 6.1.

F I G U R E 6.1: NT architecture

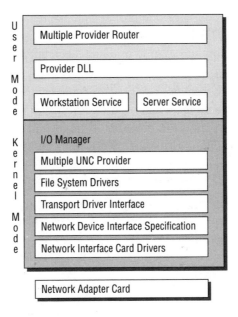

Network Interface Card (NIC) Drivers

Each type of NIC installed in your server will have a specific driver associated with it. The driver should be NDIS (network device interface specification) 4 compliant. (NDIS 3 compatible drivers will still work on an NT 4 server, but it is recommended that newer drivers be used.)

NDIS is a specification that defines how a NIC driver should communicate with the adapter, the protocols, and the operating system. Specifically, NDIS is a library of network functions that are predefined for NIC driver developers. NDIS acts as an interface layer between the driver and card, submits requests to the operating system, and allows the network drivers to receive and send packets independent of the operating system.

Typical problems at this layer of the architecture include corrupt, out-of-date, or missing drivers. Microsoft certifies all of the drivers found on the NT CD-ROM and those available for download from their Web sites. If you are using a card that is not on the hardware compatibility list, you should contact the manufacturer to determine whether they have an NT 4 driver.

Transport Protocols

The various protocols that can be used on an NT network were discussed earlier. Each of these protocols has its own tools and techniques for troubleshooting communication problems. Some of the more commonly used tools are described in Table 6.1.

T A B L E 6.1: Tools for Troubleshooting Protocols

Protocol	Troubleshooting Tool or Technique
TCP/IP	• PING the address of the remote computer. • Use IPCONFIG /ALL to check the IP configuration of the local computer. • Use IPROUTE to check the routing table.

T A B L E 6.1: Tools for Troubleshooting Protocols *(cont.)*

Protocol	Troubleshooting Tool or Technique
NWLink	• To check the IPX configuration of the local computer, type **IPXROUTE CONFIG** at a command prompt. • To view the SAP table, type **IPXROUTE SERVERS** at a command prompt. • To view the routing table, type **IPXROUTE TABLE** at a command prompt.
NetBIOS and AppleTalk	• Neither of these protocols has a set of configuration tools. To troubleshoot these protocols, use Network Monitor to capture and analyze traffic.

Transport Driver Interface (TDI)

The TDI acts as the interpreter between the protocols and redirectors, and services above them. From a developer's perspective, the TDI acts as a common interface between these two layers. This makes writing NT networking modules easier, since the APIs (application programming interfaces) are well documented.

The server has a specific set of services that it can provide, but each protocol will ask for those services in a different way. The TDI is the interpreter because each transport protocol knows how to talk to it, and it knows how to talk to each of the services.

File System Drivers

The file system drivers are above the TDI. NT supports peer-to-peer networking, so NT Server and NT Workstation provide server services. All of the network server and redirector modules are written as file system drivers. From a developer's perspective, this makes writing networked applications easier—if the program needs to open a file, it can make the same sort of call whether the file is local or remote.

Redirectors

Redirectors provide the ability to access remote computer resources. The Windows NT system redirector allows access to Windows NT, Windows for Workgroups, LAN Manager, LAN Server, and a few other types of servers. When you design the redirector as file system drivers, it allows applications to make the same sort of call for local and remote files. The redirector runs in kernel mode, so it can take advantage of other kernel-mode modules (such as the cache manager) to increase performance; it can be dynamically loaded and unloaded; and it can coexist with other redirectors.

In addition to the NT redirector, some redirectors are used to connect to other operating systems, such as Novell NetWare and Banyan Vines. This is the true benefit of using a modular design—you can add functionality as needed.

Server Service

The server service also acts as a file system driver. It handles incoming requests for files from the network. It is composed of the following components: SRV.SYS and LanmanServer.

Multiple UNC (Universal Naming Convention) Provider (MUP)

The MUP handles requests for files that have names following the UNC standard. In the UNC standard, names begin with a double backslash (\\), which indicates that the resource exists on the network. The MUP receives these requests and recognizes that the requested resource is remote. It then passes the request to each registered redirector until one recognizes the requested name.

Multiple Provider Router (MPR)

One of the registered redirectors that the MUP will hand requests to is the MPR. The MPR is specifically designed to handle requests that do not follow the UNC standard. It is made up of a series of provider .DLLs that provide the ability to communicate with a foreign system, such as NetWare or Banyan Vines.

Resolving Connectivity Problems

Now that the various components that make up the networking environment of the NT operating system have been examined, the objective for this section—how to resolve connectivity problems—can be discussed. Actually, given all of the discussion that led up to this, the resolution process is fairly straightforward.

Most communication problems will revolve around configuration errors rather than problems with specific software modules. The only two software components that might cause problems are the NIC driver and the third-party-provider .DLL files. The solution for either type of problem is simple—install a new copy, preferably the latest available version.

Troubleshooting configuration issues relies upon your knowledge of the various protocols in use on your network. The steps are simple, though:

1. Determine whether the problem is the transport protocol—for instance, if you are using TCP/IP, try using the PING utility to communicate. If this works, you can move up the OSI layers to the next step.

2. Test the NetBIOS connection by using a NET command. At a command line, type **NET VIEW** *Server Name.* This should return a list of all shared resources on that server. If it does, the problem is probably application related.

Exam Essentials

Networking is a complex yet critical piece of most NT environments. It is essential that you know the components involved and how they interact. For the exam, you should concentrate on the following items.

Know the tools used to troubleshoot protocol-related problems.   For this examination, a detailed understanding of each protocol is not required. However, it is assumed that you do at least have a firm grasp on the fundamentals. See Table 6.1 for details.

Understand the function of a redirector. A redirector is a software component that provides the ability to access remote resources. Microsoft Windows NT ships with a system redirector that allows communication with each of the Microsoft network-capable operating systems (Windows for Workgroups, Windows 95, and Windows NT), as well as LAN Manager and LAN Server. Other redirectors are used to access foreign systems such as Novell NetWare and Banyan Vines.

Understand the function of the multiple UNC provider (MUP). The MUP accepts requests in which the resource name adheres to the UNC standard. It passes the request to each register's redirector until one of them accepts it.

Understand the function of the multiple provider router (MPR). The MPR handles requests for resources in which the name does not follow the UNC standard. Usually, this will be a request for resources on a server not running Windows NT, such as a Novell NetWare server. The MPR manages a series of DLLs that are designed to talk to foreign servers.

Know the two-step process for troubleshooting connectivity problems. First, determine whether the problem is the transport protocol. Most protocols include a utility to test the ability to communicate, such as the PING utility for TCP/IP. Second, test the NetBIOS connection by using a NET command to access the remote computer.

Key Terms and Concepts

File system driver: Software designed to provide access to a file system. While this definition might seem simplistic and obvious, it is important to understand that this is really all a file system driver is for.

Multiple protocol router (MPR): A user-mode component designed to route requests to resources that do not adhere to the UNC conventions.

Multiple UNC provider (MUP):   A user-mode component that interprets UNC names, passing them along to the proper redirector.

Network interface card drivers: Software designed to allow communication between the physical network interface card and the operating system.

Redirector: A file system driver designed to allow access to remote resources.

Transport drive interface (TDI):   A component of the Windows NT networking architecture designed to act as an interpreter between the protocols and the redirectors.

Universal naming convention (UNC):   An industry standard method of naming resources on the network. All names begin with two backslashes (\\) to indicate a network resource.

Sample Questions

1. Which of the following items accepts and handles network requests that use UNC names?

   A. MUP

   B. MPR

   C. TDI

   Answer: A—MUP stands for multiple UNC provider.

2. Which of the following items accepts and handles requests not formatted using a UNC name?

   A. MUP

   B. MPR

   C. TDI

   Answer: B—MPR stands for multiple provider router.

3. Which of the following utilities is used to test a connection between TCP/IP hosts?

   A. IPXROUTE

   B. IPCONFIG

   C. PING

Answer: C

Choose the appropriate course of action to take to resolve resource access and permission problems.

Permission and resource access problems are usually pretty straightforward. They involve a yes-or-no decision—someone either can or cannot do something to something. If a user is supposed to be able to use a printer and cannot, you have a resource access problem. If a user is supposed to be able to write to a file and cannot, you have a permission problem. The tricky part comes when you try to figure out where the problem lies.

Critical Information

In the case of resource access or permission problems, it is simple to locate the problem. Finding the solution can be more difficult. For example, the problem may be that people cannot access a resource because they cannot log on. Is that a hardware, software, network, or, most likely, an SEU (stupid end user) problem?

Necessary Procedures

Your pager has beeped. You answer the call—it is a frantic end user or help-desk operator. Something isn't working! What do you do now?

Troubleshooting Resource Access and Permission Problems

When a user calls and says that they cannot access the system or a resource:

1. Ask questions. Is it just one person, or is there more than one person involved? What resource is it? Is it a hardware problem; is the printer shut off?

2. If the user cannot log on, make sure that the user is attached to the right domain, is using the right logon name, has the caps-lock key set properly to on or off (*PASSWORD* is not the same as *password*), and is supposed to be on during that time.

3. If the user cannot access a resource, can you access the resource using a different account? If so, you now have a permission problem.

4. When you have determined that the access problem is due to a permission rather than a hardware problem, the next step is to determine how the user was *supposed* to be able to access the account. Were the permissions to be assigned to a group? Can the rest of the group access the resource? If the rest of the group can access the resource, the problem lies with the individual and the group or user memberships they have been given.

TIP Be very suspicious of the no-access permission. If a user belongs to a group that is given no access to a resource, that user will not gain access to the resource, no matter what other group membership they enjoy.

---

5. Make sure that the user is spelling the name of the resource correctly. You would be surprised how fast fingered some users can be, and it is amazing how long you can look at **www.micorsoft.com** before realizing that it is not the same as **www.microsoft.com**.

6. If no one can log on, has the NetLogon service stopped? Check it by going to Start ➤ Settings ➤ Control Panel ➤ Services. While you are there, check the Server and Workstation service.

7. If this is a new server and has never been brought online before, it may not be communicating with the outside world. Check the protocol bindings and make sure you are talking the same languages as everyone else. You can check bindings by choosing Start ➤ Settings ➤ Control Panel ➤ Network.

8. Rights and permissions will take effect the next time the user logs on. If it is a new assignment, have the user log off and then on again.

9. The last place to look is the system policy editor. Is there a new system policy for the user or the user's computer?

10. Is the resource a directory subjected to both NTFS and share permissions?

Exam Essentials

Rights and permissions are favorite topics of the exam writers. Be sure that you understand how the no-access permission can make lives miserable.

Know that the most restrictive rights and permissions are the ones that apply. When you look at the rights and permissions that a user has been granted, take into account all groups the user belongs to, as well as the individual user assignments. The most restrictive rights apply.

Know the impact of the no-access assignment. If a user has been given no-access permissions to a file, folder, or share, that permission will override all others. So, the user TMENDAL may have full control through his membership in the ADMIN group, read access through his membership in the Management group, and no access through his membership in the Accounting group—TMENDAL would be out of luck. No access would override all other permissions.

Know when rights and permissions take effect. A user must log off and then on again to generate a new security identifier (SID). Once the new SID access control list (ACL) has been generated, the new rights or permissions will take effect.

Key Terms and Concepts

SID (security identifier): Code generated to identify a specific user or group to the NT security subsystem.

Sample Questions

1. The user TMENDAL has full control of a folder through his membership in the ADMIN group, read access through his membership in the Management group, and no access through his membership in the Accounting group. TMENDAL calls and says that he cannot see anything in the folder. How do you solve TMENDAL's problem?

   A. Tell TMENDAL to deal with it.

   B. Grant the group Everyone read access to the folder.

   C. Remove TMENDAL from his membership in the Accounting group.

   D. Copy the information from the folder into a folder TMENDAL can access.

   Answer: C—When you remove TMENDAL from the Accounting group, it will remove the no-access permissions and allow him to see items in the folder.

2. TMENDAL is having a *bad* day. After you removed him from the Accounting group, he still cannot see anything in the folder. Why not?

A. TMENDAL is a SEU.

B. You didn't really remove him from the Accounting group.

C. It isn't midnight, yet. All changes take effect at midnight.

D. TMENDAL has not logged out and back on to generate a new SID ACL.

Answer: D—TMENDAL needs to log out and then back on. This will generate a new SID ACL, giving him the rights to access the files.

Choose the appropriate course of action to take to resolve fault-tolerance failures. Fault-tolerance methods include:

- Tape backup
- Mirroring
- Stripe set with parity

Fault tolerance is defined as a system designed so that the failure of one component will not affect functionality. Fault-tolerance failures will not be discussed, because that phrase implies that the fault tolerance itself did not work. The steps involved in reinstating a fault-tolerant state after a component failure has caused the system to switch over to the redundant mechanism will be examined.

Of the three subobjectives, only two really deal with fault tolerance. A tape backup is not fault tolerant in the sense that server functionality is not affected by a failure. When you are forced to use your tape backup to recover from a critical failure, there will be a lapse in network services. Tape backups just allow you to re-create your system from archived data. Those data are only as fresh as the last time you backed them up—any data saved since that time will have to be re-created.

It is fairly easy to calculate the hourly cost of network downtime—count the number of people who rely upon the network to perform their job and multiply that number by an average hourly salary. The resulting figure is the tangible cost per hour of interrupted service. This number does not, however, include the intangibles that are so important in today's competitive market—such as the revenues lost when a client cannot get the service they expect and take their business elsewhere.

Critical Information

As discussed earlier, Microsoft places a lot of emphasis on the various fault-tolerance technologies on NT. Recovery from a failure is part of that emphasis.

Tape Backup

No matter what business you are in, you need a way to archive your data against loss due to hardware failure, user error, and acts of nature. The most cost-effective technology available today is tape backups. While the intent is different, tape backups offer a few advantages over the disk-based fault-tolerance technologies discussed in earlier chapters:

- The hardware and media are fairly inexpensive.

- Tapes can be stored off-site to protect against theft, fire, or flood.

- Tapes can be used for long-term archival of data. Disk-based technology is usually too expensive for long-term storage.

- A backup freezes data at a specific point. If you want an earlier version of a file, retrieve it from one of your older tapes.

- Tapes can be used to protect against mistakes when making changes to your environment. With a disk-based solution, your data are vulnerable when you are working on the server.

Most companies have a tape backup process in place. Many of those companies, however, have no plan of action in the event of a critical failure. The LAN administrators can retrieve files from the tape, but have no idea of the steps involved in recovering a complete server.

This exam objective requires you to understand the basics of server recovery from a tape backup.

1. Fix whatever physical problem is forcing the recovery. This is the step that is ignored most often when administrators put together a disaster recovery plan. If the problem is a hard drive failure, you should know which vendors to call for a replacement part and what the average turnaround time is on delivery. If your local vendor cannot deliver replacement parts within an acceptable amount of time, consider a contract with a company that guarantees their turnaround time. You should have a plan for the replacement of every critical piece of hardware on your network.

2. The next step will depend upon what piece of hardware has failed. If the disk that died is your boot device, you will have to reinstall the operating system and the partitions that existed before the disaster.

3. After the operating system is up and running, recover the registry from your backup set. Remember that any changes that were made since the backup was created will be lost. Be sure to re-create those changes before continuing with the recovery process.

4. Restore the data from your tape. Remember to check the option that restores file permissions. Once again, the tape will not contain any data created since the backup was done. Have someone from each department verify which data will have to be reentered.

The steps involved in the restoration of your data will depend upon the type of backups that you are doing. There are three main techniques for data backup:

Full backup—Each time a backup is performed, the entire server is backed up. While this method of backing up your server will take the longest amount of time, it is the easiest to use for recovery. To restore you server, just use the latest available backup tape.

Incremental backup—When using the incremental method of backup, first perform a full backup. Each evening after that, you back up only the data that have changed since the day before. This form of backup takes the least time to perform each evening, but can be the most confusing and time-consuming method of backup from which to recover. To recover, you must first restore the full backup, and then each tape, in order, since the full backup was performed.

Differential backup—Once again, start by performing a full backup. Each evening, back up all data that have changed since that full backup. The length of time that it takes to accomplish this will increase each evening until it makes sense to do another full backup and start the process again. Recovery is fairly straight-forward—first, restore the full backup, and then restore the last differential tape.

As you can see, a full recovery from tape backups can be a lengthy process. This is why most consultants suggest using both tape backups and one of the disk-based fault-tolerance technologies. The tape is used to recover from major problems (fire, flood, tornado, etc.), while a fault-tolerant disk system can protect against the more common problem of hard disk failure.

Mirroring

As discussed in Chapter 1, disk mirroring is a software-controlled fault-tolerance system that results in two disks containing the same data. If one disk fails, the other will continue to function and users will not experience any downtime. A subset of mirroring, called duplexing, provides even more redundancy by physically connecting the two disks to two different controller boards. Duplexing not only protects against a disk drive failure, it also provides redundant cabling and controllers.

Since NT's boot and system partitions can be mirrored, this process is used extensively in today's business environments. For this exam objective, you need to know how to reinstate the mirrored state if one of the disks fails.

Correct this problem in the Disk Administration utility found in the Administrative Tools (Common) group. It is a three-step process:

1. Break the mirror set.

2. Install the replacement hard drive.

3. Reboot and re-create the mirrored set.

The operating system will then copy the data from the existing drive to the new one. However, if the primary drive of the mirror set is the one that failed, it requires the extra step of rebooting the computer with a floppy disk containing a modified BOOT.INI file.

Stripe Set with Parity

As discussed in Chapter 1, a stripe set with parity is a software-controlled fault-tolerance disk system in which a series of disks are seen as one logical drive. Each time data are written to this logical drive, the operating system calculates parity information, which is stored on another physical disk in the set. You can use the parity information to re-create the data if one of the disks in the set fails.

When one of the disks in the set dies, the system will automatically begin using the parity information. In this way, the data are still available to users, although there is a performance cost—the data must be rebuilt from the parity information. The process of rebuilding the data can take a large amount of processor time and will usually decrease performance.

The steps to rebuild the stripe set with parity are as follows:

1. Replace the dead drive. On some of the more advanced servers, you can do this while the server is still running; otherwise, you will have to down your server for the installation of the new drive.

2. In the Disk Administrator utility, select the stripe set with parity. Control-click an area of free space (on your new drive), and then choose Fault Tolerance ➤ Regenerate. The regeneration process will not begin until you restart your server.

NOTE   If you have a system with hot-swappable drives (a system that allows the installation of new drives while the server is running), you should be aware of two things. First, your system probably has hardware-controlled RAID technology. Since hardware-controlled RAID is faster than software-controlled RAID, you should implement the manufacturer's version and read the manual for your server to learn about the recovery process. Second, if for some reason you do use NT's stripe set with parity technology, be aware that when you install the new drive and finish the recovery process, the system will not begin rebuilding the data on the new drive until you restart the server. This process will add a tremendous amount of overhead to your server.

Necessary Procedures

The following procedures are stressed on the MCSE exam. It is critical that you know how to recover from component failures in a fault-tolerant system.

Breaking the Mirrored Set

To break the mirrored set:

1. Highlight the mirrored partitions in the Disk Administrator utility.

2. Choose Fault Tolerance ➢ Break Mirror.

Re-creating the Mirrored Set

To re-create the mirrored set:

1. In Disk Administrator, Ctrl-click the two partitions of equal size.

2. Choose Fault Tolerance ➢ Establish Mirror.

Regenerating a Stripe Set with Parity

To regenerate a stripe set with parity:

1. Install the new hard disk.

2. In Disk Administrator, Ctrl-click the stripe set and an area of free space.

3. Choose Fault Tolerance ➤ Regenerate.

4. Restart the server.

Exam Essentials

The real "exam essentials" for this objective are found above in the "Necessary Procedures" section. Before you continue, be sure that you are comfortable with the following items.

Understand the steps involved to recover a server from a tape backup.   Fix the physical problem. Next, reinstall the operating system and restore the registry. Finally, restore the data (remember to choose the option that restores file permissions).

Know the three methods of backup.   The methods are full, incremental, and differential.

Know how to use each type of backup in a full recovery.   For a full backup, restore the entire tape. For an incremental backup, restore the full backup and then each of the tapes made since that full backup. For a differential backup, restore the full backup and then the last tape made.

Know the process used to reestablish a mirrored set if a disk fails.   Break the mirror, install the new disk, and re-create the mirror.

Know the steps involved in recovering from a failed disk in a stripe set with parity.   See the "Necessary Procedures" section above for details.

Key Terms and Concepts

Differential backup: A backup system that starts with a full backup and is followed with daily backups of the data that have changed since then.

Full backup: A tape of the entire contents of a server.

Incremental backup: A backup system that starts with a full backup and is followed with tapes of the data that have changed each day.

Regenerate: To rebuild data on a replacement disk in a stripe set with parity.

Sample Questions

1. When restoring from a backup tape, which method requires you to restore the last full backup and each tape since the last full backup?

   A. Full backup method

   B. Incremental

   C. Differential

   Answer: B—In the incremental backup method, you first perform a full backup, and then each day back up only data that have changed. This means that you must first restore the last full backup and then each tape created since then.

2. When using the differential backup method, which of the following statements describes the restoration process?

   A. Restore the full backup.

   B. Restore the full backup and then each tape created since that date.

   C. Restore the full backup and the last tape created.

   Answer: C—The differential method includes a full backup and then daily backups of everything that has changed since that full backup. This results in there being only two tapes necessary for the restoration.

3. Which of the following statements describes the method used to recover from the failure of one disk in a mirrored set?

   A. Install the new disk and the system will automatically remirror.

   B. Break the mirroring using Disk Administrator, install the new disk, and create the mirrored set.

   C. Install the new disk and restore the data from backup tape.

   Answer: B—If a disk in a mirrored set fails, you must break the mirrored set and re-create it.

Perform advanced problem resolution. Tasks include:

- Diagnosing and interpreting a blue screen
- Configuring a memory dump
- Using the Event Log service

There is no such thing as a crash-proof server—there are only servers that have yet to meet the set of circumstances necessary to bring them to their knees. When a server crashes, a complex set of circumstances have usually caused the problem. This objective set covers the actions you can take to analyze the situation.

Critical Information

Although Microsoft doesn't stress this objective too heavily on the exam, you are expected to know what to do when you have a problem on an NT computer.

Diagnosing and Interpreting a Blue Screen

When the Microsoft NT operating system encounters a fatal error, it displays a stop screen, often called a blue screen. The blue screen contains debugging information useful in interpreting exactly what was happening at the time of failure. If the system recovery options are turned on, NT will also generate a file with this debugging information.

At first glance, the blue screen can seem intimidating, but you will use only a small amount of data to determine the cause of the error. With some errors, the cause is immediately apparent from this information. With others, you might have to rely upon Microsoft technical support for assistance.

There are five distinct areas on a blue screen. Each area provides specific information regarding the error or recovery options.

Area One: Debug Port Status Indicators

Later in this section, a process that allows you to dump the debugging information out the serial port to another computer will be examined. This connection is similar to a modem connection. In the upper-right corner of a blue screen, you will see a series of indicators that display the status of this connection (see Table 6.2).

T A B L E 6.2: Connection Status Indicators

Status Indicator	Description
MDM	Modem controls are in use
CD	Carrier detected
RI	Ring indicator
DSR	Data set ready
CTS	Clear to send
SND	Byte being sent

T A B L E 6.2: Connection Status Indicators *(cont.)*

Status Indicator	Description
RCV	Byte received
FRM	Framing error
OVL	Overflow
PRT	Parity error

Area Two: Bug-Check Information

This area starts with *** Stop. The error code follows *Stop*. There are also up to four developer-defined parameters in parentheses, followed by an interpretation of the error. However, don't get your hopes up on the interpretation. Sometimes, it leads you to the solution of your problem, but more likely it is an obscure message.

Area Three: Driver Information

This area lists information about the drivers loaded at the time of the error. The three columns list the preferred load address, creation date (also known as the link time stamp), and name of the driver. This area can be useful because many blue screens list the address of the instruction that caused the problem. You can compare that information with the preferred load address to determine which driver might have caused the problem.

Area Four: Kernel Build Number and Stack Dump

This area shows two things—the build number of the operating system kernel (the presence of any service packs is not indicated) and a range of addresses that *may* indicate the failed code.

Area Five: Debug Port Information

This area confirms the configuration of the communication port used to dump information to another computer (if configured), and it indicates whether a dump file was created.

Each blue screen has a unique stop code. For information on a particular blue screen, search Microsoft TechNet for the code found in area one.

Configuring a Memory Dump

When an NT server displays a blue screen, it is your responsibility to correct the problem as soon as possible to minimize server downtime. Sometimes, the solution will be obvious from the data displayed. You might also have a good idea of what caused the problem by looking through the server change log and noting recent changes to the server's configuration. When the solution is not obvious, you might have to take more drastic measures—analyzing the memory contents at the time of the blue screen. There are three ways to accomplish this:

Local debugging—In other words, onsite analysis of memory. Two computers—the target (the server with the problem) and the host—are attached using a null modem cable. The host runs debugging software designed to analyze problems in NT.

Remote debugging—Once again, the target and host are connected with a null modem cable. The difference is that Microsoft technical support uses RAS to dial into your system and then analyze the memory contents remotely.

Crash dump—By far, the most common method is to configure NT to dump the contents of memory into a file when the fatal error occurs. You can then send this file to Microsoft technical support for analysis.

To set up the target and host computers, you must have two computers running the same version of NT, including any service packs you have installed. They should be connected by a null modem cable (or you can set up a dial-in connection from the host). The host computer must have the proper symbols files installed. The symbols file contains code used in the debug process. The symbols file must match the build, including service packs, of the target computer.

Once you have met the prerequisites, modify the BOOT.INI file on the target server. Add the /debug switch to the appropriate operating system choice. On the host computer, configure the communication port by setting environmental variables. Next, restart the target computer. When the blue screen is generated, you will be able to debug the problem from the host computer.

It is unlikely that you will actually debug a blue screen. Most administrators do not have the technical knowledge necessary to accomplish this type of task. It is far more likely that you will generate a memory dump file to be sent to Microsoft technical support.

In the System control panel, you will find a Startup/Shutdown tab. On this tab, you can configure NT to perform certain functions when a fatal error is encountered. You can have NT write a message to the system event log, send an administrative alert, write the contents of memory to a file, and automatically reboot the system.

If you choose to have the contents of memory written to a file, the system dumps the contents of RAM into the PAGEFILE.SYS file. When the system restarts, this information is written to a file named MEMORY.DMP. You can then send this file to Microsoft for analysis. Be aware that there is no compression involved in this process, so the dump file will be at least as large as your memory.

NT ships with three tools for processing memory dump files—DUMPFLOP, DUMPCHK, and DUMPEXAM. For the exam, you have to be concerned only with the latter two.

DUMPCHK.EXE—Verifies the contents of a dump file to ensure that it will be readable by a debugger. When you run this program, it can help ensure that you don't waste time uploading a corrupt dump file to Microsoft.

DUMPEXAM.EXE—Analyzes the contents of the dump file and extracts any useful information. This information is placed into a text file that can be considerably smaller than the dump file itself.

Using the Event Log Service

The two main steps in troubleshooting are gathering pertinent information and correlating that information into a plan of actions to correct the problem. A common mistake is to address the symptoms without understanding the underlying cause. NT ships with a great tool—the Event Log—for gathering information about errors on your server.

The Event Log service tracks certain activities on your server and logs information about those events into a series of log files. There are three distinct log files: system, security, and application.

Each log file is responsible for tracking different types of events. Many events will not be tracked unless the system is configured to audit those types of events. The application log tracks application-related events, such as the starting and stopping of application-related services. The security log tracks NT security events, such as logons. The system log tracks events that affect the operating system.

There are also different levels of event messages. Some are purely informational; for instance, an application might generate an event message when it is started. Others are generated when an error is encountered. Still others indicate the failure of a service. For the purpose of troubleshooting, the fatal error messages can be extremely informative.

Figure 6.2 shows the contents of a typical system log. The circle icons with an *i* in them indicate informative messages. The stop-sign icons indicate failure messages.

F I G U R E 6.2: A typical system log

Date	Time	Source	Category	Event
3/24/98	9:18:04 PM	Rdr	None	8003
3/24/98	9:05:01 PM	NETLOGON	None	5719
3/24/98	9:03:04 PM	Rdr	None	8003
3/24/98	8:50:01 PM	NETLOGON	None	5719
3/24/98	8:48:04 PM	Rdr	None	8003
3/24/98	8:35:01 PM	NETLOGON	None	5719
3/24/98	8:21:19 PM	NETLOGON	None	5719
3/24/98	8:19:44 PM	NETLOGON	None	5719
3/24/98	8:19:10 PM	EI90x	None	3
3/24/98	8:19:10 PM	EI90x	None	3
3/24/98	8:19:10 PM	EI90x	None	3
3/24/98	8:19:06 PM	EventLog	None	6005
3/24/98	8:19:10 PM	EI90x	None	0
3/24/98	8:00:16 PM	BROWSER	None	8033
3/24/98	8:00:16 PM	BROWSER	None	8033
3/24/98	7:56:13 PM	NETLOGON	None	5719
3/24/98	7:48:04 PM	Rdr	None	8003

Event Viewer - System Log on \\WSEND200
Log View Options Help

Each message will contain the date and time that the event occurred (an event ID), the service that generated the message, and a short message.

You can often use this information to determine the cause of a problem. Make sure that you look through all of the fatal messages, though, because many services depend upon other services. The last message listed might only be a symptom of the real problem.

Sometimes, the information in the event messages will give you enough information to determine the cause of your problem. In these cases, you can write down the event ID and research that particular error in TechNet. Microsoft technical support will often request the event ID of any errors when you call for support.

Necessary Procedures

The only real procedure for this objective concerns dumping memory into a file for later analysis (usually by someone at Microsoft technical support).

Configuring NT to Dump Memory into a File When a Fatal Error Is Encountered

To configure NT to dump memory into a file when a fatal error is encountered:

1. Open the System control panel.

2. Access the Startup/Shutdown tab and choose from the options listed below:

   ▪ Write an Event to the System Log.

   ▪ Send an Administrative Alert—Unless the system is unable to do so, a message will be sent to all members of the administrator group.

   ▪ Write Debugging Information to—The contents of memory will be written to the file specified.

- Overwrite Any Existing File—If a debugging file already exists, this option will instruct the system to overwrite it with the new memory dump.

- Automatically Reboot—Since most critical errors are the result of a certain set of circumstances, if you make the system restart, it will often allow processing to continue.

Exam Essentials

Knowing what to do when a problem occurs is a career and examination necessity. Be aware of the following items.

Know the five main areas of a blue screen.   The five main areas of a blue screen are as follows: debug port status indicators; bugcheck information; driver information; kernel build number and stack dump; and debug port information.

Know the three methods of memory analysis.   The three methods are local debugging, remote debugging, and crash dump.

Understand the crash-dump process.   When a fatal error is encountered, the NT server will copy the contents of memory into the PAGEFILE.SYS file. When the system is restarted, the information is copied into another file. You can send this file to Microsoft for analysis.

Know what options are available when configuring the recovery options for an NT server.   Options include writing an error to the event log; sending an administrative alert; writing the contents to a file; having that file overwrite an existing memory dump file; and restarting the server automatically

Know the three logs in the Event Viewer.   The three logs are system, security, and application.

Understand the type of information that you might find useful in an event log message.   Useful information includes the date and time the event occurred; the event ID; the name of the service that generated the event message; and the short description of the error.

Know the use of the event ID. You can use the event ID during research of a problem. When using Microsoft TechNet, for instance, you can query the database for articles that contain the event ID.

Key Terms and Concepts

Crash dump: A process in which the contents of memory are dumped into a file for later analysis.

DUMPCHK.EXE: A utility designed to verify the format and contents of a memory dump file.

DUMPEXAM.EXE: A utility designed to analyze a memory dump file and extract any pertinent information into a small text file.

Host computer: When debugging a fatal error, the machine running the debugging software.

Link time stamp: The creation date and time of a driver.

Preferred load address: The base memory address that a driver requests when loaded.

Target computer: When debugging a fatal error, the machine that is encountering the error.

Sample Questions

1. In the driver information section of a stop screen, which of the following items are included in the data shown?

    A. IRQ of the offending device

    B. Preferred load address

    C. Creation date

    D. Name of the driver

    Answer: B, C, D—The driver information section shows information about drivers loaded—not the hardware that they might control.

2. Which of the following parameters must you add to the BOOT.INI file to implement a memory dump?

   A. Com:x

   B. Crashdebug

   C. Mem:xx

   D. Basevideo

   Answer: B

3. Into which file is memory written during memory dump?

   A. MEMORY.DMP

   B. PAGEFILE.SYS

   C. MEMDUMP.TXT

   Answer: B—This is really a trick question because memory is dumped into the paging file first, and then transferred to MEMORY.DMP on the next restart. Read the questions carefully!

Index

Note to the Reader: First level entries are in **bold**. Page numbers in **bold** indicate the principal discussion of a topic or the definition of a term. Page numbers in *italic* indicate illustrations.

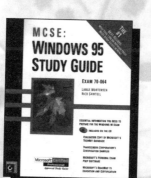

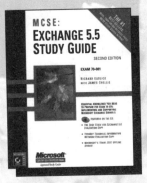

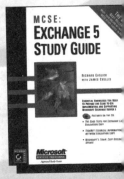